EXPEDITIONARY EAGLES

OTHER TACTICS AND INTEL. SUPPLEMENTS FROM POSTERITY PRESS:

THE LAST HUNDRED YARDS: THE NCO'S CONTRIBUTION TO WARFARE
ONE MORE BRIDGE TO CROSS: LOWERING THE COST OF WAR
PHANTOM SOLDIER: THE ENEMY'S ANSWER TO U.S. FIREPOWER
THE TIGER'S WAY: A U.S. PRIVATE'S BEST CHANCE FOR SURVIVAL
TACTICS OF THE CRESCENT MOON: MILITANT MUSLIM COMBAT METHODS
MILITANT TRICKS: BATTLEFIELD RUSES OF THE ISLAMIC MILITANT
TERRORIST TRAIL: BACKTRACKING THE FOREIGN FIGHTER
DRAGON DAYS: TIME FOR "UNCONVENTIONAL" TACTICS
TEQUILA JUNCTION: 4TH-GENERATION COUNTERINSURGENCY
HOMELAND SIEGE: TACTICS FOR POLICE AND MILITARY

EXPEDITIONARY EAGLES

OUTMANEUVERING THE TALIBAN

ILLUSTRATED

H. JOHN POOLE

FOREWORD BY

MAJ.GEN. RAY L. SMITH USMC (RET.)

POSTERITY
PRESS

Published by Posterity Press
P.O. Box 5360, Emerald Isle, NC 28594
(www.posteritypress.org)

Cataloging-in-Publication Data
Poole, H. John, 1943-
Expeditionary Eagles.
    Includes bibliography and index.
    1. Infantry drill and tactics.
    2. Military art and science.
    3. Military history.
I. Title.   ISBN: 978-0-9818659-2-8   2010   355'.42
Library of Congress Control Number: 2010923107

Cover art © 2010 by Michael Leahy
Edited by Dr. Mary Beth Poole
Proofread by William E. Harris

First printing, United States of America, July 2010

For all who have served in Afghanistan.

(Source: Corel Gallery, Totem Graphics #06D031)

Contents

Illustrations

Chapter 13: *Drug Interdiction Tactics*

Chapter 14: *New Techniques on Offense*

Chapter 15: *New Techniques on Defense*

Chapter 16: *The Village Contingent Option*

Foreword

Expeditionary Eagles should prove invaluable to all who want to win in Afghanistan. To show how U.S. theater commanders might be the first to do so since Tamerlane, it pulls out all the stops. After respectfully pointing out that war has been most successfully waged in a Christian manner, it makes a good case for going after the drugs instead of the Taliban. Then, it painfully suggests that the U.S. military must be less protective of its procedural heritage and bold in its utilization of infantry squads.

Active-duty military leaders may be tempted to disregard such talk. At this point in their history, that would be a mistake. Poole is only trying to convey what—in many circles—has already been accepted as fact. After the Baghdad Surge, the Pentagon fully realized that small units would be the key to winning the low-intensity conflicts of the 21st Century. But with any stratified bureaucracy, that big a paradigm shift takes time. Poole points out that time is not one of our current luxuries. The Commander in Chief has given the theater commander one year to sufficiently "protect the Afghan population" for Afghan security forces to take over. According to the author, that can only be accomplished by experimentally instituting certain changes to U.S. procedure. Though thoroughly tested in the Eastern world, many are well outside the Pentagon's political comfort zone. Instead of continuous perimeters around Kabul and Kandahar, he says there must be a tiny NATO contingent in every village/neighborhood along major roads and at border crossings. The job of those contingents would be collectively to impede the movement of enemy reinforcements, supplies, and fund-raising opiates.

Because 90% of the world's heroin comes from Afghanistan, no combination of military sweep, mayoral/police infusion, and construction aid will be enough to override the endemic corruption. That will take grassroots supervision that can only come from hundreds of U.S. squads locally participating in Combined Action

Platoons (CAPs). Instead of looking for Taliban to kill, each contingent of 20 or so GIs would help a sister squad of Afghan soldiers and another of police to maintain some semblance of order. As such, they would be more like "foreign-aid workers in the security sector" than "occupiers." Their nonviolent demeanor would so differ from Taliban bullying that civilian ire against the latter could only mushroom.

This document offers the best blueprint for final victory that I have seen. It greatly details what must concurrently happen in Pakistan. Then, it simply shows how more extensively to implement the President's ongoing guidance. For those who have not kept up with the evolution of small-unit tactics, such a widespread deployment of junior enlisted personnel may seem overly risky. Unfortunately, war is inherently risky. Unless, it has a good chance of finally succeeding, any number of casualties is too many. I also have seen the potential of this generation of young Americans. And I too can confirm the success of the CAP program in Vietnam. The author knows that some bitter fighting may occur at isolated locations. As such, he has provided some very lethal defensive techniques in Chapter 15. Those techniques should be enough to dissuade any number of Taliban from following through on their ground assault. And they will do so without any chance of collateral damage to civilians. As with all of Poole's previous intelligence and tactics supplements, *Expeditionary Eagles* should be required reading at every level throughout the U.S. security establishment.

M.Gen. Ray L. Smith USMC (Ret.)

Preface

This researcher has made the assumption that the most dubious of man's inventions—war—is still most successfully prosecuted with Christian ethics. For that to be true, peace must be the goal, and that peace must derive from something other than the martial law that now suppresses all dissent in Chechnya. Next, "how to fight in Christian manner" must be clearly defined. Pope John Paul II stipulated that to "most morally" defend against an aggressor, one must kill as few of his soldiers as possible.[1] In Matthew 5:44 and Luke 6:26 of the Christian Bible, Jesus says to love one's enemies. But how can one love the potential instrument of his own destruction? It's quite simple really. Don't do anything to him that wouldn't be personally acceptable. After being drafted, Sgt. Alvin C. York's religious beliefs initially prevented him from participating in World War I (WWI). Then, he found Matthew 22:21. In that Biblical passage, Jesus advises, "Render . . . unto Caesar the things that are Caesar's, and to God the things that are God's." York must have interpreted that to mean "do what you can to stop evil," because he soon dropped his request for "conscientious objector" status. During the Meuse-Argonne Offensive of 1918, he and two of his subordinates then proceeded to kill 20 Germans and capture 100 more to save their own patrol from annihilation.[2] When asked why he did it, he said it was to save lives. That's not the same as fighting evil with evil, or doing what one side deems morally reprehensible (like urban bombardment) to counter what the other side similarly disdains (like suicide bombing). It may assuage the craving for vengeance, but it does little to break the cycle of violence. It therefore works against the overall mission—namely, peace.

Some within the United States (U.S.) military consider war too "pragmatic" a subject to be discussed in the context of religion. Unfortunately, the two are already linked in the minds of fundamentalist Muslims. Ignoring the connection will only make things worse. If Islamists want to combine combat with religion, then

Christians should do likewise. However, they cannot then violate their own ethics or denigrate Islam. Instead, they must take the moral high ground, while embracing the world's next largest Abrahamic religion. To accomplish both at once, U.S. troops have only to more closely follow their own Christian principles in battle. At some point, mainstream peace-loving Muslims will notice the similarity of intentions and disavow any warmongering from within their own ranks. But, make the mistake of thinking that God loves only Christians or that "eyes in the sky" gives one the right to dispense summary justice, and peace in Afghanistan may become as elusive for devout Americans as it was for atheistic Soviets.

H. JOHN POOLE

Introduction

Initial Research

Finding enough new information to allow American forces to "snatch victory from the jaws of defeat" in Afghanistan was no easy task. The world's most tactically proficient army would have trouble protecting a society this fragmented. Much of the Afghan terrain is so precipitous as to defy conventional defense and resupply. And its inhabitants have been fighting technologically superior foes for so long that they make perfect guerrillas. Add to this the fact that the U.S. military has traditionally relied more on firepower than small-unit maneuver, and one starts to see the magnitude of the challenge.

While there is no shortage of enemy intelligence, its most vital particulars have mostly been buried in reams of minutia or otherwise deemed unworthy to ascend the chain of command. Expert opinions also abound. However, most—through their patently Western outlook—offer traditional "fixes" to parts of the problem, with too little concern for whether they might mesh with those for other variables. As convoluted as the situation was in Iraq, that in Afghanistan is worse. One would have to be a longtime student of tribal and smuggling hierarchies to make much of a dent in the power balance. That level of research is well beyond the capabilities of this author. Instead, he has focused on the interaction between neighboring-state players, factions within what is now collectively called the "Taliban," Hekmatyar's *Hizb-i-Islami Gulbuddin (HIG),* and various organized crime elements.

With U.S. defense, justice, and intelligence communities now fully committed to the Afghan conflict, its prognosis is still not good. For what might be enough to reverse this trend, one must view that conflict as a manifestation of 4th-Generation Warfare (4GW). 4GW is that which is waged simultaneously in the political, economic, psychological, and martial arenas. For political and operational insight, the author reviews what was unsuccessfully tried by the last occupier. For current enemy intelligence, he relies heavily on Indian and Pakistani news reports. For martial technique, he extrapolates from 44 years of off-and-on exposure to Eastern tactics.

Historical Perspective

Except for the immigration-oriented Mongols and their Turkic offspring (Tamerlane), no foreign power has ever successfully occupied Afghanistan. Among those who have tried are Greek, Persian, British, and Soviet empires.[1] After failing in Vietnam and only coming close to succeeding in Iraq, America's Armed Forces will have their work cut out for them in this strategic crossroads of South Asia. They must do something markedly different from what those four empires attempted. Now complicating the issue is the technological advent of overhead surveillance and precision munitions. Whether those "arms industry money-makers" have changed warfare enough to permit the surgical removal of a society's radical elements is doubtful. More probably, they will only create the illusion of progress while doing too little to build popular support. This book is about doing what no one else has been able—winning through small-unit maneuver and nonviolent interdiction, rather than overwhelming force.

While all Americans hold dear the lives of their young soldiers, too much emphasis on the survival of each individual can lead to wars being unnecessarily forfeited. Casualties are always painful (and politically embarrassing), but military commanders have the implicit obligation to risk enough of their subordinates to ensure victory. Otherwise, all losses are in vain. Among the ways to reduce friendly casualties are preliminary bombardment and robotics. Both have pitfalls. Just as a well-aimed bullet from 50 feet will cause less collateral damage than a smart bomb from 10,000, so will a self-sufficient squad be more effective than a remotely controlled division. Rank has nothing to do with it. To arrive at the most timely and humanitarian decisions, one must logically defer to the most senior person at the scene of each incident. There are those within the U.S. military who obviously feel that their junior noncommissioned officers (NCOs) cannot be trusted to arrive at moral decisions. Most have never been enlisted themselves, nor have they previously commanded U.S. troops in combat. Then, there are those who claim

U.S. squads lack the tactical potential to operate alone. Most have never personally participated in small-unit aggressor operations against a Western military unit. Nor do they see any need for "unconventional warfare" training for their troops. Nor have they ever allowed their NCOs collectively to arrive at their own tactical techniques (like football plays).

Situational Perspective

To limit friendly casualties, Soviet and now North Atlantic Treaty Organization (NATO) forces have tried to conduct a war in Afghanistan from standoff distance. Much of that country is highly mountainous. That means all but the most sophisticated of smart munitions will not hit their intended targets. Even on a slope that perfectly aligns with each shell's trajectory, a horizontal error of 50 meters can easily translate into 200 along the ground.

From a tactical standpoint, the missing ingredient in any stand-off decision is microterrain. As most commissioned officers have never been part of a squad, they don't fully realize the importance of ground undulations and foliage to surprise-generating maneuver. Without that surprise, they cannot hope to minimize friendly casualties. Most Eastern armies and insurgencies operate—with no shortage of manpower—from the "bottom up." It does little good to go after their leaders; and for every fighter killed, ten more quickly appear. To win the 4GW conflict in Afghanistan, widely dispersed U.S. forces must closely interact with citizenry and opposition alike (like the Marines did in Anbar Province and the Army did during the Baghdad Surge). Only then will they be able to befriend enough of the Afghan population to dry up a rebellion. To do this safely (and without a lot of collateral damage), those U.S. contingents must be trained in "unconventional warfare"—how to hide when too badly outnumbered. While not as effective as the Mongol tactic of marrying into opposition tribes, "disappearing" at will also makes a widespread presence possible.

Competing Factors

Any discussion of U.S. involvement in Afghanistan must necessarily consider neighboring-country intentions. That's because

xix

several have a vested interest in Afghanistan—most notably, Pakistan, Iran, and China. The present Afghan regime grew out of the Northern Alliance, with Iran as its primary mentor.[2] The original Taliban had Pakistani sponsorship.[3] China has mostly supported the Taliban,[4] but it is also close friends with Iran. Of the three countries mentioned, the People's Republic of China (PRC) is by far the most clever, expansionist, and dangerous.

According to "conventional U.S. wisdom," China is now expanding its navy to discourage any Western intervention during a large-scale military adventure (like the invasion of Taiwan). China's true intentions are more apparent to the residents of South Asia. That's because they share the same holistic thought processes. The PRC wants to control world trade and the maritime approaches to its own shores to ensure a sufficient supply of natural resources during time of war. That's why it has been developing a bigger navy, not for conventional aggression against Taiwan or any other Western ally. Once it controls the major trade routes, it can more easily manage the political subversion of all countries along the way. Most of the commercial port facilities now being built with Chinese "foreign-aid money" will eventually host a Chinese naval presence. Within just the Indian Ocean alone, those joint facilities already include the following: (1) Gwadar, Pakistan; (2) Trincomalee and Hambantota, Sri Lanka; (3) Chittagong, Bangladesh; (4) Coco Islands (Myanmar-owned north of the Andamans); and (5) Site-tway and Rangoon, Myanmar. By 2020, China will also have several sequels to its new high-speed rail link to Lhasa, Tibet. They will come from Beijing, Chengdu, and Lanzhou. From Lhasa, the PRC already has an all-weather road through the areas seized from India in 1962 to its high-altitude borders with Pakistan and Afghanistan.[5] As was demonstrated in the massive military exercise of August 2009, this road/rail network will allow China rapidly to project military force to its border with India. It will also complete the conduit for Iranian oil that China has been helping to construct from Herat to Peshawar through Afghanistan's Bamian Province.[6]

The Book's Limitations

To achieve adequate detail, this work has necessarily been restricted to the largest threads of evidence concerning the Afghan resistance. While those threads represent every 4GW arena, they may not adequately depict the whole picture. In assessing an Eastern threat, this researcher has also made little attempt to conform with "conventional Western wisdom." Whenever an erroneous statement or conclusion is suspected, U.S. readers should take the time conclusively to disprove it through additional research. In a war this convoluted, military professionals can no longer rely on past impressions of hazy origin.

The Book's Utility

Throughout U.S. history, other-nation perspectives have seldom played much of a role in U.S. government decision making. Because of the cultural gap between victim and rescuer in Afghanistan, more attention to foreign perspectives may be in order this time around. The most reliable U.S. ally in the region is India. Now facing an assault from both and Communist and Islamist extremists, India provides helpful insights into the Pakistani source of Taliban reinforcement and resupply. Having drawn from these insights, *Expeditionary Eagles* should constitute a useful supplement to U.S. intelligence efforts. Still, no amount of intelligence will do U.S. forces much good unless it is first sorted by an authority on Eastern small-unit tactics. In Asian wars of "national liberation," almost all strategic goals are realized "from the bottom up." Within Afghanistan, that same warfighting methodology has been described as "death (to all occupiers) by a thousand razor cuts."[7] Through a somewhat "backwards" military career and many years of subsequent study, this author has the perfect background for prioritizing Taliban intelligence. With more situational clarity comes the chance for specially tailored tactical technique. To the latter, Part Three of this book is dedicated.

Acknowledgments

Thanks be to God for any wisdom herein. All U.S. military leaders who genuinely want victory in Afghanistan must find a way to morally override the chronic inertia of their respective bureaucracies. Should they fail to deviate from "established procedure," they will almost certainly neglect their sacred responsibility to America and the world. For all U.S. service personnel, the correct order of allegiance is to God, Country, and—only then—to Corps.

Part One

The Full Extent of the Problem

"They're on our left, they're on our right, they're in front of us,
they're behind us. . . . [T]hey can't get away this time."
— U.S. Marine Hero "Chesty" Puller

(Source: Attributed to most famous U.S. Marine leader, Lt.Gen. Lewis B. "Chesty" Puller USMC [Ret.])

1 __ What Lies behind All the Afghan Turmoil?

● Of what interest is Afghanistan to China?

● Which Afghan resource does China not want for itself?

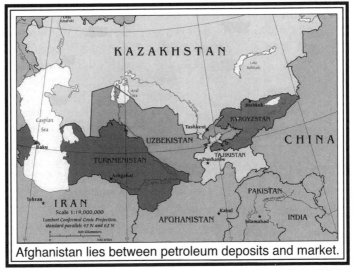

Afghanistan lies between petroleum deposits and market.

(Source: Courtesy of General Libraries, University of Texas at Austin, from their website for map designator "caucasus_cntrl_asia_pol_2003.jpg")

The Crossroads of South Asia

Afghanistan is where East meets West, and North meets South. For centuries, many powerful invaders have tried to add it to their empires. Its latest ordeals seem more ideological in origin, with the current one being over the choice between Western-style democracy and Taliban despotism. Before that, Pakistan and Iran vied through proxies for whether Afghanistan would become a Sunni or Shiite theocracy. Still, one should never mistake political preference for overall agenda. As with most of the world's other highly contested regions, the underlying issue here is trade.

3

The Most Obvious Trade Commodity

Since the first internal combustion engine, Afghanistan has occupied a "geo-strategically important" location. It lies between the oil-rich Middle East and Asia's biggest petroleum markets. Now, it also provides the easiest access to the vast natural gas reserves of the Caspian Basin. That's why Michael Moore's "Fahrenheit 9/11 Documentary" so heavily focused on America's "UNOCAL" (Union Oil Company of California) pipeline. Its job was to transport gas from Turkmenistan's Dauletabad-Donmez basin via Afghanistan to one of Pakistan's Indian Ocean ports. UNOCAL had been laying the diplomatic groundwork for this project since 1995. In Afghanistan, those efforts ceased in August 1998 when America began to take more direct military action against *al-Qaeda* and the Taliban. Since the fall of the Taliban, the proposal for a Trans-Afghan pipeline has been rekindled. Afghan President Hamid Karzai signed the necessary protocol in December 2002 between the governments of Afghanistan, Turkmenistan, and Pakistan.[1] As evidenced by Map 1.1, a slightly different route is now envisioned. Under the original scheme, the gas was to go to Gwadar by pipeline and then on to India for further distribution by ship.[2] The current configuration takes it alongside the road from Herat to Kandahar and then from Quetta overland through Multan, Pakistan, to Fazilka, India. Its $7.6-billion construction will not be completed until 2014. A Gas Pipeline Framework Agreement was then signed by representatives of the project's participating nations on 25 April 2008. It committed those parties to initial fabrication by 2010. First, of course, the whole southern part of Afghanistan will have to be cleared of land mines and Taliban forces. Then, the Afghan army and local security elements will be enough to protect the pipeline. Revenues from it should increase Afghanistan's annual income by approximately a third.[3]

This project has been wrapped in controversy since *Le Monde* alleged on 9 December 2001 that Mr. Karzai had been a consultant for UNOCAL on the Trans-Afghan pipeline prior to his assignment as interim president.[4] While that accusation was never substantiated, the first U.S. ambassador to Karzai's regime—Zhalmay Khalilzad—did briefly consult for Cambridge Energy Research Associates, while it was doing a risk analysis for UNOCAL on the same Turkmen gas conduit.[5] As might be expected, America was not the only nation interested in the endeavor. It was the PRC that built

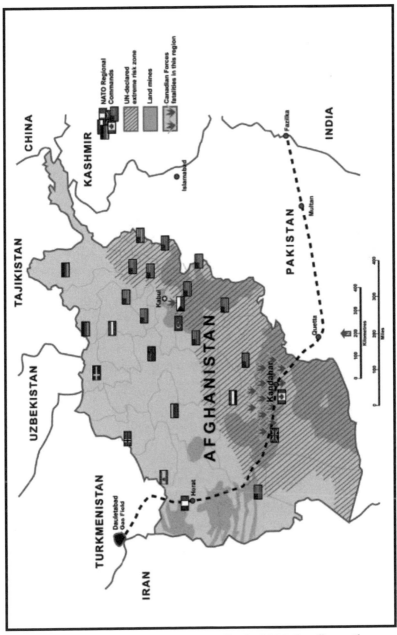

Map 1.1: The Trans-Afghan Pipeline's 2008 Configuration
(Source: Courtesy of www.globalresearch.ca, map designator "TAPI pipeline.jpg," copyright © 2008 by Travis Lupick, straight.com)

the Gwadar port facility, and it was the PRC that tried to outbid Chevron for UNOCAL in the summer of 2005.[6] Therefore, one can clearly see that the competition over Afghanistan is not just about style of governance.

China's Back-Up Plans for Petroleum Access

Aspiring superpowers require great quantities of oil and natural gas. As a result, China's current road-building "assistance" in Afghanistan's Bamian Province has more to do with the movement of Iranian petroleum from Herat to Peshawar than good will.[7] To complete the link, the PRC has also helped Pakistan to complete the southern portion of the high-altitude Karakoram Highway.[8] A lot of oil can be moved by limited-access road. Railways and pipelines are also much easier to build alongside of one. As of 28 January 2005, a new highway has also existed between the Dogharoun region of northeastern Iran and Herat.[9]

To handle the massive flow of natural gas from the Caspian Basin, the PRC also has plans for its own pipeline along a different route. (See Figure 1.1.) Spanning the entire distance between Turkmenistan and the PRC, it will first run north along the Caspian Sea to Atasu, Kazakhstan, and then east to Alashankou, China.[10] (See Map 1.2.) Understandably, it will be named the Central Asia Gas Pipeline.[11]

Iran's Own Bid for an Oil Conduit

The Trans-Afghan pipeline is obviously a Western initiative. However, that initiative carries with it no particular stigma. The West has just as much right to Caspian Basin petroleum as China. And someone has to counter the spread of Communism. Like China, Iran has a revolutionary government and expansionist agenda. It also sits astride considerable petroleum reserves. Accordingly, it has been planning its own transportation conduit to India. Called the "Peace Pipeline," it will pass through Pakistan's Baluchistan Province south of the Afghan border. In May 2009, the leaders of Iran and Pakistan agreed to their respective portions of that arrangement. India has yet to endorse its part, because Washington legitimately discourages all dealings with Iran.[12]

Figure 1.1: Caspian Petroleum Rig
(Source: Corel Gallery, Totem Graphics, Miscellaneous #31F038)

American Intentions on the Caspian Gas

The U.S. would probably like to access Turkmen gas through

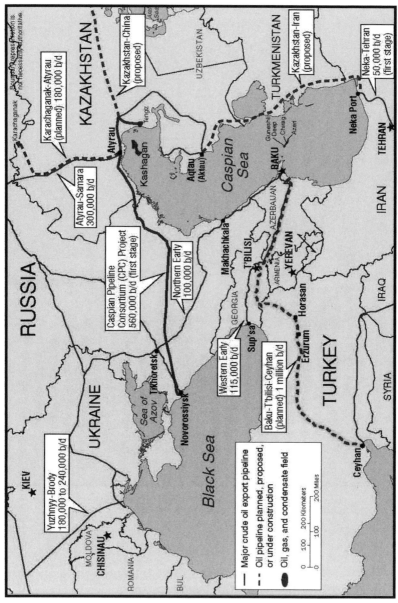

Map 1.2: The Only Western Pipeline through Georgia in 2002
(Source: Courtesy of General Libraries, University of Texas at Austin, from their website for map designator "caspian_pipelines_2002.pdf")

Afghanistan, but it wouldn't invade that country to get it. The West's only existing non-Russian pipeline runs from Azerbaijan (on the western shore of the Caspian), through Georgia, and on into Turkey. (Look again at Map 1.2 [pipeline capacity in barrels per day].) After Russia forcefully annexed part of Georgia in 2008, one could safely say that this Caucasus route would be extremely tenuous in time of war. The only other pipelines to Europe are through Russia. In 2006, Europeans from France to Finland experienced shortages when Russia cut the natural gas supplies to Ukraine after that nation refused to accept a price hike.[13]

The Kashmir Dispute May Also Have Been about Oil

As Pakistan had done in 1947,[14] China seized part of Jammu-Kashmir from India in 1962. It did so after building an unauthorized road (through Indian territory) from Tibet to its Xinjiang Province. One year later, Pakistan ceded the Trans-Karakoram Tract (along the northern frontier of Gilgit-Baltistan agency to the PRC. The Pakistani-occupied part of Jammu-Kashmir is now called Azad Kashmir and the Northern Areas, whereas the Chinese-occupied part is called Aksai Chin.[15] (See Maps 1.3 and 1.4.) In essence, the PRC had clearly demonstrated a willingness to use force to extend its western trade routes.

Contrary to popular opinion, the Karakoram Highway was not built to further friendship between China and Pakistan. It was built to transport Middle Eastern oil to China via the Gwadar seaport. In recent years, China has become so worried about a wartime blockade of the Malacca Straits that it has been developing several alternative routes.

The Pakistani government has already embarked on several projects (with the financial and technical assistance of China) to exploit Gwadar's strategic potential. The new port will have conversion facilities for the further transport of pipeline-delivered natural gas. There will be a new coastal highway (financed by the Chinese) connecting Gwadar to Karachi and all points north. Gwadar will then serve as the port of entry for all ship-borne oil and gas heading up the Karakoram Highway to the western-most regions of China (or via Tibet). China has been promised sovereign guarantees for the use of the Gwadar port.[16]

Within this context, it's much easier to see how China's new

9

road from Peshawar to Herat helps it to access Iranian oil. This new stretch of asphalt is quite simply the culmination to an energy network that has been under construction through Iran, Pakistan, Tibet, and Chinese-seized portions of India for over 50 years. (Look again at Map 1.4.)

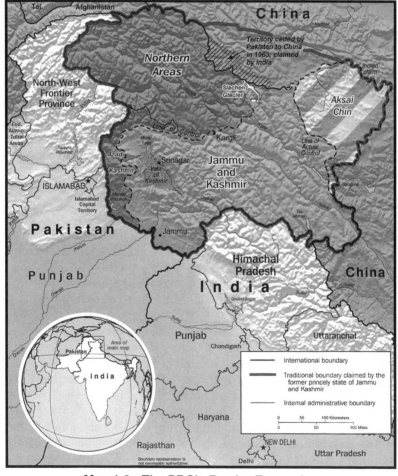

Map 1.3: The PRC's Border Expansion
(Source: Courtesy of General Libraries, University of Texas at Austin, from their website, for map designator "kashmir_region_2004.pdf")

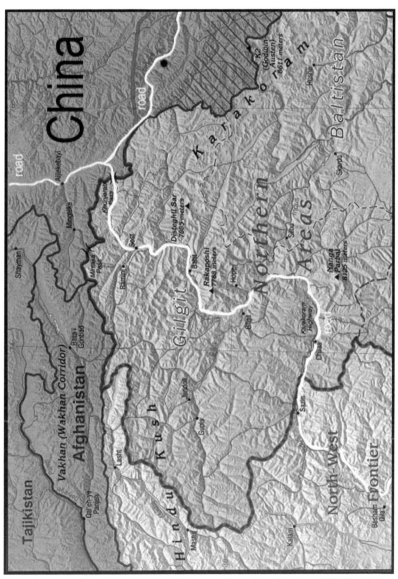

Map 1.4: One End of the Chinese Road to Iranian Oil Fields
(Source: Courtesy of General Libraries, University of Texas at Austin, from their website for map designator "kashmir_region_2004.pdf")

Commodities That Come from Afghanistan and Pakistan

While Washington has shown no particular interest, southwest Asia has its fair share of strategically important minerals. According to NPR (National Public Radio) News on 22 October 2009, the U.S. may help China to open its narrow border with Afghanistan. The PRC wants to build a rail link to one of the biggest copper mines in the world through the Wahkan Corridor.[17] (Refer back to Map 1.4.) As of 7 October 2009, American troops were providing security for a PRC-owned company exploiting the Aynak copper reserves. Worth tens of billions of dollars, those reserves are in Logar Province just south of Kabul.[18]

Ostensibly for the minerals, China is also very interested in Baluchistan. Its new naval base at Gwadar is common knowledge, but its forward operating base at Quetta is only rumor. Everyone has hastily assumed that both have only to do with the transport or extraction of petroleum and minerals. According to *Asia Times*, the Chinese have directed most of their Pakistani investment toward Baluchistan. Besides an oil pipeline and rail link to the Karakoram Highway (Gwadar-Dalbandin railway through Rawalpindi[19]), they plan to improve the transportation corridor from Gwadar to Quetta.[20] The Chinese companies at work in Baluchistan are Metallurgical Construction Corporation (MCC), its subsidiary MRDL, and a Chinese petroleum outfit—the Bureau of Geophysical Prospecting (BGP).[21] Baluchistan is home to Pakistan's largest gas discovery at Sui, with gas reserves in excess of 10 trillion cubic feet (the energy equivalent to 1 billion barrels of oil).[22]

> MCC acquired the 18 billion-rupee (U.S. $223 million) Saindak copper and gold project on a 10-year lease in September 2002. It has been operated by MRDL. . . .
>
> [In 2002], MCC also agreed to invest $74 million to exploit and develop lead and zinc deposits, estimated at over 14 million tons, at the Duddar Lead and Zinc Project, northeast of Gwadar. . . .
>
> Zhuzhou Smelter, China's second-largest zinc producer by capacity, plans to import 50,000 tons of zinc concentrate and 20,000 tons of lead a year from Duddar. The company owns less than 40% of the Duddar mine but plans to take its entire output.

The Chinese are also engaged in petroleum exploration in Baluchistan. BGP was awarded a $1 million contract in 2001 to survey an area in Dera Bugti, in the province's heartland.[23]
— *Asia Times Online*, 26 March 2009

The PRC's ruling political party has never been the least bit shy about going outside host-country channels to establish local agreements. Its Consulate General in Karachi visited the Governor of Baluchistan in Quetta on 5 September 2007. With him were representatives from MCC. Ostensibly seeking security guarantees for MCC workers, he offered a "contribution to improvement of [the] local economy and living standard."[24] From a big-business standpoint, it looked more like a local payoff to more easily hijack national assets. The only threat to the extraction of natural resources in this part of the world is the Baloch Liberation Army (BLA).[25]

The Chinese have also been playing a . . . role in the efforts of the Army to crush the independence struggle, by providing the Pakistani military units deployed in Baluchistan with arms and ammunition and by sharing with them the intelligence collected by Chinese intelligence officers posted in Gwadar and other places under the cover of engineers.[26]
— *India Defence* (New Delhi), 14 March 2006

Now Afghanistan Has Another "Strategic" Commodity

As an agricultural nation with limited governmental controls, Afghanistan currently has an exportable "crop-derivative" that is of tremendous strategic significance. (See Figure 1.2.) That's because this particular derivative will generate huge profits for whoever helps with its distribution. When shipped to the United States, it would also serve to destabilize the only society still capable of opposing Islamist and Communist expansion. Most often accused of such a scheme is the Taliban.[27] Still, with over 90% of the world's opiates now coming from Afghanistan, any number of other national and non-national players could be interested in curtailing U.S. interference.

One of the first steps in the Communist takeover method is to

THE FULL EXTENT OF THE PROBLEM

destabilize the targeted nation. According to an American Foreign Policy Council report, "there is a well-documented history of both Russian and Chinese organized crime organizations working as tools of their governments.[28] It should come as no surprise then that the Central Intelligence Agency's (CIA's) *World Factbook* still describes Mainland China as "a major trans-shipment point for heroin . . . [and] source country for methamphetamine and heroin chemical precursors."[29] One of its Hong Kong Triads—Sun Yee On—is a known "business" extension of the People's Liberation Army (PLA).[30] And another of the PLA's extensions—China Ocean Shipping Company (COSCO)—has been often accused of international drug smuggling.[31] Considering all of these things together, one gets a brief glimpse of the PRC's underlying stake in Afghanistan.

> [The triads'] powerful influence is felt worldwide in counterfeiting, arms dealing, alien smuggling and money laundering. Hong Kong is a key transit point for the Southeast Asian heroin and methamphetamine that pour into the United States, and triads play a key role in the drugs' transshipment.[32]
> — *The New Republic* (Washington, D.C.), 1997

If Hong Kong was the key transit point for Southeast Asian heroin pouring into the U.S. in 1997, then it may also be for Southwest Asian heroin in 2010. Yet, in 2004, President Karzai rejected a U.S. proposal to end poppy production in Afghanistan through aerial spraying of chemical herbicides. He was afraid it would adversely affect the economic situation of his countrymen. That, in itself, speaks only of poor judgment. Unfortunately, Mr. Karzai's younger brother—Ahmed Wali Karzai (who helped to finance the presidential campaigns)—has been credibly linked with the heroin trade.[33]

America's Belated Response to the Drugs

Finally realizing the danger, Washington permitted its expeditionary forces to modify their approach to the Afghan insurgency in early 2009. Wars are largely won through limiting the enemy's strategic assets. If heroin has been both funding the foe and undermining the home front, than one is obligated to stop its flow. The

Figure 1.2: The Opium-Producing Poppy
(Source: Corel Gallery, Totem Graphics, Miscelaneous #31F038)

original Taliban came up from Quetta, so Kandahar would have been the logical province to flood with U.S. Marines. Yet, Helmand was chosen instead—probably because 70% of Afghanistan's export opium (a full two-thirds of the world's total supply) comes from Helmand Province.[34] (See Map 1.5.)

Concurrently Lowering the Ideological Interference

Regional historians readily agree that Iran and Pakistan have long competed over Afghanistan through surrogate armies. The

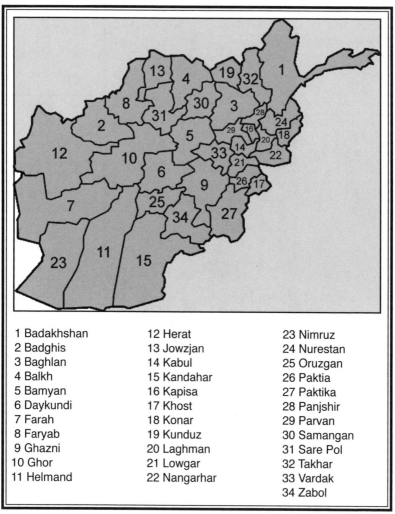

1 Badakhshan	12 Herat	23 Nimruz
2 Badghis	13 Jowzjan	24 Nurestan
3 Baghlan	14 Kabul	25 Oruzgan
4 Balkh	15 Kandahar	26 Paktia
5 Bamyan	16 Kapisa	27 Paktika
6 Daykundi	17 Khost	28 Panjshir
7 Farah	18 Konar	29 Parvan
8 Faryab	19 Kunduz	30 Samangan
9 Ghazni	20 Laghman	31 Sare Pol
10 Ghor	21 Lowgar	32 Takhar
11 Helmand	22 Nangarhar	33 Vardak
		34 Zabol

Map 1.5: The Many Provinces of Afghanistan
(Source: Wikipedia.org, s.v "Afghanistan," under provisions of GNU Free Documentation License, map designator "Afghanistan_pro…es_numbered.png")

Iranian proxy's method must have been similar to that of Lebanese *Hezbollah,* whereas the Pakistani proxy's method was initially that of Hekmatyar and then of the Taliban. After the Soviets' departure, the Northern Alliance continued to pursue Iran's strategic interests while controlling the northern part of the nation. When the Pakistani-backed Taliban came up from Quetta, civil war ensued. Since that time, Afghanistan has experienced both Maoist subversion and a strong *al-Qaeda* presence.

To stop this ideological tug of war, NATO will first have to persuade Afghanistan's closest neighbors to stop interfering with its internal affairs. (See Maps 1.6 and 1.7.) The next two chapters will investigate only the Pakistani side of this philosophical scrum (that most influenced by Wahhabism). Then, the illicit drug trade will be revisited in earnest.

Map 1.6: Shiite Iran on One Side
(Source: CIA, *The World Factbook*, map designator "iran.html")

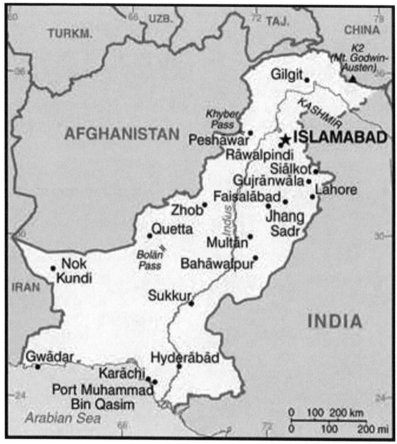

Map 1.7: Sunni Pakistan on the Other Side
(Source: CIA, *The World Factbook*, map designator "pakistan.html")

2 The Afghan Taliban's Karachi Home

- From where do most Afghan resistance fighters come?
- How can this flow of enemy reinforcements be slowed?

A city's courtyard walls can hide a lot of militant activity.

(Source: DA PAM 550-175 [1989], p. xxxvii)

Afghanistan's First "Taliban" Came from South Pakistan

The word "taliban" translates into "students." The students that joined *mujahideen* leader Mullah Mohammed Omar in 1989 were predominantly Pashtun and from refugee *madrasas* just inside Baluchistan. Then, in 1996, Omar's Taliban got more help. According to the South Asia Analysis Group, "cadres of the *Sipah-e Sahaba (SSP), Lashkar i-Jhangvi (LeJ), Lashkar-e-Toiba (LET),* and *Harakat ul-Mujahideen (HUM),* encouraged by the [Pakistani] Inter-Service Intelligence [ISI], entered Afghanistan in . . . thousands to help the Taliban in its successful assault on Jalalabad and Kabul."

19

They stayed on to fight the Iranian-backed Northern Alliance, with their infrastructure possibly becoming that of Osama bin Laden. When the Taliban was evicted from Afghanistan in 2001 by what was now also a U.S.-backed Northern Alliance, that infrastructure moved back into Pakistan.[1] It has since contributed as much to Pakistan's volatility as to Afghanistan's insurrection. Like before, *madrasa* graduates still figure prominently in the equation.

Pakistan's Alternative Way of Educating the Poor

The word *madrasa* means "center of learning" in Arabic. In a Muslim country, the term is generally applied to grade schools that teach Islamic doctrine. As of 2004, one million Pakistani youths were purportedly studying in 20,000-50,000 *madrasas* (or *madaris*).[2] Now, over two million children attend more than 50,000 programs. There are different denominations of *madrasas*. A local source claims up to 60% are Deobandi, 17.5% Barelvi, 2% Ahle Hadith, 2% *Jamaat-i-Islami,* and 2% Shia.[3] Those that are Deobandi and Ahle Hadith follow to varying degrees the same ultra-conservative Wahhabi principles as *al-Qaeda,* whereas the Barelvi majority do not. For educating the poor, *madrasas* have traditionally offered free tuition, room, and board to their students. Many sprang up to service the Afghan refugee camps. During the 1980's, Pakistan's *madrasas* were mostly in its Northwest Frontier and Baluchistan provinces.[4] However, by 1997, Punjab also had over 2500. That province's Lahore division accounted for 323, while its Bahawalpur division had 883. Of the combined total, 972 were Deobandi and 174 Ahle Hadith. Throughout the rest of the country, there were many more Deobandi and 200 more of the Ahle Hadith.[5]

There are few restrictions on who may teach at these religious schools. As a result, many of the combatants in Kashmir and Afghanistan have been their graduates.[6] *Madrasas* along the Baluchistan-Afghan border have purportedly provided the Taliban with most of its replacements, but others have contributed.[7]

At the time of independence in 1947, there were only 137 Madrasas in Pakistan. According to a 1956 survey, there were 244 (Ahmad's survey in Malik, "Colonialization of Islam," 1996). . . . Since then . . . the number of madrasas has doubled every ten years, with current estimates as high as 45,000 (Singer, "Pakistan's Madrasas," Brookings Inst., 2001, 3).[8]

— U.S. Institute of Peace Report, 2005

Several *Madrasa* Networks Support the Afghan Resistance

Radical elements within Pakistan's two largest religious parties—*Jamaat-i-Islami (JI)* and *Jamiat Ulema-i-Islam (JUI)*—support America's enemy in Afghanistan. Whereas at least part of *JI* supports Hekmatyar,[9] *JUI/F* (Fazlur Rehman faction) supports the Taliban.[10] *JUI/F's* military wing has returned to its original name—*HUM*.[11] *JI's* military wing is still the *Hezb (Hezb-ul-Mujahideen)*, but both deny the connection.[12]

Other supporters of the Taliban are *Jamaat-ul-Dawa (JuD* with *LET* as its military wing) and *SSP* (with *LeJ* as its military wing).[13] Like *al-Qaeda, JuD* is strictly Wahhabi in belief. It and *LET* are not Deobandi, but rather Ahle Hadith.[14] *SSP* and its military wing are Sunni-Deobandi and radically anti-Shiite.[15] Both *LeJ* and *LET* are thought to provide *al-Qaeda* with suicide commandos and bombers (to include women and children).[16] *HUM* and *LET* may together furnish up to 30% of the Afghan Taliban's overall manpower.[17]

Not only do *JUI/F* and *JI* have extensive strings of Pakistani *madrasas*,[18] but so does *SSP* (43 in Karachi alone as of 2002).[19] Many of these schools were established for Afghan refugees with Saudi money. With that money came Wahhabi influence.[20] Whereas most *JI madrasas* are near refugee camps in northern Pakistan,[21] *JUI/F* has many at Quetta in Baluchistan Province and Karachi in Sindh Province. In fact, Karachi's Binori Mosque is known as a "*JUI*-Taliban stronghold."[22] Not surprisingly, it was *JUI madrasas* that originally spawned the Taliban.[23]

As of 2003, every one of the above-mentioned militias had been banned by Pakistan's central government except for *LET*. Having enjoyed a proxy relationship with ISI in the war against India in Kashmir, it and its political parent were moved to a "watch list" in 2003 instead of being rebanned.[24]

The Pakistani Sects That Defended Afghanistan in 2001

More that just the Afghan Taliban resisted the U.S. invasion of

Afghanistan in October 2001. There was also *al-Qaeda's* Brigade 313. It had the following five components: (1) *Harakat ul-Jehad i-Islami (HUJI,* a Deobandi affiliate of *JUI/F);* (2) *Jaish-e-Moham-med (JEM,* an offshoot of the merger between *HUM* and *HUJI* [25]); (3) *Harakat ul Mujahideen al-Alami (HMA,* another offshoot of the same merger);* (4) *LET;* and (5) *LeJ.* There was another coalition of 35,000 Pakistani fighters formed by *al-Qaeda.* Called the International Islamic Front (IIF), it included contingents from *LET, JEM, HUM, LeJ, and HUJI.* Some 30,000 of its fighters survived the U.S. airstrikes and moved back to Karachi, Lahore, Faisalabad, Rawalpindi, and Azad Kashmir (Pakistan-occupied Kashmir).[26] The leaders and some cadres of *HUJI* took refuge in South Waziristan of the Federally Administered Tribal Areas (FATA). Other *HUJI* cadres went to the Buner part of Pakistan's Northwest Frontier Province (NWFP).[27] It is from such places that much of Pakistan's internal turmoil now springs.

That turmoil depends—for its life blood—on powerful networks of militant *madrasas.* Since the Soviet-Afghan War, Pakistan has become progressively infused with the more codified and strict Wahhabi form of Islam from Saudi Arabia. In the early 1980's, President Zia-ul-Haq decided to establish *madrasas* instead of modern schools in the Afghan refugee camps. He did so for a natural supply of "resisters" to Western influence. That trend has carried over into modern-day Pakistan. By 2002, as many as 1.0 million Pakistani students were studying in *madrasas,* compared to 1.9 million in government-run primary schools.[28]

Karachi's Binori Town Seminary

Karachi has been widely portrayed as a lawless refuge for Islamist extremists, but a recent visitor to that city detected no anti-American sentiment at its center. Its people were as polite as any he had met, and its paramilitary police acting more like allies in a joint struggle. (See Map 2.1.) That's probably because Karachi has long been beset by powerful fringe elements. With payoffs and threats, those elements easily blend into the sectarian backdrop of a huge city. Then, as regularly reported, they reaffirm their presence.

Besides being the probable debarkation point for 90% of the world's total supply of heroin, Karachi is home to much of its Deo-

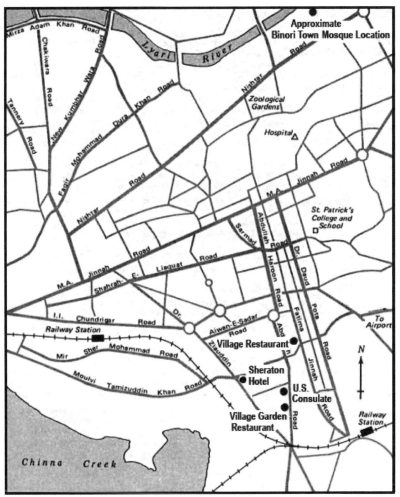

Map 2.1: Karachi's Hotbed of Extremism
(Sources: General Libraries, University of Texas at Austin, from their website for map designator "karachi.jpg")

bandi Sunni extremism. That makes some of its outlying neighborhoods as unhealthy for nosy Shiites and Christians, as they
are for drug agents. At the center of Karachi is an area that has
been variously called New Town, Binori Town, and Gurumandar.

Here exists Pakistan's second largest *madrasa*-system university (or seminary) in Pakistan—"Jamia Uloom."[29] The Binori mosque complex lies on the western side of a busy street (possibly Jhangir Road before it turns into the Hyderabad highway) about a half mile north of the distinctive Mausoleum of Quiad-e-Azam. (Refer back to Map 2.1.) More like a sprawling compound than a place of worship, this complex is completely screened by low storefronts and only distinguishable from the street by the huge red minarets that spring from its interior. It appears only accessible through one or two narrow openings in the commercial facade. At the main entrance in May 2010 stood two non-uniformed sentries who, though quite menacing, would luckily prove indecisive. Also emerging was a man with the khaki trousers and swagger of a *jihadist* combatant.[30] Westerner visitors would be wise to stay well clear of this site. Satellite images do show Binori Town's most famous mosque—Kanz-ul-Eemaan (or Kunzul Eemaan)—to be just north of the Quiad-e-Azam Mausoleum on Jhangir Road, but whether it is Deobandi could not be confirmed.

The Binori mosque was founded many years ago by Allama Yusuf Binori and Maulana Mufti Mahmood. Mahmood was the head of *JUI* at the time. Among Binori's more famous professors, graduates, and honorees have been the following: (1) Maulana Masood Azhar, the hijacker of Indian Airlines Flight 814 and founder of *JEM* in 2000;[31] (2) Mullah Omar, current head of the Afghan Taliban;[32] (3) now assassinated Maulana Azam Tariq, leader of the *SSP*;[33] (4) now assassinated Mufti Nizamuddin Shamzai, tutor of Mullah Omar and Osama bin Laden;[34] (5) Maulana Fazlur Rehman, founder of *JUI/F*;[35] and (6) Qari Saifullah Akhtar, founder of *HUJI* and then top Taliban leader.[36]

> The [Binori] madrasa also teaches "jihad" to its students and its seminarians regularly go to Afghanistan to train in the art of warfare. A large percentage of the Taliban's upper-crust leadership has been students of [the] Binori mosque. . . .
> "This institution produces over 1,000 Mujahids every year. Each one of them is fully committed to religious teaching and jihad," says one of the teachers at the madrasa.[37]
> — *The Friday Times* (Pakistan), 25 February 2000

In mid-September 2003, *Time Magazine* concluded that Islam

doesn't get any more radical than the version taught at the Binori town mosque and seminary. It educates more than 9,000 students at branches across the city. In the emotion-filled days following 9/11, its sermons reviled George Bush and lauded Osama bin Laden. *Time* went on to say the school has top Taliban commanders for alumni and serves as a stopover for *al-Qaeda* personnel *en route* to Afghanistan.[38] There are thought to be two convalescent centers for wounded Taliban insurgents near that Binori seminary.[39]

> Officials confirm the mosque has often been used by sectarian outfits as a "safe haven.". . .
> Leaders from Afghanistan's Taliban militia frequently visit the mosque and its madrasa.[40]
> — *The Friday Times* (Pakistan), 25 February 2000

Unfortunately, the Binori's reputation gets worse. *JEM* was founded there,[41] and *JEM* operatives have been connected to the death of Daniel Pearl.[42] In March of 2009, Binori's powerful Deobandis started taking over Barelvi mosques in the Karachi area.[43]

What Karachi's Police Have Been Doing about the Problem

On 26 June 2009, authorities raided the hideout of a radical faction in Karachi, seizing a large arms cache.[44] Local officials guard against extremism in theory but regularly overlook the ultra-conservative variety. While Binori's rhetoric is now supposedly monitored by plainclothes policemen,[45] it probably still lauds the Taliban and *al-Qaeda*. The Binori mosque complex enjoys so much religious and political clout within Pakistan that no government agency can move against it. The problem, of course, is that Pakistan is in many ways an Islamic state, in which all *madrasas* are viewed as places of education. Sadly, some of Binori's graduates may now believe suicide bombing to be an acceptable medium of change. According to prestigious PBS (Public Broadcasting System) in May 2009, *madrasas* north of Karachi (presumably in Quetta) have been preparing children as young as five to become suicide bombers.[46]

If anything, Karachi is becoming less stable. The number of people assassinated there over the years is staggering. Poorer parts of the city are now heavily Talibanized. As of June 2009, unveiled women were being publicly threatened, and coeducational schools told to segregate the sexes or else. Many of those poor neighborhoods have become rest and recreation havens for veteran Taliban fighters and recruiting sites for new ones. Sohrab Goth is one of Karachi's Pashto-speaking enclaves in which active militants are known to seek shelter.[47] When guerrillas find a "base area" that is off limits to any kind of military action, they become much harder to defeat.

The Seminary at Akora Khattak

Akora Khattak is a massive "refugee-camp-turned-town" that is 31 miles east of Peshawar on the road to Rawalpindi. Here lies Pakistan's largest *madrasa*-system university—"Dar-ul Uloom Haqqania" (sometimes called the "University of Jihad"). Together with Jamia Uloom at Binori, this school has provided doctrinal instruction to most of the *madrasa* staffers along the border and Taliban leaders inside Afghanistan. Its namesake is more probably the founder—Maulana Samiul Haq, a *JUI* leader who had served in the National Assembly and Senate—than Mawlawi Jalaluddin Haqqani—the legendary guerrilla leader. As such, this seminary's orientation is almost certainly Deobandi. Its graduate roster of Taliban leaders and documented dislike for the Northern Alliance makes *JUI/F* its most likely sponsor.[48]

Lahore's Seminaries

In 2001, a South Asia Analysis Group paper described "Jamiya Ashrafiya" in Lahore as doing the same kinds of things as the seminaries at Binori Town and Akora Khattak. Like the former, Jamiya Ashrafiya is Deobandi.[49] Also located in Lahore is the Ahle Hadith seminary of "Jamia Muhamaddia." *JuD* is its most likely sponsor, as *JuD* is also Ahle Hadith.[50]

Key *Madrasa* Locations

Wherever there are Afghan refugees, there will be extremist *madrasas*. Many of Binori's graduate "seminarians" undoubtedly teach at *madrasas* around Quetta. Similarly, Akora Khattak alumni almost certainly staff the Peshawar *madrasas*. Both towns are so close to the border that they easily recruit Taliban fighters. Of course, there are extremist *madrasas* in other parts of Pakistan as well. Many are near the militant-wing headquarters and training sites of the other religious parties. (See Map 2.2.) At some *madrasas*, military training has been added to the religious curriculum.[51]

Where *Madrasa* Graduates Go for Military Instruction

After leaving the Islamic-doctrine-oriented *madrasas*, some Pakistanis receive military training in Afghanistan while others learn how to fight in their own country. Much of this instruction occurs along the Baluchistan or FATA boundary with Afghanistan. (During the Soviet-Afghan War, these camps were reportedly run by the Pakistani religious parties themselves.[52]) Other instruction takes place in the loosely governed areas of Central Pakistan and occupied Kashmir.

As of June 2009, what has been loosely called "the Taliban" controlled both Waziristans, Bajaur, and Orakzai agencies (just below Peshawar) in FATA. It also controlled the Lower Dir, Shangla, Swat, and Buner districts of NWFP.[53] Its presence in NWFP should come as no surprise, because until 2008, *Muttahida Majlis Amal (MMA)* ran the government of that province. *MMA* is a confederation of religious parties that include *JUI/F, JI, Jamiat Ahle Hadith, Tehrik-e-Islami* (Shiite), and *Jamiat Ulema-e-Pakistan* (Barelvi). (Decidedly anti-American and pro-*sharia*, the *MMA* has also governed Baluchistan for a while since 2001.[54]) Thankfully, Swat and Buner are now back in federal hands.

Below are the cities in which affiliates of Taliban and Hekmatyar are trained (or based) inside Pakistan. (See Map 2.2.) Most of this information has come from the Pakistani literature and private intelligence-gathering agencies within India. Wherever there are training sites or bases, there will also be contributing *madrasas*. The biggest of the *madrasa* chains belong to *JUI/F, JI, SSP, JuD,* and *Jamiat Ahle Hadith*. They will require the most supervision.

Karachi

One source claims *LET* trains right in Karachi. Another says

Figure 2.1: Northeastern Baluchistan Is Trackless Desert
(Source: FM 90-30 [1977], p. 2-7)

LeJ does as well. As a teeming metropolis of some 17 million, that city certainly has enough walled courtyards to hide a few terrorist academies. *HMA* is also based at Karachi. *JEM* was born there and probably does at least some of its military training within its city limits. Additionally, this former Pakistani capital hosts a considerable *SSP* presence. That presence is enough to support 43 *SSP madrasas.*[55]

Quetta

As of late 2004, there were no fewer than six Taliban training camps in Baluchistan.[56] (See Figure 2.1.) In all likelihood, most are part of the *JUI/F* network around Quetta. That would link them to *HUM*. Quetta is quite near the Afghan border. As such, there are many refugee camps nearby. Each would have its own

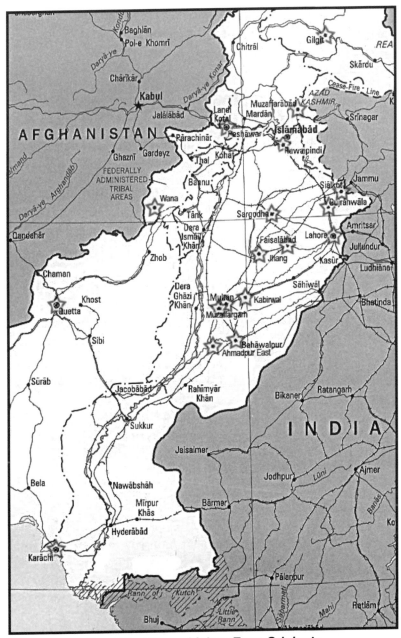

Map 2.2: Where Afghan Foes Originate
(Source: General Libraries, University of Texas at Austin, from their website for map designator "pakistan_pol_1996.pdf")

madrasas tasked with Taliban recruiting.[57] Many senior Taliban are believed to live in Quetta and the nearby tribal regions. *LET* also has a training center in Quetta.[58]

Wana

The capital of South Waziristan—Wana—is supposed to have its own militant training camp. While that camp may be affiliated with *LeJ*, there is no absolute proof of that. It is known that *HUJI* leaders and cadres went to South Waziristan after being evicted from Afghanistan in 2001.[59] That same year, the *JEM* camp of *"Balakot"* was reported to be somewhere in FATA.[60]

Peshawar

It is *LET* that maintains a training center in the capital of NWFP—Peshawar. *JEM* is also based there.[61] Because of the many refugee camps around that city, other militant organizations undoubtedly operate in its vicinity.

In the Sandhar District of Sindh

North of Karachi, *LET* has the *Markaz Mohammed bin Qasim* training camp in the Sanghar District of Sindh Province. That camp is most likely in one of the towns along the main highway to Sukkar.[62] (Refer back to Map 2.2.)

Ahmadpur East

Ahmadpur East is a town about half way to Islamabad from Karachi. It contains not only a regional headquarters of *JEM*, but also an *SSP* stronghold.[63]

Sargodha, Jhang, Multan, Bahawalpur, and Muzaffargarh

Strongholds of the *SSP* have been reported in all five of these towns, with its home headquarters being in Jhang.[64] Just north of Ahmadpur East, Bahawalpur hosts a *JEM*-sponsored *madrasa* called *Usman-o-Ali*, a *JEM* training base in its Model Town neighborhood, and quite possibly *JEM's* central headquarters. According to Britain's *Sunday Telegraph* in September 2009, *JEM* has also just established a new fully enclosed 4.5 acre training site about 5 kilometers out of Bahawalpur at Chowk Azam.[65] Then, as one heads north toward Faisalabad, he encounters Muzaffargarh, Multan, and finally Jhang. *LET* also has a training center in Multan.[66] Just to the northwest of Faisalabad, Sargodha hosts both an *SSP* stronghold and *LeJ* unit.[67]

Kabirwal

LeJ operates a training site in Kabirwal. This town is in the Khanewal district of Punjab and just northeast of Multan.[68]

Murdikhe

For the initial training of recruits, *LET* has long maintained the *"Markaz-e-Taiba"* complex some 35 kilometers north of Lahore near Murdikhe.[69] Murdikhe lies astride the main road between Lahore and Gujranwala. It is in the vast area between these two cities that *JuD* has created its own fundamentalist "state." While the government of Punjab now administratively controls *"Markaz-e-Taiba"* in accordance with U.N. Resolution 1267 against *JuD,* the complex still continues to operate.[70] Not surprisingly, *JuD's* impromptu state still has up to 20 Islamic institutions, 16 *madrasas,* and 140 of its own secondary schools.[71] It also has access to its own *madrasa* system seminary (possibly the same one as cited for Lahore).

SSP is also based at Murdikhe and near here runs a training camp for *LeJ*. *SSP* operates 28 *madrasas* in the province of Punjab, so many may be in, or just north of, Lahore.[72]

One cannot help noticing the physical proximity between the *HUM, HUJI, HMA, JEM, LET,* and *LeJ* training bases mentioned so far. Very possibly, the members of some, if not all, of these militant factions have been receiving military instruction at the same facilities (sharing camps). That is known to be the case for *LeJ, HUM,* and "other Deobandi terrorists from Pakistan."[73]

Lahore

While Karachi is often called the source of Muslim extremism, it can barely compete with Lahore. Lahore contains the headquarters and working infrastructure for two of Pakistan's largest radical organizations: (1) *JI;* and (2) *JuD* (formerly *MDI).* Many of those "Punjabis" running around Afghanistan and laying siege to Islamabad come from Lahore and its sister cities. Whereas *JI* has Deobandi roots, *JuD* is Ahle Hadith (Wahhabi).[74] Besides having large *madrasa* systems in Lahore, both actively pursue their Islamist agenda at Punjab University near Anarkali Bazaar on Mall Road. There, the *JI's* youth wing—*Islami Jamiat Talaba (IJT)*—competes with its *JuD* counterpart—*Tubala Jamat-ud Dawa (TJD)*—for the hearts and minds of 24,000 Pakistani college students.[75]

JI has its headquarters on Multan Road in the Lahore suburb of Mansoora (with its armed wing training in Azad Kashmir).[76] But, *JuD's* armed wing—*LET*—has its immense "Murdikhe" complex just 35 kilometers north of Lahore in Sheikhupura District near the town of Narang Mandi (probably inside *JuD's* self-proclaimed state).[77] In 2002, *JuD* started calling itself a charity organization, so as to disassociate itself from this armed wing. That same year, *LET* reportedly moved its main offices to Chauburgi Markaz in Lahore.[78] Most of Lahore's 323 *madrasas* must be associated with its largest seminaries. As "Jamiya Ashrafiya" is Deobandi,[79] *JI* is its most likely sponsor. "Jamia Muhamaddia" is Ahle Hadith, so probably part of the *JuD* system.[80] There are also a smattering of *madrasas* from *JUI/F* and *SSP.* An *LeJ* unit is supposed to be in Lahore as well, but no training base.[81]

Gujranwala

LET is known to have a training camp in Gujranwala.[82] At the north end of *JuD's* impromptu "state," this town would be the logical place for one. *LeJ* has a unit in Gujranwala, but no reported base.[83]

Rawalpindi

LET allegedly operates a training facility in Rawalpindi.[84] In the past, *HUM* has also had a regional headquarters in this raucous blue-collar city right next to Islamabad.[85] There is no telling how strong *HUM* still is there, but somebody did a pretty good job of blowing up Islamabad's Marriot hotel in September 2008. *HUJI*, a close affiliate of *JUI/F*, is one of the groups suspected.[86] Like *JEM*, the present-day *HUM* is an offshoot of the merger between the original *HUM* and *HUJI*.[87] *LeJ* has a unit in Rawalpindi but no reported training center. It is the prime suspect in the Marriott explosion (and most probably put up to it by *al-Qaeda*).[88]

Sialkot and Gilgit

Sialkot is a medium-sized town in the northeastern corner of Punjab, whereas Gilgit is deep in the Northern Areas of Pakistan-occupied Kashmir. *LET* is supposed to have training camps in both places.[89]

Something Out of the Ordinary at Muzaffarabad

HUM and two of its offshoots (one *JEM)* have all been based at Muzaffarabad (in Azad Kashmir).[90] They are not alone there. *LET* has also trained at Muzaffarabad in camps named *Muaskar-e-Toiba, Muashar-e-Aqsa, Muaskar Umm-al-Qura, Muaskar Abdullah bin Masood,* and *Muaskar Abu Bashir.*[91] In early December 2008, the Pakistani army raided another *LET* camp by the name of *Shawai Nullah.* It is only about five kilometers from Muzaffarabad.[92]

Here's the paradox. In 2004, *Hezb* was also training at Muzaffarabad.[93] As many as 20,000 of its cadre fighters were being instructed there at camps called *Tarbela* and *Haripur* (two municipalities just across the NWFP border). Other *Hezb* camps in the area are *Kotli, Mirpur, Oggi, Jungal-Mangal,* and *Gadhi-Dupatta.*[94]

One would not expect the collocation of *Hezb* with the other factions. *JUI/F* was formed along the Saudi Wahhabi model,[95] as was *JuD* (formerly *MDI*). That means *JUI/F* and *JuD* think largely alike. However, *JI* and *Hezb* followed the Egyptian Moslem Brotherhood model.[96] Thus, *Hezb* would not train next to the others unless it enjoyed the same ISI proxy status as *LET* in Kashmir. Further research does show *Hezb* to have been an ISI proxy.[97] Many of these camps may still be operational.

A Possible Reason for the Mixture of Philosophies

According to India's South Asia Analysis Group, Pakistani military-intelligence set up its clandestine "Army of Islam" from competing sects to pose less of an internal threat to Pakistan. As a part of this same army in Afghanistan, *HUM* and *LET* first helped the *mujahideen* to defeat the Soviets and then the Taliban to resist the Northern Alliance. "After the collapse of the Najibullah Government in Kabul in April 1992, the ISI shifted its Army of Islam to Jammu and Kashmir." There it started working in tandem with *Hezb* against the Indians. In 1999, *JEM* also joined the ISI's surrogate army.[98]

Unfortunately, some of those factions also joined bin Laden's IIF in 1998. Additionally, there were representatives of *HUM, LET,* and *JEM* in *al-Qaeda's* Brigade 055.[99] One worries about their dual allegiance (to both ISI and *al-Qaeda).*

Political Offices and Funding

Because *LET* was only on Pakistan's "watch list" until August 2009, it may still have as many as 2200 offices across Pakistan.[100] The banned *SSP* has 500 more branch offices in all 34 districts of Punjab.[101] According to India's *Friday Times,* even the banned *HUJI* may maintain branch offices in 40 districts and revenue divisions across Pakistan, including Sargodha, Dera Ghazi Khan, Multan, Khanpur, Gujranwala, Gujrat, Mianwali, Bannu, Kohat, Waziristan, Dera Ismail Khan, Swabi, Peshawar, and Islamabad.[102] That last location might help to explain the September 2008 Marriott explosion.

According to the Central Intelligence Agency's (CIA's) *World Factbook, JUI/F, JI,* and *Jamiat Ahle Hadith* are all still legal political parties within Pakistan. As such, they too would have their own "offices" throughout the country. That presents a problem. More than just recruiting may go on at these locations. *JEM* has stated that its offices would serve as schools of *jihad.*[103]

Almost all the militant factions mentioned in this chapter have been accused of linkages to either the ISI or *al-Qaeda.* Under Pakistan's new president, the first institution is much less likely to involve religious-party militias in its foreign escapades. However,

JEM and *LeJ* still look very much like *al-Qaeda* partners. Both are known to be receiving much of their funding from Saudi Arabian "benefactors."[104]

Pakistani Taliban Want More Than Just Afghan Victory

It was Mufti Nizamuddin Shamzai who first established the "pro-Taliban movement" inside Pakistan. While at Karachi's Binori seminary, he was the vital link between the Afghan Taliban and *JUI/F*. Most of Mullah Omar's first fighters were Pashtun refugees from border *madrasas* near Quetta, Baluchistan. Then, he began to get an infusion of native Pakistanis from interior-province *madrasas*. Of late, Baitullah Mehsud in the Waziristans has headed up a militia that is closely allied with Mullah Omar. Made up almost exclusively of Pakistani tribesmen, that ally of the Afghan Taliban is called *Tehrik-i-Taliban Pakistan (TTP)*.

Recently operating in the Swat Valley is another Pakistani affiliate of the Afghan Taliban (to be named in the next chapter). One of the first things it did was to destroy 200 coeducational government schools.[105] That fact would not be too worrisome, if on 14 April 2009, *Frontline World* had not reported Pakistan's state educational system to be virtually in shambles, with only *madrasas* left. There are 80 million children in Pakistan, with one fourth below the poverty line. That puts 20 million children at risk of extremist brain washing.[106]

By every indication, these northern manifestations of what has become known as the "Pakistani Taliban" intend to take over cities like Peshawar and eventually the Pakistani State. By creating alternative educational systems, they may be well on their way to realizing that goal.[107] Afghanistan's *madrasas* are now generating many of their own resistance fighters.[108] That will leave more of the Pakistani *madrasa* graduates at home to contest their own government.

The Pakistani, Indian, and Western media now make little distinction between these various kinds of Taliban. To make any sense of their reporting, one must remember that different groups are operating in different geographical areas and that all are using *madrasa* students to accomplish their goals. "Students," after all, is the local definition of the word "Taliban."

Mounting Evidence of the Unthinkable

Earlier in this chapter, there was mention of five-year-olds being trained as suicide bombers in Quetta. According to a regional news source, hundreds of children are undergoing instruction at several "suicide nurseries" run by *TTP* in FATA as well. This source also claims that Baitullah Mehsud was buying children specifically for this purpose.[109] This particular trend must be nipped in the bud.

What Must Now Be Done by the Pakistani Government

Pakistan must now make some very difficult internal choices. Not only its welfare, but also that of the free world, may hang in the balance. If everything comes out alright will largely depend on whether the U.S. and Pakistani defense establishments now see more promise in books than bullets. To modernize Turkey in 1934, President Kemal Ataturk ordered all Islamic *madrasas* closed. (He also banned the veil and allowed women to vote.[110]) Still, Ataturk was an avowed agnostic.[111] Not all Pakistani *madrasas* need to be closed. Only those that sow hatred stand to damage Pakistani society. That society has clearly indicated it would rather be a state for Muslims, governed by civilian institutions and secular laws, than an Islamic State, governed by clerics and *sharia* law.

Pakistan's public education system must be somehow rejuvenated, so that there will no longer be any need for *JUI/F* or *JI madrasas*. Also closed must be those from *SSP, JuD*, and *Jamiat Ahle Hadith*.[112] Of course, most worrisome are those belonging to *SSP*. With influence in all four provinces of Pakistan, this religious party is now considered by some to be the most powerful extremist group in the entire country. The *SSP* reportedly receives significant funding from Saudi Arabia through wealthy private sources in Pakistan.[113]

Most of these extremist *madrasas* are likely located in, or around, Quetta, Wana, Peshawar, Akora Khattak, Rawalpindi, Muzaffarabad, Gilgit, Sialkot, Gujranwala, Murdikhe, Lahore, Sargodha, Faisalabad, Jhang, Multan, Muzaffargarh, Bahawalpur, Ahmadpur East, Kabirwal, and Karachi. (Refer back to Map 2.2.) If these *madrasas* are not closed, Hekmatyar and Mullah Omar will continue to enjoy an unlimited supply of replacements for their Afghan resistance, and the Pakistani government may be in trouble.

3 The Pakistani Taliban's _ Islamabad Offensive

- What's behind all the trouble in Central Pakistan?
- How close did the militants get to the Pakistani capital?

JI-affiliated "Taliban" had hilltop outposts in Swat District.

(Source: DA PAM 550-65 [1986], p. 285)

Taliban Strongholds in Northern Pakistan?

According to British Broadcasting Corporation (BBC) News, only 38% of FATA and NWFP remained under Pakistani governmental control on 22 June 2009. There were "Taliban strongholds" in the following: (1) Bajaur, Orakzai, North Waziristan, and South Waziristan agencies within FATA; and (2) Lower Dir, Swat, Shangla, and Buner districts within NWFP. (See Map 3.1.) One cannot help noticing the two pincers converging on Islamabad—one from the south and the other from the north. With the possible exception of Nowshera, Charsadda, and Karak Districts in NWFP, all other agencies and districts between the stronghold areas have also suffered a "Taliban presence."[1] As that presence grows, one wonders how long Pakistan can remain a U.S. ally.

What Are These "Taliban" Trying to Accomplish

As will be shown later in the chapter, most of these northern "Taliban" have been pushing for a stricter application of *sharia* law within FATA and NWFP. For a while in early 2009, the Swat invaders were appeased by replacing all civil law with *sharia* in surrounding regions.[2] Thus, this new Taliban's degree of legitimacy within Pakistan has ebbed and flowed with its battlefield fortunes. While in varying degrees linked to the original Taliban of Mullah Omar, most of these northern factions appear only peripherally interested in what happens to Afghanistan. Henceforth, they will be called either "Taliban" (with quotation marks to denote the media's catch-all definition) or their factional name (to distinguish them from Omar's Afghan Taliban). Without a short history of *sharia* in Pakistan, there is no way to quantify the new threat.

Sharia Is Already Part of the Pakistanis' Heritage

Pakistan's Constitution specifies Islam as the "state religion." As a result, the Islamic Republic of Pakistan operates as an Islamic State in many ways. According to the CIA's *World Factbook,* Pakistan's legal system is "based on English common law with provisions to accommodate Pakistan's status as an Islamic state."[3] General Zia-ul-Haq, the country's third military president, suspended its Constitution in 1978 and introduced the *sharia* legal code as part of his "Islamization" policy. The very next year, "Zia decreed the establishment of *shariat* courts to try cases under Islamic law."[4] Though that original Constitution has since been reinstated, Zia's "Federal *Shariat* Court" survives to this day as an amendment.[5]

It lies within the discretion of the court of first instance [the local court] to decide whether to try a case under civil or *sharia* law. If the latter, then the appeals process goes to the Federal *Shariat* Court, rather than to the high courts.[6]
— Library of Congress Country Study, 1995

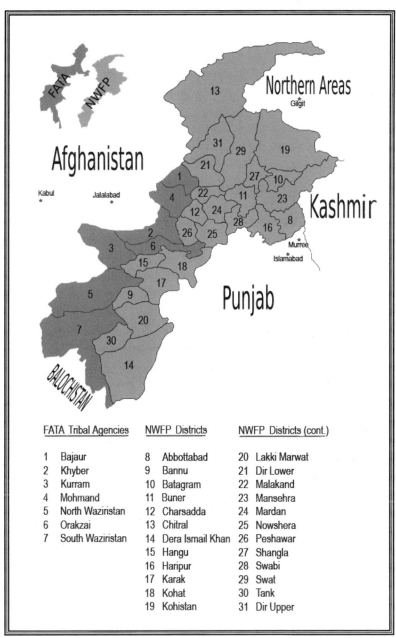

Map 3.1: Subdivisions of FATA and NWFP

(Source: Wikipedia.org, s.v "NWFP," by provision of GNU Free Documentation License, as adapted from nwfp.gov.pk by pahari sahib, map designator "NWFP_FATA.svg")

While the term *"sharia* law" is nowhere to be found in Pakistan's Constitution, a roughly equivalent phrase—"the teachings and requirements of Islam as set out in the Holy Quran"—is.[7] Thus, one could safely say that a loose interpretation of *sharia* has already been applied throughout the country. The same types of activities are illegal, but the more draconian of the Islamic punishments (like stoning and amputation) have been withheld.[8] Yet, the "degree-of application" debate still goes on in many Pakistani circles. A few government agencies, most notably the nearly autonomous ISI, may still pursue Zia's stricter version of *sharia*.

The implications are clear. Part of the Pakistani government may secretly support the Pakistani Taliban, just as it once did the Afghan Taliban. However, that possibility will take many chapters to assess. First, the Pakistani Taliban's power by region must be considered.

Bajaur

Bajaur is a place where Afghan rebels could hide. It adjoins their highly volatile Kunar Province. A continuous line of rugged hills separate it from the Kunar Valley. Those hills form a barrier that can only be penetrated at one or two points. Across this barrier ran the old road from Kabul to Pakistan before the Khyber Pass was adopted as the main route. For centuries, the Kunar River Valley has been the invasion route into Afghanistan.[9] Of course, attack in the opposite direction is equally possible.

Bajaur has been long suspected of hosting *al-Qaeda's* regional headquarters. Maulvi Faqir Mohammad supposedly commands the "Taliban" contingent in Bajaur and has 10,000 armed fighters. A year-long Pakistani operation ended there early in 2009 with a peace agreement. That agreement has since broken down. As a result, the so-called "Taliban" are back in control of most areas outside the district capital of Khar. "Taliban" camps are reported at various places inside Bajaur, including Salarzai and Dasht.[10] Who these so-called "Taliban" really are will be discussed later in the chapter.

North Waziristan

North Waziristan is administratively divided into three areas—Miranshah, Mir Ali, and Razmak. The "Taliban" control all three. In every part of the agency, they mount daily patrols into town centers, hold summary courts, and settle disputes from rented office spaces. While "Taliban" leader Gul Bahadur runs North Waziristan, Baitullah Mehsud's successor commands three "Taliban" camps. Two are located in Miranshah, and the third in Razmak.[11]

Orakzai

Orakzai tribal agency has been divided into two administrative areas. Lower (southern) Orakzai is largely Shia, but mountainous Upper (northern) Orakzai is dominated by Sunnis and Taliban sympathizers. Just south of Peshawar, Orakzai is of great strategic importance to both sides. Even before Baitullah Mehsud's death, Haikimullah Mehsud was the commander for Orakzai, Kurram, and Khyber agencies. Until being killed himself, he was Baitullah Mehsud's successor and cousin to Qari Hussain, the mastermind behind the training of suicide bombers.[12]

South Waziristan

South Waziristan is the largest of the FATA tribal agencies, with two big Pashtun tribes—the Mehsud and the Wazir. The Waziris have historically settled on both sides of the Pak-Afghan border, whereas the Mehsuds live only in South Waziristan. Until just recently, the Pakistani government had very little control over South Waziristan, with its Army garrison largely restricted to Wana. An Army contingent had to evacuate the Mehsud-dominated area of South Waziristan in 2008 when 300 troops were taken hostage. Most northern parts of South Waziristan were under the direct influence of Baitullah Mehsud's successor—Haikimullah. They contained as many as seven camps where suicide bombers were trained (at Makeen, Shaktoi, Kanigaram, Dela, Kot Kai, Shawwal, and Badar). Another "Taliban" leader Mullah Maulavi Nazir is believed to be running two other training centers at Shikai and Baghar. Many of his followers are based in the northern end of Baluchistan Province, just south of Wana. In October 2009, Pakistani forces moved back into South Waziristan. After four days of fighting, they captured

Kotkai—Haikimullah Mehsud's hometown and probable headquarters for the Mehsud tribe. Qari Hussain, organizer of Taliban suicide squads, is also from Kotkai.[13]

Other Tribal Agencies Targeted by These "Taliban"

The "Taliban" are moving into the Khyber Agency to attack convoys carrying NATO supplies into Afghanistan. They are now in almost total control of two of its three sub-divisions, to include Jamrod and Bara.[14] The "Taliban" are also present in all three sub-divisions of Mohmand Agency. They are under the command of Omar Khalid of the Safi tribe of Pashtuns. He and 5,000 militants have been resisting attempts by security forces to clear them from the southeastern parts of Mohmand.[15]

Lower Dir

The "Taliban" have found many hideouts in Lower Dir. In April 2009, the Pakistani Army acknowledged that the "Taliban" had dug in on the regions's high ground. The biggest mountaintop strongpoint matrix appeared to be in the area of Maidan. That is also the hometown of a radical cleric who brokered the now-defunct Swat "peace deal"—Sufi Mohammad.[16]

Swat

Known as the Switzerland of Pakistan, Swat has been a tourist destination for decades. For a time in the spring of 2009, it came under almost total "Taliban" control when militants targeted security forces, police, secular politicians, and government-run schools. By early April 2009, *sharia* law had been imposed as part of a peace agreement. However, the militants failed to disarm as promised, and an army offensive against them ensued in early May. The main city of Mingora was retaken by government forces later that month. Unfortunately, the "Taliban," under their leader Maulana Fuzlullah, had already extended their control throughout Swat. Many may have now melted away into the northern part of the district where they previously enjoyed almost total control.[17]

Shangla

Shangla is said to be under partial control of the "Taliban." Recent reports speak of militants taking over emerald mines and a possible army operation in the offing. The "Taliban" captured Shangla Top, a strategic point, in early 2008 and have since taken over many police stations in the district. The occupants of those stations had little choice but to run for their lives. Other government buildings in Shangla have since been alternately in and out of "Taliban" control.[18]

Buner

As Buner is only 65 miles from Islamabad, its control would greatly help anyone trying to replace the central government of Pakistan. As soon as the Swat "Taliban" moved into Buner, the Pakistani military decided to put a stop to the ever-deepening incursion. It launched an operation against those so-called Taliban in April 2009.[19]

Other "Taliban-Besieged" NWFP Districts

The Swat River forms the boundary between Malakand district of NWFP and Bajaur agency of FATA. Malakand was where the Pakistani government first offered to replace all civil law with *sharia* to achieve a cease fire with the "Taliban" in February 2009.[20] It soon became clear that this *sharia* deal extended into the Swat District as well.[21] (Refer back to Map 3.1.) As Bajaur abuts Afghanistan's Kunar Valley, one can see why the Swat River Valley constitutes an entrance route for the Afghan Taliban or Hekmatyar into the heart of Pakistan.[22] After leaving Malakand, the Swat River runs through Charsadda and Nowshera Districts before reaching the Indus River.

Though not technically a "Taliban" stronghold, Hangu District was believed to be under the direct control of Haikimullah Mehsud, the right-hand man of (and successor to) "Pakistani Taliban" leader Baitullah Mehsud.[23]

An entire volume could be dedicated to all the militant intrigue that has occurred in the district of Peshawar. Therein are refugee camps, *madrasas,* and recruiters of almost every Pakistani militant organization. As of June 2009, at least 400 vehicles carrying supplies to the NATO forces in Afghanistan had been destroyed in the Peshawar district.[24]

Baitullah Mehsud's fighters from South Waziristan started making incursions into the adjacent NWFP district of Tank in 2005. Their primary targets were the music stores, barbers' shops, and police stations of Tank's main city. Its police initially offered some resistance but have since become more careful. They now mostly stay inside their heavily barricaded police stations. The civil administration is almost completely paralyzed by the threat.[25]

Original Taliban Did Not Participate in "Swat Offensive"

More than one Pakistani faction is actively involved in the Afghan resistance. All seem to be currently allied with Mullah Omar's Afghan Taliban, but not all are actually part of it. Take Hekmatyar's *Hizb-i-Islami Gulbuddin (HIG)* for example. Much of its wherewithal comes from *JI,* whereas that of the Taliban comes from *JUI/F.*[26] *JI* has always wanted Pakistan to become an "Islamic State," whereas *JUI* was willing to let the community of learned men "expand traditional Islamic education, reform the teaching of Islamic law, and promote that law's application in contemporary Muslim society."[27] The difference may be in the degree of power and strictness of law enforcement. *JI* has followed the Egyptian Muslim Brotherhood model, while *JUI/F* prefers the Saudi Wahhabi model.[28]

Not surprisingly, the so-called "Taliban" invasion of Swat District was actually carried out by a radical offshoot of *JI* — namely, *Tehreek-e-Nafaz-e-Shariat-e-Mohammadi (TNSM).*[29] The TNSM was founded by a former leader of *JI* — Sufi Muhammad — in 1992 with the goal of more strictly enforcing *sharia* law. After dispatching thousands of *jihadist* fighters to contest the U.S. invasion of Afghanistan in 2001, *TNSM* was banned by the Pakistani government on 12 January 2002.[30]

The *Tehreek-e-Nafaz-e-Shariat-e-Mohammadi (TNSM)*

TNSM has since been active along the Afghan border in the

Bajaur and Mohmand agencies of FATA (Hekmatyar is extremely popular in the former). With its headquarters in the Maidan region of Low Dir (near the Bajaur Agency boundary),[31] *TNSM* has been progressively expanding its area of operations through Malakand and into Swat District.[32] Often overlooked in the history of Afghanistan, *TNSM* has been recently described as "one of the most dangerous religious militant groups in Pakistan."[33] When its founder was imprisoned in 2002, his son-in-law—Maulana Fazlullah—assumed leadership of the group. That founder—Sufi Muhammad—was released from prison in 2008 after promising nonviolence. He then managed to broker the now-defunct Swat "peace deal."[34] In the aftermath of the 2007 Lal Masjid *madrasa* raid in Islamabad, *al-Jazeera* claims that Fazlullah's forces formed an alliance with Baitullah Mehsud's group. While they are certainly cooperating, there is no evidence of any alliance or merger.[35]

In July 2007, *TNSM* took over much of the Swat District and then held on to it for almost four months. In November, Pakistani forces ousted Maulana Fazlullah and his followers from a large encampment in the village of Imam Dheri. By then, *sharia* law had been authorized and operating in Malakand since 16 February, and in Swat since 13 April.[36] The *TNSM* is not the same as what the media now calls the "Pakistani Taliban." Neither are its links to Mullah Omar as great.

The *Tehrik-i-Taliban (TTP)*

The official name for the Mehsud's "Pakistani Taliban" is the *Tehrik-i-Taliban (TTP)*. The *TTP* had started to take shape in 2002 when Pakistan's military conducted incursions into the tribal areas to combat "foreign militants." Many local veterans of the Afghan fighting took exception to these incursions. In December 2007, the *TTP* officially formed under the leadership of Baitullah Mehsud.[37] On August 25, 2008, the Pakistani government banned it. In late December 2008 and early January 2009, Mullah Omar sent a delegation to persuade the region's most prominent militia leaders to put aside their differences, reduce hostilities with the Pakistani military, and aid the Afghan Taliban in combating the American presence in Afghanistan. Baitullah Mehsud, Hafiz Gul Bahadur, and Maulavi Nazir all agreed to this in February and formed the *Shura Ittehad-ul-Mujahideen (SIM)*. (Notice that *TNSM* chief

45

Maulana Fazlullah was not included.) In a written statement, the three affirmed that they would put aside any differences to fight American-led forces. The statement also included a declaration of allegiance to both Mullah Omar and Osama bin Laden.[38]

Most Aggressive of the *al-Qaeda* Affiliates

LeJ, JEM, and *TNSM* now appear to be the most aggressive of the fundamentalist militias within Pakistan. *LeJ, JEM,* and *LET* are all part of Osama bin Laden's IIF. Though somewhat hard to believe, even *JI*-affiliated *TNSM* is now supposedly part of the Wahhabi IIF. Of the group, only *LET* has avoided attacking Pakistani security forces (possibly because of ISI proxy status). Unlike the others, *LET* additionally harbors no ill will against Shiites. *JEM* is thought to have actively supported *TNSM* in its fight against the government security forces in the Swat Valley.[39]

The Pakistani Military's Latest Moves against *TNSM*

TNSM has been aggressively contesting the Pakistani judicial system in Malakand District since 1994. In April 2001, it demanded that a "true Islamic judicial system" replace the government setup. When it was banned after sending people to defend Afghanistan later that year, things got ugly. Pakistani authorities suspect it was *TNSM* that launched a suicide bombing at Dargai in November 2006 to avenge a U.S. missile strike at Damadola. Forty paramilitary recruits died in that Dargai attack. Maulana Liaquat, a prominent *TNSM* leader, had just been killed during an "aerial" strike claimed by the Pakistani military on a *madrasa* at Chingai village in Bajaur Agency on 30 October 2006. The Pakistani government later stipulated that this particular *madrasa* was being used to train militants.[40]

By early April 2009, *sharia* law had been imposed as part of a deal between the authorities and *TNSM* in Swat. However, the militants failed to disarm completely in line with the accord and their fighters spread to neighboring districts, prompting international consternation. A Pakistani army offensive was launched in Swat District in early May. The main city, Mingora, was retaken later that month.[41]

On 20 July 2009, the Pakistani army attacked the *TNSM's* Maidan headquarters. That assault included five villages— Sherkhanay, Shedas, Misrikhanay, Sangolai, and Saparay—and two mountaintop strongholds (Saparay Top and Point 1260). These locations are near Timergara in Lower Dir District. Though 100 militants were killed, their top leaders—Commander Hafizullah (possibly a *nom de guerre),* Qari Shahid, Dr. Wazir, Muftahuddin and Abdus Salam—all got away.[42]

Maulana Faqir Mohammad is a *TNSM* leader often associated with Bajaur.[43] He must be one in the same with the Agency's supposed "Taliban" commander—Maulvi Faqir Mohammad. That would make *TNSM* the force from the Kunar Valley corridor that tried to envelop Islamabad, and not the *TTP* or Mullah Omar's original Taliban. As the *TNSM* is a *JI* offshoot, one suspects a Hekmatyar connection. Kunar is where Hekmatyar first joined the Afghan resistance in 2004.[44] Since the Soviet-Afghan War, Kunar has also been a favorite hangout for Osama bin Laden.[45] During the 1990's, *al-Qaeda* had a close working relationship with Hekmatyar's Kashmir-oriented militia—*Hezb.*[46] Afghan fighters were seen crossing over into Pakistan from Afghanistan to help with the Swat fighting. They could be from Hekmatyar's Afghan army—*HIG.* Al-Qaeda has long been suspected of being based in Bajaur. According to the *Christian Science Monitor,* Hekmatyar "is also believed to be operating from Pakistani soil in the northern tribal areas."[47] *TNSM and JEM* are among the most active of *al-Qaeda's* current partners.[48] Thus, one minimally suspects the hand of *al-Qaeda* on the envelopment of Islamabad. To the extent that Hekmatyar was also involved, Iran may also have a stake in the outcome.[49] Within Pakistan, there has already been talk of a foreign power being behind the move on its capital through Swat. Unfortunately, Iran is not the nation suspected. Both *TNSM* and *JEM* are supposedly anti-Shia.[50]

Swat's Earlier History Also Suggests an *al-Qaeda* Presence

There have been *TNSM* fighters in the Swat District of NWFP for quite some time. By January 2003, militant groups led by radical cleric Maulana Fazlullah had already started to attack police checkpoints and local residents there. In 59 villages, those militants set up a "parallel government" with Islamic courts that imposed *sharia* law. At the end of a four-month truce in late September

47

2007, fighting with local authorities resumed. The paramilitary Frontier Constabulary was deployed to the area, but was initially ineffective. On 16 November 2007, militants captured the Alpuri sub-district headquarters in neighboring Shangla. Local police fled without resisting a force that included Uzbek, Tajik, and Chechen volunteers.[51]

In late November 2007, Pakistani regulars ejected Maulana Fazlullah's *TNSM* from a base in Imam Dheri (eight kilometers from the Swat Province's main city of Mingora). This base had been established long enough to have its own mosque and *madrasa*. Among the dead defenders of one of its outlying strongpoints were two foreigners (one Uzbek).[52] Later, it was discovered that many more Uzbeks were with *TNSM* at the time. Government troops and government-allied tribesmen drove "*al-Qaeda*-affiliated" Uzbeks out of South Waziristan in 2004 (killing some 300 of them).[53] Ever since that occurred, this region's Uzbeks have been generally associated with *al-Qaeda*.

> The pro-Taliban insurgents broke out of the semi-autonomous FATA in 2007, briefly taking control of the six districts of the normally peaceful Swat Valley before being cleared out by . . . [over] fifteen thousand Pakistani troops. . . . The insurgent fighters consisted mainly of local Taliban, but Pakistani officials as well as locals who fled the area said they were commanded by *several hundred foreign fighters linked to al-Qaeda — mainly Uzbek fighters* (italics added).[54]
> —Associated Press/ABC News reporter, May 2009

President Karzai's military chief of staff (former warlord and CIA operative Dostum) also commands large numbers of Uzbeks.[55] Still, *TNSM* is more likely to have had military advisors from *al-Qaeda* during its envelopment of Islamabad through the Swat Valley.

Then Came the Move on Islamabad from the Southeast

With the possible exception of Benazir Bhutto's assassination, all of Rawalpindi's incidents have looked like random acts of terrorism. Yet, the edge of teeming Rawalpindi is a scant 15 miles from Pakistan's more ordered capital — Islamabad.[56] On 10 October 2009, nine or so terrorists disguised as Pakistani soldiers shot their way through the main gate of Pakistan's National Army Headquarters in Rawalpindi, seizing its security building, taking some 44 people hostage, and only succumbing after a 19-hour siege. *LeJ* was suspected of the atrocity, but Rawalpindi is a long way from *LeJ's* home turf. While generally viewed as a warning by the *TTP* not to renew the offensive in FATA, this attack may have had more far-reaching implications. Only part of FATA is controlled by the *TTP*. The northern part is controlled by *TNSM*.[57]

This Army Headquarters assault is highly reminiscent of the suicide squad attack against Pakistan's Intelligence Agency Headquarters in Lahore on 28 May 2009. That incident was considered to be revenge for the Swat Valley intervention.[58] As the first part of this chapter has demonstrated, the Swat Valley culprit was undeniably *JI*-affiliated *TNSM*.

In mid-October 2009, NPR radio carried another short piece about the Army Headquarters siege in Rawalpindi. It gave two hints as to the assailants' identity, but those hints did not correlate. The attack was supposedly conducted by "Punjabis" with the probable intention of "avenging the death of Baitullah Mehsud."[59] Baitullah Mehsud was head of the Mehsud tribe in South Waziristan.[60] Most of his *TTP* are from that part of FATA. To which residents of Punjab Province did the article refer? There are also some unidentified Punjabis fighting in Afghanistan.[61] Might they be from *JI's* armed wing? *JI* has its headquarters in Mansoora (a suburb of Lahore).[62] That's in Punjab Province.

Because Mullah Omar's Taliban came from *JI*-rival *JUI/F*, no one seems to think that *JI* could be involved with Pakistan's internal struggle. They would be wrong. During the government assault on the Waziristans in 2004, there were *JI* flags flying all along the Afghan border.[63] On 19 June 2009, *JI* chieftain Syed Munawar Hussan told the British Embassy's political councilor Chris Senath and First Secretary George Hudson that "the military operation [against the radicals] was launched on the directives of [the] U.S. government, and it is destabilizing the state."[64] In April 2009 right after being sworn in as fourth Ameer of *JI*, he told his party's members that "the U.S. policies are anti-human and its terrorism has turned the whole world into hell, but we will resist it till the last drop of blood."[65] That means *JI* is also opposed to any government, foreign or domestic, that sides with America. Still, it is highly doubtful that its militia conducted the attack on Army Headquarters.

The Most Likely Culprit at Pakistani Army Headquarters

After the assault on Pakistani Army headquarters in Rawalpindi, BBC News also released series of articles on this subject. While none openly identified the culprit, one implied the Punjabis responsible had done the following: (1) been encouraged by *al-Qaeda;* (2) been reached in the labor pool through *SSP;* (3) been from around Sargodha; and (4) been former members of a government proxy in Afghanistan and Kashmir.[66] There does exist an *SSP* "stronghold" and *LeJ* unit in Sargodha.[67] *SSP* and *LeJ* were sent to Afghanistan by the ISI to help the Taliban in 1996.[68] "After the collapse of the Najibullah government in Kabul in April 1992, the Pakistani military-intelligence establishment did shift its Army of Islam to Jammu and Kashmir."[69] Of all the militant groups in Punjab Province, *LeJ* is also the most probable surrogate of *al-Qaeda.* It is known to receive much of its funding from Saudi Arabian "benefactors."[70]

Another of the BBC articles stated that the "Taliban" had attributed the Rawalpindi Army Headquarters attack to one of its own Punjabi factions. It named the Taliban spokesman as "Azam Tariq." Azam Tariq just happens to be the founder of *SSP.*[71] Thus, *SSP's* militia—the *LeJ*—would seem to be the most likely attacker of Army Headquarters. *LeJ* has also been named the culprit by more than one Pakistani newspaper.[72] A faction calling itself the Amjad Farooqi Group took credit for the attack, demanding an end to military operations against the Taliban.

> The Amjad Farooqi Group is . . . a mish-mash of Pakistani jihadi groups from all regions of the country. . . While the Amjad Farooqi Group is largely made up of members from the Harkat-ul-Jihad-Al-Islami [not the same as HUJI], members from the Taliban, the Lashkar-e-Jhangvi [LEJ], the Lashkar-e-Taiba [LET], and other groups can be called on to fill out the ranks.[73]
> — *Long War Journal,* 10 October 2009

Fedayeen-e-Islam Has Taken Much of the Other Credit

After a ground assault by 25 terrorists on Lahore's Police Training Center in March 2009, *Fedayeen-e-Islam* said it had launched the attack to keep federal forces out of South Waziristan. Like the Amjad Farooqi Group, *Fedayeen-e-Islam* appears to be in the *JUI/F* camp.

The *Fedayeen-e-Islam* is believed to be comprised of members of the *Jaish-e-Mohammad [JEM]* . . . a banned terror group that operates in South Waziristan. The *Fedayeen-e-Islam* has direct links to . . . Baitullah Mehsud as well as to *al-Qaeda*. The *Fedayeen-e-Islam* claimed it carried out the devastating Marriott Hotel suicide attack [in Islamabad] in September 2008. . . .

The *Jaish-e-Mohammed* was implicated along with the *Lashkar-e-Taiba [LET]* as being behind the Dec. 13, 2001, military assault on the Indian Parliament building in New Delhi.[74]

— *Long War Journal,* 30 March 2009

As the Pakistani Army's Waziristan Offensive Started

In October 2009, Pakistani forces went in after the 1,000 to 2,000 *al-Qaeda*-linked Uzbeks still thought to be in South Waziristan.[75] Expecting also to meet resistance from the *TTP* of Haikimullah Mehsud, it struck deals with his closest allies to keep them out of the fight—namely, Maulvi Nazir and Hafiz Gul Bahadur.[76] It is Bahadur who controls North Waziristan.[77] Nazir is based south of Wana.[78] This deal must have come as quite a shock to Haikimullah. His predecessor had agreed with Bahadur and Nazir in February 2009 to form the *SIM* to help Mullah Omar and Osama bin Laden defeat the Americans.[79]

Right after the government offensive into South Waziristan kicked off, an Army Brigadier and his driver were gunned down inside Islamabad.[80] Then, on 2 November 2009, a suicide bomber attacked a queue of people waiting to cash pay checks at a Rawalpindi bank. Among the dead were nearly 30 soldiers from the nearby Pakistani Army Headquarters.[81] On 4 December, six militants struck the mosque near military headquarters in Rawalpindi. They threw grenades and opened fire, killing 27 civilians and nine soldiers, one a major general and another a brigadier.[82]

As the terrorist events near Islamabad were interspersed with some in Lahore, not everyone concluded that the Pakistani capital was again under attack. Considering the number of terrorist outfits based in and around Lahore, that city would also make a good place for a diversion.

Southeastern Pincer on Islamabad May Come from Lahore

In mid-March 2010, after a relative lull in Pakistani city attacks, there were two major bombings in Lahore over a span of five days. The first came against the government's "Special Investigation Agency" and was claimed by the "Pakistani Taliban." The second was directed at Army patrols.[83] One possible explanation was that Pakistani authorities had been homing in on the Punjabi Taliban, and the Punjabi Taliban didn't like it. *JI* has its headquarters in a Lahore suburb.[84] *LET* has its Murdikhe training center in a vast *JuD*-controlled area just north of Lahore.[85] That makes Lahore the perfect "headquarters" for the Punjabi Taliban. With an *LeJ* unit already stationed there,[86] it could have easily arranged for *LeJ* attacks on Rawalpindi and Islamabad.

The Bottom Line

On 11 February 2010, Haikimullah Mehsud had succumbed to wounds he incurred in a January drone attack.[87] Thus, not only South Waziristan, but also Orakzai, Kurram, and Khyber agencies were temporarily without a *TTP* leader.[88] As have the assassinations of many claimants to the title of "top *al-Qaeda* operations officer," Haikimullah's death will make little difference to a "bottom-up" insurgency. Sadly, Western generals may never see how nonessential their Eastern counterparts are to an overall war effort.

This chapter has shown factions other than the *TTP* to be more involved with the double-envelopment of Islamabad. Many have been virtually ignored by the latest government offensive. One can only wonder how much influence *al-Qaeda* really has over the proceedings.

4

Al-Qaeda's Hidden Influence

- Why isn't *al-Qaeda* more in the news?
- Can *al-Qaeda* operate through other-sect infrastructures?

Arabs are hard to distinguish from Pakistani tribesmen.

(Source: DA PAM 550-21 [January, 1985], p. 459; DA PAM 550-25 [December, 1988], chapt. 4)

Al-Qaeda's Continuing Influence on the Region

By every indication, it was *al-Qaeda* behind the militant move on Pakistan's capital through the Swat and Buner Districts of NWFP in the Spring of 2009. In July 2009, *al-Qaeda's* second in command menacingly told the Pakistani people that they must back Islamic militants to counter the influence of the United States on their own country.[1]

> I believe that every . . . Muslim in Pakistan should seriously contemplate . . . Pakistan's present state and expected fu-

53

ture, because the blatant American crusader interference in Pakistan's affairs . . . has reached such an extent that it now poses a grave danger to Pakistan's future and very existence.[2]
— Ayman al-Zawahiri, July 2009

According to a U.S. Congressional study, Hekmatyar's *HIG* is only an *al-Qaeda* "affiliate," whereas *HUM, JEM* (a *HUM* offshoot), *LET,* and *LeJ* are all *al-Qaeda* "partners." That study goes on to say that *"al-Qaeda* has always been more a coalition of groups than a unified structure."[3] As U.S. pressure has mounted, *al-Qaeda* may have reverted to its former umbrella status in which allied factions conduct all operations. Prior to 2001, it primarily worked through the infrastructure of *HUM, LET, LeJ,* and *SSP (LeJ's* parent).[4] As *al-Qaeda* changes from an organization back into a "movement," killing its "purported leaders" will do less good. That's because movements tend to offer more support (e.g., training and funding) than operational direction. The only trace of *al-Qaeda's* contemporary influence would then be in the form of "Saudi money from undisclosed sources" and "tiny contingents of foreign trainers."

The Lashkar-e-Jhangvi (LEJ), the militant wing of the anti-Shia Sipah-e-Sahaba Pakistan (SSP), is emerging as the new Trojan Horse of Al Qaeda to carry out operations on behalf of Al Qaeda. . . .
In the past, this role was being performed by the Lashkar-e-Toiba (LET). Both the LET and the LEJ are members of Osama bin Laden's International Islamic Front (IIF) for Jihad Against the Crusaders and the Jewish People. Both are strongly Wahhabi organizations, but whereas the LEJ is strongly anti-U.S., anti-Israel, anti-India, anti-Iran and anti-Shia, the LET is only anti-U.S., anti-Israel and anti-India, but not anti-Iran or anti-Shia.[5]
— South Asia Analysis Group, November 2007

As for the Reports of *al-Qaeda* Training Bases in Pakistan

In July 2009, Associated Press (AP) carried a story about an American who claimed to have been recently trained at *"al-Qaeda* camps" in Pakistan.[6] There may be *al-Qaeda* cells or even an *al-Qaeda* headquarters detachment in the Waziristans, but a full-fledged training base exclusively run by *al-Qaeda* personnel is hard to believe. Yet, the possibility still exists. When the Pakistani military moved into the Waziristans in early 2004, they encountered fierce resistance from forces that included Arabs, Uzbeks, Chechens, and Uighurs.[7] At that time, Pakistani officials claimed 400-500 *al-Qaeda* militants were involved in the fighting, and that they had recruited and trained some 2,500 local tribesmen who the locals were calling "The Men of al-Qaida."[8] In October 2009, the Pakistani military went again into South Waziristan after a group of "al-*Qaeda*-linked Uzbek militants." It was also prepared to deal with any local *al-Qaeda* backers—most notably the *TTP* of Baitullah Mehsud's successor, Haikimullah Mehsud.[9] During the previous assault on South Waziristan, the Islamic Movement of Uzbekistan (IMU) was thought to be providing security for Osama bin Laden.[10] It is certainly possible that some semblance of *al-Qaeda* headquarters or training facility has now returned to the region.

> The report [July 2007 National Intelligence Estimate] assessed that the organization *[al-Qaeda]* was regrouping and regaining strength in Pakistan's tribal areas along the border with Afghanistan. . . .
> Rohan Gunaratna of the International Centre for Political Violence and Terrorism Research in Singapore says bin Laden's group is training most of the terrorist groups in Pakistan's tribal areas. "Al-Qaeda considers itself as the vanguard of the Islamic movement," Gunaratna says, and it has introduced its practice of suicide bombings to both the Afghan and the Pakistani Taliban.[11]
> — Council on Foreign Relations, April 2008

There is no telling how much instruction *al-Qaeda* now personally provides to Pakistani citizens. However, during the Soviet-Afghan War, most of its training on Pakistani soil was not done at *al-Qaeda* bases *per se,* but rather at religious-party facilities with a few visiting *al-Qaeda* instructors. *HUM, JEM, LET,* and *Hezb* all had their own military training camps along the Afghan border.[12] In 2001, there was a *JEM* facility at Balakot in FATA.[13] By 2003, only the *HUM* camps were officially recognized as still being in existence.[14] Yet, *al-Qaeda* has at times shared its instructors with

LET and *HUJI* camps.[15] That is what more probably happens today. *Al-Qaeda* would then have instructors at, and provide funding to, some of the religious-party (militant-wing) training bases mentioned in Chapter 2. That the repatriated American was being trained in suicide bombing is implicit evidence of an *al-Qaeda* instructor.[16] Suicide bombing was totally unknown to Afghanistan before legendary Northern Alliance leader—Massoud—was killed a few days before 9/11.[17] Now suicide bombings happen all the time in both Afghanistan and Pakistan. This unfortunate development has undoubtedly sprung from the Salafist cooperation between *al-Qaeda* and Lebanese *Hezbollah.*[18]

What Pakistan Must Now Do about the Threat

The new president of Pakistan is more genuinely supportive of Western interests than was the last. However, Pakistan's government is still not completely free of Islamist or corrupt factions. Because Mr. Zardari's now assassinated wife was a veritable saint, he may finally be persuaded to remove all hidden support for *al-Qaeda* from his beleaguered country. To do so, he must first gain total control over the largely autonomous and heavily Islamized ISI. Then the following would be appropriate: (1) keeping *LET* banned this time;[19] (2) countering all Wahhabi and Saudi influences on Pakistani soil (to include monetary donations); (3) closing all military training facilities of *HUM, JEM, HUJI, HMA, LET, LeJ,* and *TNSM*; (4) closing all *madrasas* run by *JUI/F, JuD, SSP, Jamiat Ahle Hadith,* and *JI*. *JUI/F, JI,* and *Jamiat Ahle Hadith* are still legal as political parties within Pakistan, so their offices must be allowed to remain open. However, all such offices must be monitored for the recruiting and training of militant wing fighters. Additionally, the *LET, HUJI, JEM,* or *SSP* offices must be permanently closed. For some reason, *SSP* did not seem to be on the list of radical organizations banned in August 2009.[20] Though previously banned, *SSP* has somehow managed to maintain 500 branch offices in Punjab Province alone.[21] While this little anomaly may not mean much, it still evokes memories of *LET*'s "watch list" interlude and the possible reasons for it (like ISI proxy status). That *SSP* and its militant wing *LeJ* both receive significant funding from Saudi Arabia does little to quell those fears.[22]

Reports of a "Shadow Army"

Al-Qaeda has reportedly now reformed Brigade 055 (that helped to maintain the Taliban regime in Afghanistan) as part of its new *Lashkar al Zil* or "Shadow Army." Elements of that army are most easily identified by their appearance. They wear masks, new clothes (possibly black with pant legs ending six inches above the ground), sneakers, and web gear. Some were spotted in the NWFP District of Swat when it was still under "Taliban" control. Within Afghanistan, the Haqqani Network may be also involved with the Shadow Army.[23]

Originally, Brigade 055 was made up of fighters from *HUM, JEM, LET,* and other religious-party factions (presumably *JUI/F* affiliated).[24] As *Hizb-i-Islami* has also been spotted on joint operations with this new Shadow Army,[25] Hekmatyar may be contributing to another of its brigades. (See Figure 4.1.)

A Hidden Mentor Appears in the U.N.

Al-Qaeda's persistence in the region may not be wholly due to religious preference and Saudi money. The PRC has, on more than one occasion, been caught providing help to *al-Qaeda.* Below are two of the most credible examples:

> DEBKAfile was the first publication to reveal that China had sent thousands of armed men into Afghanistan in support of Osama bin Laden and the Taliban. . . .
> Follow-ups, verified by other media, appeared on October 20 and November 15. In the first, we reported 15 Chinese fighters found dead in Kandahar. They were part of an escort convoy for one of bin Laden's senior lieutenants, Basir al-Masri, commander of the Arab contingents in Jalalabad, which came under U.S. bombing as it left Kandahar. . . .
> Now comes the CNN report, which confirms that Beijing sent to bin Laden, not only men but also quantities of weapons.[26]
> — Israeli Intel. Periodical, 17 December 2001

U.S. intelligence agencies stated in classified reports last year that China continued to supply arms to al-Qaeda ter-

rorists after the September 11 attacks. A week after the attacks, Beijing supplied a shipment of Chinese-made SA-7 shoulder-fired missiles to Osama bin Laden's terror network, according to senior U.S. officials.[27]
— *Washington Times,* 12 April 2002

In July 2009, India introduced a proposal to sanction *JEM* chieftain Maulana Masood Azhar under the "Al Qaida and Taliban Sanctions" Resolution 1267 in the United Nations. The Peoples Republic of China put a hold on that proposal, forcing India to muster more diplomatic support.[28] One would think that the world's next superpower would have better things to do with its time. Still, *JEM* is often called the Pakistani representative in *al-Qaeda's* worldwide network.[29]

Figure 4.1: Arab Trainer
(Source: Courtesy of Michael Leahy, © 2005)

5 The Drug Barons

- To what extent have drugs corrupted the Karzai regime?
- Which international cartels distribute the Afghan drugs?

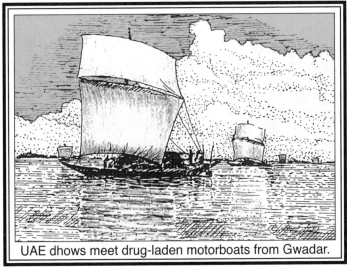

UAE dhows meet drug-laden motorboats from Gwadar.

(Source: DA PAM 550-175 [September, 1988], cover)

The "Golden Crescent's" Opium Heritage

Throughout recorded history, opium-producing poppies have flourished in the inverted crescent formed by Afghanistan, Pakistan, and Iran. They may have been introduced to the region by Alexander the Great around 330 B.C. During most of the 20th Century, both the Afghan and Pakistani opium harvests were sent to Iran for further export, with Afghanistan's ruling family controlling much of that trade. When Afghan King Zahir Shah was overthrown in 1973, the Pakistani tribal areas became the region's biggest producer of opiates. By the time the Soviets' occupied Afghanistan in 1979, the Pashtun tribes in Pakistani FATA were growing more poppy than all of their Afghan cousins put together. The product of their illicit endeavors was trucked down to Karachi for further shipment. Soon, that city's Pashtun waterfront slum of Sohrab Goth contained immense underground bunkers of the stuff.[1]

Then, as the West came to Afghanistan's assistance, its poppy equation began to change. By the end of the Soviet-Afghan War, the head of the Drug Enforcement Administration (DEA) was telling the U.S. Senate Intelligence Committee that drug labs along Afghanistan's southern border were producing more than half the heroin sold on U.S. streets. Whether or not that quantification was absolutely correct, the announcement implied something very interesting. It meant that the heroin conduit through Baluchistan eventually led to the United States. (See Map 5.1.) About that same time, a CIA assessment confirmed the following: (1) 11 "one-ton" heroin storage vaults in the Sohrab Goth neighborhood of Karachi; (2) three tons of heroin awaiting shipment to the U.S. or Western Europe at any give time from that city; and (3) the heroin heading westward by boat.[2] Why then, do most Americans still believe that all Asian heroin comes to their country from the "Golden Triangle" of Burma and Laos?

For the last 30 years, Iran has professed to be blocking the overland portion of that Baluchistan conduit. Yet, as a revolutionary theocracy opposed to almost every Western influence, its claims are suspect. *Hezbollah*—the Lebanese offspring of the Iranian Revolutionary Guard—has long supported itself through drug trafficking.[3]

Al-Qaeda's Links to This South Asian Drug Trade

Through Western aid in the 1990's, Pakistan was able to reduce its drug addiction problem. It did so through poppy crop substitution. At that point, Pakistan became more of a trans-shipment point for Afghan opiates than its own source of supply. The dope generally followed the same transportation networks out that—a decade earlier—had funneled war supplies in to the *mujahideen*. Although the poppy fields and processing labs had since moved across the border into Afghanistan, their command and control remained in Pakistan.

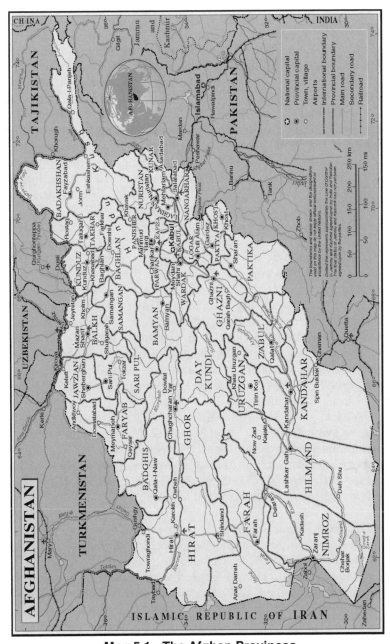

Map 5.1: The Afghan Provinces
(Source: Courtesy of the United Nations, Department of Peacekeeping, Cartographic Section, Map No. 3958, Rev. 5, October 2005, © n.d.)

Most of the drugs now coming out of Afghanistan still move southward into Baluchistan. They appear to fund only the Taliban, and not *al-Qaeda.* Since the mid-1990's, the Taliban's principal contact in this regard has been the "Quetta Alliance." In fact, a joint U.S. Intelligence report has described the Quetta Alliance as being the "dominant [drug] trafficking organization in Southwest Asia." (Whether that is entirely true has yet to be determined.) Not surprisingly, the Taliban's top military council and central ruling *Shura* also reside in Quetta. Openly presiding over them until the late summer of 2009 was Mullah Abdul Ghani Baradar. (He was finally arrested in Karachi in mid-February 2010.) According to *Newsweek,* "he controls the Taliban's treasury." For all practical purposes, he also functions as Mullah Omar's chief of staff.[4] All the while, the Taliban's overall commander (Omar) was still in hiding.

Historically, there has also been a northern drug conduit out of Afghanistan. While traditionally destined for Europe, some of its contraband now ends up in Russia. Herein is a warning for any who might want to occupy the place. This northern conduit has carried product from the fields and labs of former Northern Alliance chieftain Abdul Rashid Dostum, among others. After the U.S. invasion, Dostum became President Karzai's Deputy Defense Minister. Until 2004, he controlled Balkh, Jowzjan, Sar-e Pul, Samangan, and Faryab Provinces with a large Uzbek militia. That militia has now been partially disarmed and Dostum relegated to running his new political party, *Junbish-i-Milli,* from Kabul. However, he still holds the symbolic post of "chief of staff to the commander in chief" and remains a disturbing presence.[5] Perhaps it's only a coincidence that Uzbek rebels from the former Soviet Republics are now deeply involved with running the northern conduit. To what degree this involvement funds *al-Qaeda* is not known.

The 9/11 Commission later concluded that donations from rich Arabs and Muslim charities contributed the bulk of al-Qaeda's funding. "We have seen no substantial evidence," the panel added, "that al-Qaeda played a major role in the drug trade or relied on it as an important source of revenue either before or after 9/11." To this day, there's no smoking gun to prove bin Laden's link to the opium trade, officials say. . . . However, there is widespread evidence Uzbek insurgents linked to al-Qaeda are heavily tied to drug smuggling

and control as much as 70 percent of the multibillion-dollar heroin and opium trade [to the north of Afghanistan] through Central Asia [Rashid, Jihad, 165; Catseel, "Narco-Terrorism"; Makarenko, "Central Asia's Opium Terrorists."] [6]
—Associated Press/ABC News reporter, May 2009

The above mentioned Uzbeks are, of course, one and the same with the Islamic Movement of Uzbekistan (IMU). After first forming in the 1990's where Uzbekistan, Tajikistan, and Kyrgzstan converge, the IMU has established a network of fighters throughout those former republics, northern Afghanistan, and Pakistan's tribal areas. As such, they have long been associated with *al-Qaeda*. It was an IMU contingent that was forced by local tribesmen and Pakistani troops to leave South Waziristan in 2004 after presumably providing bin Laden's outer-security perimeter.[7] It was also IMU fighters who in 2008 accompanied *TNSM* on its Swat Valley envelopment of Islamabad.

Pakistani officials say that Uzbek fighters have numbered among those captured and killed in the government's offensive to retake the Swat Valley. One Pakistani newspaper claims that local Taliban forces include up to 4,000 foreign fighters, most of them members of the Islamic Movement of Uzbekistan (IMU).[8]
— *The Economist,* 11 June 2009

It would certainly appear, then, that the two biggest narcotics conduits out of Afghanistan are being run by separate organized crime factions, each having its own insurgent force as protection. One has to wonder who fills those roles on the smaller exits to the east and west. On the Eastern leg, Hekmatyar must somehow be involved.

Afghanistan's Traditional Drug Routes

Narcotics trafficking and its resultant corruption are nothing new to Afghanistan. Besides northern drug routes through Turkmenistan and Tajikistan,[9] there are three smuggling conduits through southwestern Afghanistan. (See Maps 5.2 through 5.5.) One goes directly into Iran from Nimroz and Farah Provinces. As late as 2004, the desert highway between Baramcha and the tri-border area of Rabat-e-Jali was a notorious gateway for smugglers. Another route dips down from Helmand into Pakistan's Baluchistan Province before heading west into Iran and eventually Turkey. Near the end of the Soviet occupation, Stinger-protected convoys regularly ran this passage under the joint auspices of the Iranian Revolutionary Guards and rogue elements of the Pakistani government. A third smuggling conduit goes by truck to Pakistan's Makran Coast and then by ship to the Persian Gulf. Powerful motorboats leave Gwadar to rendezvous with larger dhows in the Arabian Sea. Speedboats also make the crossing between Qasm, Iran, and Por Sha'am, United Arab Emirates (UAE).[10]

Much of the region's opium growing and heroin manufacture has now shifted into Afghanistan. But back in 1984, 70 percent of the world's supply of high-grade heroin was either produced in, or

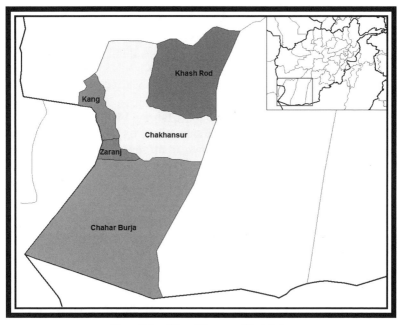

Map 5.2: The Nimroz Districts
(Source: Wikipedia.org, s.v. "Nimroz," under provisions of GNU Free Documentation License, map designator "Nimroz_districts.png")

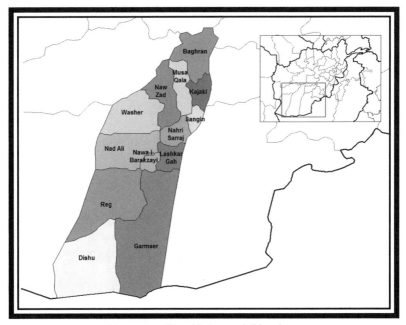

Map 5.3: The Helmand Districts

(Source: Wikipedia.org, s.v. "Helmand," under provisions of GNU Free Documentation License, map designator "Helmand_districts.png")

smuggled through, Pakistan. Its most controversial conduit ran from NWFP to the port city of Karachi. Trucks brought heroin out and war supplies in (for the Afghan resistance). Two *mujahideen* leaders—Gulbuddin Hekmatyar and Mawlawi Jalaluddin Haqqani—had already turned to drugs for additional funding.[11] Behind the trucking scheme were rogue elements of the Pakistani military. The amount of corruption within Pakistan's government was so high at the time that an embedded heroin syndicate seemed likely.[12]

Then, there were the more northern mountainous crossings between Afghanistan and Pakistan that are still used for narcotics smuggling today. Not all are tiny and obscure—e.g., the major highway across the Khyber Pass. The Soviets never successfully interdicted *mujahideen* resupply routes into Afghanistan. Very possibly, that means two things: (1) those resupply routes were one

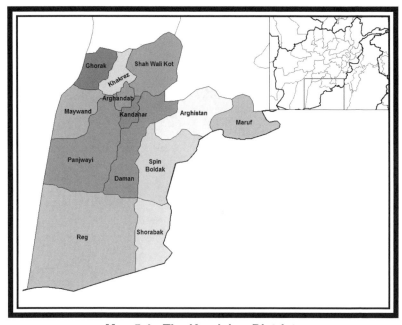

Map 5.4: The Kandahar Districts
(Source: Wikipedia.org, s.v. "Kandahar," under provisions of GNU Free Documentation License, map designator "Kandahar_districts.png")

in the same with the biggest drug-smuggling routes; and (2) much of the *mujahideen's* ordnance was being smuggled "in composite pieces" over public roads as opposed to being mule-packed "in tact" along hidden trails. Please note the similarity in location between the above-mentioned drug routes and the known resupply routes on Map 5.5.

Haqqani and Hekmatyar still command insurgent forces in the vicinity of the Khyber Pass. The former operates a series of camps in the border districts of Paktiya Province, from which he moves drugs eastward into Pakistan. Many of those drugs have come to him from Hekmatyar areas to his north and labs in Nangarhar Province. Neither war lord personally takes part in the smuggling to maintain some measure of deniability.[13]

Past Attempts to Monopolize the Afghan Drug Trade

During the Soviet-Afghan War, Hekmatyar was the ISI's favorite in its coalition of seven *mujahideen* leaders. That's why he routinely got more than his share of military aid from the West. At the time, Mullah Nasim Akhundzada was the most powerful war lord in Helmand Province and already harvesting opium to help fund the fight against the Russians.[14] (Refer back to Map 5.3.) Then, for control of Helmand's poppy fields, Hekmatyar launched a two-year internal war against Akhundzada.[15] By the end of the Soviet occupation, Hekmatyar had a series of heroin labs along the Afghan border and was tied in with Pakistani smuggling networks.[16] He next became the ISI's principal instrument for determining the future of post-occupation Afghanistan. After the interim government collapsed in 1992, rival militias began to vie with each other for supremacy. In 1993, those factions agreed upon a coalition government with ethnic Tajik and *mujahideen* hero Rabbani in charge. By 1994, the ISI had grown tired of waiting for Hekmatyar to overthrow Rabbani's regime in Kabul. So, it created the Taliban (Pashto for "students"). It did so by arranging for hundreds (if not thousands) of *JUI / F madrasa* graduates from Quetta to join *mujahideen* leader Mullah Omar in Kandahar.[17] (Refer back to Map 5.4.) When those Taliban contingents first moved across the Afghan border, they were contested by Hekmatyar's militia.[18] Their direction of attack coincided with their southern origins, but just as many "students" could have come into Afghanistan from Peshawar's refugee camps to the east. Clearly, Hekmatyar was being stripped of his greatest heroin assets. And, because the *JUI / F* was opposed to drug use, the ISI may have also been shifting to a different proxy to reduce Afghan heroin production. In 1996, it reinforced the Taliban with thousands of radical *LeJ* (from *SSP), LET* (from *JuD)*, and *HUM* (from *JUI / F)* so that Kabul could finally be captured. At that point, Rabbani escaped to fight with the Northern Alliance.[19] While the Taliban did eventually ban poppy cultivation in 2000,[20] it would soon justify opium harvesting as a way to weaken its new adversary—NATO and the West.

The Largest Afghan Stashes

After the ban on poppies, Western observers noticed that the

Taliban made no attempt to seize drug stocks or arrest traffickers. In fact, it continued to tax the trade in opium, enjoying higher revenues as its price increased.[21] Then, key Taliban officials began to hoard huge quantities of opiates as a hedge against any shortage. Among those suspected of such hordes were Haji Bashir Noorzai and Mullah Omar. As the tribal leader and drug kingpin whom the Taliban made "mayor of Kandahar" during their December 2001 departure, Noorzai is now in U.S. prison. Like Baradar before his 2010 capture, Noorzai may have been the Taliban's banker.[22] Overall Taliban leader Omar is also rumored to have 3,800 tons of opium buried somewhere outside Kandahar. Counternarcotics officials believe other Taliban leaders have similar stashes that together function as a type of "federal reserve."[23]

Omar's Regional Commanders Also Deal in Drugs

While Hekmatyar's army is not technically part of the Taliban, it still participates in the Afghan resistance. Neither is Haqqani from the original Taliban. A member of *JI*-supported *Hizb-i-Islami*, he defected to the Taliban in 1996.[24] In 2003, Mullah Omar asked Hekmatyar to lead the eastern flank of the resistance from the mountainous provinces of Kunar and Nuristan. At the same time, he directed Haqqani to control the southeastern region from a rear-area headquarters in North Waziristan.[25] He still does so, though his son Sirajuddin Haqqani has now assumed many of the same responsibilities.

Today, Hekmatyar's *HIG* constitutes a full-fledged narco-terrorist organization.[26] Its commanders are said to have massive schemes to smuggle timber, gemstones, and heroin out of their respective areas of operation. Because the Afghan Province of Kunar abuts the FATA agency of Bajaur (a suspected hideout of al-Zawahiri), Hekmatyar is believed to have links to *al-Qaeda*. In truth, Hekmatyar has links to almost everyone, including the Iranians.[27]

Haqqani operates in the Afghan border region to the south of Hekmatyar. His Paktiya Province camps now include Jaji and neighboring Dand Wa Patan. During the Soviet Afghan War, he frequented Miram Shah (the capital of North Waziristan). (See Maps 5.5.) In addition to Paktiya Province, he currently operates in Khost and Paktika provinces.[28] Because the latter abut the loosely administered Waziristans, he can smuggle some of Hekmatyar's product along with his own. Fully to appreciate Haqqani's mixed affiliations, one must consider his background. Between the Afghan border provinces of Kunar and Paktiya lies Nangarhar. Poppies have been grown there for centuries. It is where another of the original seven *mujahideen* leaders became interested in drugs. His name was Mawlawi Mohammad Yunis Khalis. Along the Afghan border during the Soviet-Afghan War, he operated several of his own heroin labs (at least seven at Ribat al Ali) and smuggling conduits. As one of the four "fundamentalist" chieftains (like Hekmatyar and Rabbani), Khalis formed an Afghan offshoot of Hekmatyar-controlled and Pakistan-based *Hezb i-Islami (HI,* a forerunner of *Hezb).*[29] At the end of the Soviet occupation, Khalis and Rabbani had the closest ties to Iran. (It was Khalis who was to sell Stinger missiles to the Iranian Revolutionary Guards.[30]) Hekmatyar's affiliation with Iran only became apparent later. (He was to help the Rabbani government and Iranian-backed Northern Alliance resist the Taliban takeover of Kabul in 1996.[31]) When *HI* subdivided, Haqqani followed the Khalis instead of Hekmatyar to later become one of *HIK's* best field commanders.[32]

Hekmatyar and Haqqani Have Great Influence in Pakistan

Hekmatyar is Pakistani. Both of his paramilitary extensions—*Hezb* in Pakistan and *HIG* in Afghanistan—are supported by *JI. TNSM* is a radical offshoot of *JI.* Thus, there is a good chance that *HIG* and *TNSM* having been sharing resources across the northern part of border in support of *al-Qaeda* or some other player. Hekmatyar has known ties to Iran. In this part of the world, ties to Iran and *al-Qaeda* need not be mutually exclusive. The above-mentioned player may even be a political party or drug syndicate. From the Bajaur Tribal Agency, *Hezb* now takes the narcotics south to Karachi.[33]

Jalaluddin Haqqani is Afghan by birth but has spent considerable time in North Waziristan in pursuit of his drug trafficking agenda. As such, he has developed many Pakistani connections. In fact, he has become so influential in Pakistan that some reports have Baitullah Mehsud's *TTP* cooperating with him. From the Waziristans, it is the *JUI/F*-aligned *JEM* that transports drugs south to Karachi.[34]

The Taliban's Former Drug Manager

Haji Bashir Noorzai is generally thought to have been the overseer of much of the Afghan drug trade. He was found guilty in the fall of 2008 of conspiring to smuggle millions of dollars worth of heroin into the United States. The Bush Administration has called this Afghan tribal leader the "Pablo Escobar of heroin trafficking in Asia" and "one of the world's most-wanted narcotics dealers." Why, then, haven't the details of this chronic flow of Southwest Asian heroin into the U.S. been more fully reported? In the last few years, the agency "drug threat assessments" have only loosely described a Southeast Asian conduit. So, Karzai may not be the only one turning a blind eye to the problem. According to a 2004 U.S. intelligence report, Mr. Noorzai maintained 18 drug refineries in Registan alone. (Refer back to Map 5.3.) He also provided explosives, weapons, and militia to the Taliban in exchange for protection of his poppy fields, opium laboratories, and transportation routes.[35]

Who Used to Be in the Quetta Alliance?

Haji Bashir Noorzai's father, Issa, was a leading member of the Quetta Alliance in the mid 1990's according to a declassified DEA (Drug Enforcement Administration) document. While there are some indications of a tribal coalition, that same document indicates the Quetta Alliance was the union of "three interrelated heroin and hashish smuggling groups" that regularly exported "multi-ton shipments of heroin and morphine base." Another alleged member of the Quetta Alliance was "Sakhi Jan" Dost Notezai. Today, his son—Amanullah Notezai—is a provincial minister in the government of Baluchistan.[36]

The Current Pakistani Connection

In May 2009, Associated Press and American Broadcasting Company (ABC) News correspondent Gretchen Peters made a tremendous contribution to the overall conduct of the Afghan War. Much of this chapter has been derived from her book *Seeds of Terror*.[37] Among other things, it shows most events in Afghanistan to

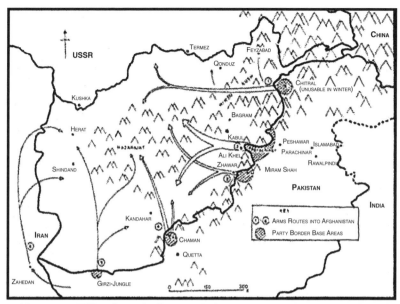

Map 5.5: "War Supply Routes In" Were "Heroin Routes Out"
(Source: Bear Trap, by Brigadier Mohammad Yousaf and Maj. Mark Adkin, © n.d. by Leo Cooper)

be now more about dope than insurgency. If not quickly abated, that dope could cause the Pakistani government to fail, and the U.S. criminal justice system to become ruinously overloaded.

As of early 2008, the Quetta Alliance was still firmly in control of the narcotics' flow out of southern Afghanistan.[38] Its current members are hard to identify. One person was either a prominent member or successful challenger before being just recently jailed— Haji Kuma Khan. His authority came to rival that of Noorzai at the end of the Taliban regime. He may have been number three in that hierarchy.[39] Until his apprehension in October 2008, Khan maintained one of many residences in Quetta and ran a drug empire that moved as much as $1 billion worth of opium and heroin a year in support of the Taliban.[40] According to a senior Afghan police official, he did not work for the Taliban or *al-Qaeda*. Instead, they worked for him.[41]

Khan was from the Brahui people who inhabit the desolate tri-border area (where Pakistan, Afghanistan, and Iran all meet).

71

Here drug smuggling is a common livelihood.[42] Khan was behind the vehicle convoys from Nimroz into Iran and boat shipments from Karachi to the UAE.[43]

Khan also ran a massive opium refinery and maintained huge underground storage depots in Baramacha, the dusty smugglers' town straddling the border between Helmand and Baluchistan.[44] When Baramacha was attacked by Pakistani forces, he created refineries and stashes in the remote Chahar Borjak district of southern Nimroz and along the mountainous border with Iran. Then, he developed mobile labs that could function out of Toyota trucks or private homes. At the Girdi Jungle refugee camp on the border of Baluchistan, he is said to have had more underground bunkers for the storage of opium.[45] (Refer back to Map 5.5.) He maintained a personal force of 1500 men who were known locally as Taliban. He also funded a large *madrasa* in Pakistan from which he drew militia replacements.[46] His fighters were not there just for show. One British Special Air Service (SAS) commander said that, whenever a lab was raided in the Deshu area of Baramcha, the resulting ambush would require NATO airstrikes.[47]

However, Khan's real strength appears to have come from his ability to build networks and corrupt officials. In Afghanistan, his many networks extended to provincial governors, security agents, regional military commanders, senior members of the Highway Police, and even to the President's inner circle.[48] Khan also played a key role in supplying the Taliban with Iranian made Improvised Explosive Devices (IEDs) and shape charges in 2007.[49]

Karzai's Reluctance to Contest the Drug Traffickers

President Karzai came to power as an appointee of the Bush Administration and leader of a Northern Alliance coalition. He was then "prompted" by defense issues and U.S. time lines to leave various war lords in place as provincial governors.[50] Others, he added to his cabinet. Many had drug connections. Since that time, Ismail Khan and Abdul Rashid Dostum have both been relieved of their official control over the Herat and Mazar-e-Shariff regions. Mohammad Qasim Fahim, (successor to Ahmad Shah Massoud as head of the Northern Alliance), has been relieved as Defense Secretary.[51] Hazrat Ali was in charge of Nangarhar Province, but now only has a seat in the Afghan Parliament.[52] Sher Mohammed Akhundzaha, a nephew of Nasim Akhundzada, was relieved as governor of Helmand under British pressure in 2006 after nine tons of opium and heroin were discovered in his basement.[53]

In September 2008, President Karzai wanted to restore Sher Mohammed Akhundzada and another provincial governor sacked for heroin dealings. The British did not agree with his proposal. Believing that Akhundzada's powerful militia could beat back the Taliban, Karzai supposedly said that "his drug associations could be overlooked."[54] In July 2008, one of the U.S. State Department's senior counternarcotics officials accused Karzai of protecting drug lords for political reasons.[55]

Karzai also raised eyebrows in 2007 when he appointed Izzatullah Wasifi as his anti-corruption czar. Wasifi was convicted in the late 1980's for trying to sell $2 million worth of heroin to an undercover cop in Las Vegas.[56] Now there are reports that Karzai "has been unwilling to assert strong leadership" on the narcotics issue "in his home province of Kandahar," and that members of his Popalzai tribe have been posted to positions along various drug-trafficking conduits.[57] Evidence is mounting that his half-brother—Ahmed Wali Karzai—is deeply involved in the drug trade. That evidence consists of the following: (1) a personal admission to a European envoy;[58] (2) a British MI6 document claiming Haji Juma Khan used Wali as a go-between with governors;[59] (3) human-rights and U.S government reports of drug ties after Wali was appointed to a senior provincial position in Kandahar;[60] and (4) an ABC News report in 2006.[61] It would appear that President Karzai still has considerable corruption inside his administration.[62]

Afghanistan's Drug Laboratories

There are initially two steps in the poppy refinement process. First, the raw opium is mixed with lime and boiling water. It is then poured into molds to make morphine bricks. Then, those bricks have to be cooked with acetic anhydride and hydrochloric acid to create heroin base, a coarse granular substance known locally as "brown sugar." The further transformation into pure white heroin takes more cooking with chloroform and sodium carbonate, followed by elaborate charcoal filtration. This latter process requires a skilled chemist and used to happen at the Turkish border. Some of it may now occur just across the Pakistani border in FATA's Khyber Agency.[63]

Modern-day opiate refiners undoubtedly try to keep the locations of their drug labs secret. Still, history has a way of repeating itself. By 1988, more than a hundred heroin labs were operating just inside Afghanistan, across from Pakistani FATA.[64] In 1989, raw opium was also being refined into low-grade heroin in the hilly Chaghi District of Helmand Province. Hekmatyar's factories (at least six) were in Koh-i-Soltan.[65] They weren't very sophisticated in appearance. Each consisted of a pair of mud huts with a few barrels of chemicals outside.

How the Drugs May Now Be Leaving Afghanistan

Well-respected Pakistani journalist Ahmed Rashid made the following assessment in March 2001: "The same dealers, truck drivers, *madrasa* and government contacts and the [same] arms, fuel, and food supply chain that provided the Taliban with its supplies also funneled drugs—just as the *same* [italics added] arms pipeline for the *mujahideen* had done in the 1980's."[66] Herein may lie a clue to how most opiates are now leaving Afghanistan. The first half of his statement simply concludes that the drugs are being smuggled out the same way war materials are being smuggled in. It is in the second part (or "aside") to his statement that the real hint may lie. Most of the *mujahideen's* war supplies were coming from the West through Pakistani government logistics channels. Prior to 9/11, part of the Pakistani government was still supporting the Taliban, but Rashid might not have wanted to openly implicate it with the drug trade. He does, after all, still live in Lahore. Thus, one must try to read between the lines a bit. As a whole, his statement suggests the same Pakistani conduits that supplied the *mujahideen* are still bringing out the drugs. What if some of those same conduits are now suppling NATO? After all, Afghanistan is still awash with buried ordnance from past conflicts, and the Taliban should be able to buy any food or fuel it needs locally. Then, Rashid's statement might mean that the same trucking companies that supplied the *mujahideen* then and NATO now are carrying hidden drugs on their way back to Karachi.

In the desert regions of southern Afghanistan, there would also be convoys solely dedicated to drugs. If properly protected, they would not need to hide their cargos. Along the Afghan routes into Baluchistan as early as 2004, Taliban units were occasionally doing the following: (1) attacking security checkpoints so drug convoys could get through; (2) launching diversionary attacks to draw Western forces away from major consignments; and (3) accompanying those consignments.[67] On the routes into Iran, a motorcycle scout would precede each convoy by three to ten miles. At the Iranian border, Iranian intelligence agents would then move the dope without interference to Tehran or all the way to the Turkish border.[68] In 2005, those same agents were sending IED's back to the Taliban in Haji Kuma Khan's empty trucks.[69]

The drug route to Karachi from northwestern Pakistan may still run in much the same way it did in 1988. Trucks coming from NWFP (most notably Peshawar) could drop their loads at various places along the main highway north of Karachi. Then, private vehicles may ferry composite parts of those loads the rest of the way into the city.[70]

Some drug conduits running eastward out of Afghanistan may still be man or mule oriented, only shifting to vehicles inside Pakistan. After all, that border is highly mountainous and crisscrossed by hundreds of trails and tunnels. But other conduits (like the one through the Khyber Pass) are so large that they undoubtedly rely on vehicles the whole way.[71]

On all these routes, deception is possible. There may be secret compartments in fuel tankers, bus seats, carpets, timber, building materials, or produce. In one instance, cabbage heads had been grown up and around packets of heroin.[72]

The Taliban's Evolving Role in the Drug Trade

At first, the Taliban taxed every part of the drug operation in southern Afghanistan. They collected revenues from farmers, truckers, and laboratories—in return, offering protection.[73] They also supported massive drug bazaars in the following places: (1) Ghani Khel in Nangahar Province; (2) Sangin in Helmand Province; and (3) Maiwand in Kandahar Province.[74] Then, the Taliban started taking a more active role in the operation. They established quotas for farmers, set up their own refineries, and created their own caches.[75] Soon they were escorting consignments and threatening farmers who didn't grow poppy.[76]

There is evidence that the Taliban may now handle all of the smugglers' transportation needs. That would necessarily entail keeping Afghan and NATO forces away from all opiate-laden convoys.[77] In July 2004, Kandahar's top narcotics cop made the claim that "the smugglers now get the terrorists (Taliban and *al-Qaeda*) to move their drugs.[78] That's the same as saying that the Taliban work for the smugglers and their hidden international syndicate bosses.

How FATA-Delivered Drugs Now Get to the Coast

According to Western intelligence officials, Karachi-based *JEM* and northern-Punjab-based *Hezb* were transporting heroin from FATA to the Pakistani coast in 2005.[79] While roadway vehicles need not necessarily be their mode of transportation, that still seems likely. All Western-arms flow into Afghanistan is now more closely monitored than during the Soviet-Afghan War, so the previous (Pakistani army) trucking scheme from NWFP to Karachi may no longer be in operation.[80] Yet, something similar must be. The Khyber Pass road does, after all, run right through the NWFP capital of Peshawar.

JEM is an offshoot of *HUM* and closely aligned with the Taliban.[81] *Hezb* was created by *JI* and Hekmatyar.[82] Thus, radicals from *JUI/F* and *JI* are either cooperating or competing on Karachi "transpo." While *Hezb* could be the shipper and *JEM* the receiver, each more probably runs its own operation. After all, *JEM* does have its "Balakot" camp somewhere in FATA.[83]

Unfortunately, *JEM* and *Hezb* have both been ISI proxies. At one time, both were also members of *al-Qaeda's* Brigade 055. As discussed in the last chapter, a reconstituted version of that brigade may now form the nucleus of the so-called "Shadow Army." Drug runner Haqqani is somehow involved with that Shadow Army.[84]

An Unpleasant Possibility

Haji Juma Khan was also smuggling drugs north through Uzbekistan and Turkmenistan.[85] That could mean the Quetta Alliance, Taliban, Hekmatyar, IMU, and *al-Qaeda* are all cooperating—with or without a hidden facilitator. Not only are they cooperating on the export of opiates from every side of Afghanistan, but also on the takeover of Pakistan. How else can one explain the dual presence of the IMU in the Waziristans with the *TTP*, and in the Swat Valley with *JI*-affiliated *TNSM?* It's not likely that rogue elements of the Pakistani ISI could be generating that much internal mayhem. One may have to look elsewhere for that facilitator. Leading the list of likely suspects is China. For more access to Iranian oil and the Indian Ocean, it would welcome the destabilization of both countries.

Unsettling Parallels with Columbia

In Colombia, *FARC* has no intention of taking over its central government.[86] Its attack objective percentages from 1968 to late 2007 more than adequately support this paradox: (1) government—27%; (2) utilities—22%; (3) transportation—9%; (4) private citizens and property—9%; (5) police—8%; (6) businesses—7%; and (7) military—1%.[87] From inside that nation, *FARC* can make all the money it wants from locally grown narcotics and still enjoy a "relatively" safe haven from which to subvert the rest of Latin America. As of 2003, *FARC* was taxing every stage of Colombia's drug business, from the chemicals needed to process the crop to various shipping channels.[88] In return, it offered protection to the fields and routes of the Colombian cartels. *FARC* has since expanded. While making no attempt to take over the regional drug trade, its operatives are now active in no fewer than eight other Latin American countries.[89] Most worrisome are the *FARC* operatives in Mexico. They may be just showing the Mexican cartels and Salvadorian *maras* how best to protect the conduit into the U.S. Or, they may be training revolutionaries. As the *FARC*'s goals and tactics are now both Maoist,[90] its hidden sponsor is no great mystery. That sponsor's middlemen in the subversion of the Western Hemisphere are Cuba and Venezuela. Its link to regional organized crime factions is, in all likelihood, a Hong Kong triad that has been proven to be a business extension of its armed forces.[91]

In Afghanistan, the insurgents now seem more interested in protecting poppy fields and drug convoys than taking Kabul.[92]

FARC's sponsor is right next door and has a long (though seldom-mentioned) history of supporting both the Taliban and *al-Qaeda*.[93] Thus, one wonders if that same aspiring superpower may be also trying—through an Afghan proxy—to subvert other parts of South Asia. In this context, the 2008 envelopment of Islamabad through the Swat Valley takes on added significance. And one would like to know which Pakistani organized crime element arranges for the further shipment of Afghan heroin from Gwadar and Karachi. Once that element has been identified, he could look for any associations with Hutchison Whampoa port facilities, COSCO shipping, or the Sun Yee On triad. Somehow or other, the undisputed boss of the Karachi underworld—Dawood Ibrahim—is involved. That's the same former resident of Mumbai who lent materiel support to the perpetrators of that city's 1993 bombings and 2008 hotel seizures.[94] In the latter incident, a close *al-Qaeda* affiliate—*Lashkar-e-Toiba (LET)*—was used as the assault force.

With all of these unexpected connections between crime, trade, and politics, one can't help suspecting an overall scheme to first destabilize and then later control the region. Mumbai has just recently been added to the "attack corridor" for Eastern India's Maoist rebels.[95]

As early as 2000, a U.N. panel concluded the following: "Funds raised from . . . heroin are used by the Taliban to buy arms . . . and to finance the training of terrorists and support the operation of extremists in neighboring countries and beyond."[96] Dawood has already helped *LET* to wreak havoc in India. What if *al-Qaeda* and an unseen international backer were working through the Taliban and Dawood to destabilize not only South Asia, but also its Western trading partners? Then, like Colombia (with extremists controlling the majority of countryside), Afghanistan and Pakistan would become a self-supporting safe haven for an expansionist militia that exported both drug dependency and revolution.

More About the History of the Karachi Connection

About 1965, Pakistan signed an agreement with landlocked Afghanistan that would allow the duty-free import of goods through Karachi. At the beginning of the Afghan resistance, Pashtun tribes on both sides of the border figured out how to make this arrangement work for them. (See Map 5.6.) With the "U-Turn Scheme," legitimate goods were trucked into the Afghan tribal areas and then smuggled back across the border to avoid Pakistani tariffs. The trucks would then return to the coast laden with Pakistani opiates. Karachi is Sindhi with Baloch areas to its north. It is therefore no coincidence that those drugs ended up in Karachi's waterfront Pashtun slum of Sohrab Goth.

After the above-mentioned Afghan Transit Trade Agreement, crime syndicates began to take over Karachi. Before long, a smuggling outfit known as the "Quetta-Chaman Transport Mafia" (Chaman is at the border on the road to Kandahar) took over the Afghan contraband trade. (There may have been another "transport mafia" in Peshawar). Trucks laden with foreign goods ran from Karachi to Kandahar or Jalalabad, and then recrossed the border with the same or other goods. Later, during the Soviet-Afghan War, the National Logistics Cell (NLC)—a Pakistani-Army-run trucking company—took weapons supplied by the West from Karachi to Quetta or Peshawar and then returned with heroin for export. Somehow or other the two trucking schemes got meshed. By 1991, tons of heroin were passing through Karachi *en route* to various international destinations. Pakistan's illicit drug industry was reportedly making U.S. $10 billion a year, or a full fourth of that country's Gross Domestic Product (GDP).[97]

Since that time, the Karachi drug lords have increased their influence—thanks largely to political and military connections. Karachi's main syndicate is that of Dawood Ibrahim. Reports of another "Memon" syndicate are probably false. Jamal "Tiger" Memon still works for Dawood, and Memon is one of Dawood's aliases.[98] When the Indian government demanded the extradition of Dawood and the Memon brothers for the 1993 Mumbai serial bomb blasts, the former escaped arrest by making a huge loan to Pakistan's struggling central bank.[99]

Today, "criminal syndicates" reportedly run the trucking companies that first transport opium to laboratories in the frontier regions of Pakistan (like the Khyber Agency where Chinese chemists refine raw opium) and then on to Karachi from where the heroin is either sent by ship or air-freighted to the West.[100]

As of August 2001, *SSP* members were joining the syndicate of Dawood Ibrahim (also known as Sheik Dawood Hassan).[101] So, not just *JEM* has been helping with the Karachi drug trade. *SSP* and its military wing—*LeJ*—are too. In August 2009, the members of one *LeJ* cell were arrested in Karachi with suicide vests and over

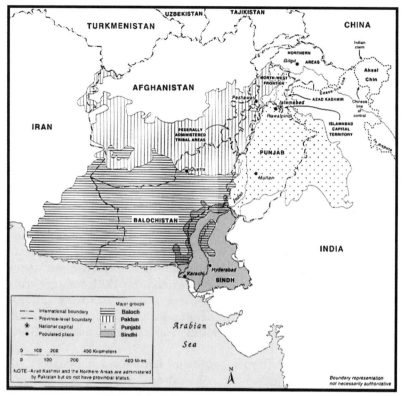

Map 5.6: The Pashtun Corridor
(Source: DA Pam 550-48 [1996], fig. 7)

four pounds of heroin.[102] While Ibrahim also supports the activities of *LET,* the merger of the two organizations has only been speculated.

According to Interpol, Dawood still maintains a house at "White House, near Saudi Mosque, Clifton, in Karachi."[103] Prior to being arrested, Haji Juma Khan also had a home in Karachi's Defense Colony neighborhood.[104] Khan's nephew Haji Hafiz Akhtar now runs the family business from just inside the Pakistani border at Baramcha.[105]

Up to a hundred *al-Qaeda* terrorists may also be hiding in the Defense Housing Society and Korangi sections of Karachi. One author hypothesizes that many of those *al-Qaeda* personnel are now members of the Federal Bureau of Investigation's (FBI's) newly discovered *Harkat-ul-jihad-al-Aalami. Newsweek* has also reported that Mullah Omar and many other senior Taliban officials may openly live in Karachi with fake Pakistani identity cards. There, they would be safe from drone missile attacks. Omar's first wife and seven children have been safely living in one of Karachi's Pashtun neighborhoods since 2003.[106]

Thus, Karachi may now serve as the coordination center for three destabilizing endeavors: (1) Afghan resistance; (2) Afghan drug trade; and (3) *al-Qaeda* expansion. From the Gulzar-i-Hjiri part of that teeming metropolis, ethnic Afghans reportedly export weapons and explosives to insurgents in Kashmir and other parts of the world. It's in this very neighborhood that the mutilated remains of American investigative journalist Daniel Pearl were found a few months after 9/11. He had been pursuing the ties of Richard Reid (the infamous "shoe bomber") to terrorist groups with known connections to the Pakistani ISI. In the process, he must have discovered how closely the two were meshed with the Afghan heroin trade. After asking too many questions about a certain Karachi-based drug lord, he—like others before him—ended up dead (more on that in Chapter 7). That this little footnote of history is not more widely known in the United States is quite troubling, and those would safeguard America from "all enemies foreign and domestic" should take a look at *The Most Dangerous Man in the World,* by Gilbert King.[107] The man to whom it refers is not Osama bin Laden, but rather Dawood Ibrahim.

Thankfully, Washington finally did take the overlords of the Afghan heroin trade to task in August 2009. That is when it first published a list of 50 Karachi drug smugglers to be either arrested or killed.[108]

The Other "Transport Mafia"

While the whole southeastern quadrant of Afghanistan is Pashtun, another "transport mafia" may have worked out of Peshawar in NWFP. In 2003, there were reports of over two tons of processed heroin reaching that city every two months. Those same reports indicated this conduit was separate from the one through Kandahar.[109]

A smuggler by the name of Haji Ayub Afridi did run a massive heroin empire that controlled the Khyber Pass. Instead of a civilian trucking conglomerate, he is known to have used NLC trucks.[110] As the NLC was a Pakistani Army operation, this is no small revelation. Minimally, it implies that some of those NLC trucks crossed the border. Inside of Pakistan, Quetta and Peshawar are where most drug deals are transacted.[111] They were generally thought to be the NLC's final destination.

Quetta's "Transport Mafia" Is Not the Same As Its Alliance

In South Asia, nicknames can be extremely misleading. Here's what a noted historian says about the Quetta-Chaman Transport Mafia.

> Another major Pakistani influence on the Taliban was the truck transport smuggling mafia based in Quetta and Chaman in Balochistan. Made up largely of Pakistani but some Afghan Pushtuns, drawn from the same tribes as the Taliban leadership and closely knitted to them through business interests and intermarriage, this mafia had become frustrated by the warring war lords around Kandahar, who prevented the expansion of their traditional smuggling between Pakistan and Afghanistan further [sic] afield into Iran and Central Asia. By contrast, the transport mafia based in Peshawar had been relatively successful in being able to trade between Pakistan, northern Afghanistan and Uzbekistan, despite the continuing war around Kabul.
>
> The Quetta-Chaman mafia funded the Taliban handsomely. Initially the mafia gave the Taliban a monthly retainer, but as the Taliban expanded westwards they demanded more and more funds—and received them. In March 1995, witnesses said the Taliban collected Rs 6 million (US $150,000) from transporters in Chaman in a single day and twice that amount the next day in Quetta as they prepared for an attack on Herat. Meanwhile the one-time,

all-inclusive customs duty the Taliban charged trucks cross-ing into Afghanistan from Pakistan became the Taliban's major source of official income. . . .

Within a few weeks of the Taliban takeover of Kandahar, not only had the volume of smuggling expanded dramatically but also the area. From Quetta, truck convoys were travel-ling to Kandahar and then southwards to Iran, westwards to Turkmenistan and from there onwards to other Central Asian republics and even Russia. Within a few months the Quetta transporters were urging the Taliban to capture Herat in order to take full control of the road to Turkmeni-stan. . . .

. . . The attack [on Herat] turned into a rout. It was the Taliban's first military defeat and they were pushed back all the way to Kandahar with over 3,000 casualties.

Despite this setback, as business opportunities grew for the Taliban families, so did the clout of the transport mafia that now expanded in Spin Boldak, Kandahar and Herat. Many Taliban bought trucks themselves or had a relative who was directly involved in trucking. Moreover, by 1996 influential heroin smugglers also began willingly to pay a "zakat" tax of 10 per cent to the Taliban exchequer for per-mission to transport heroin out of the region. The heroin trade was officially condoned by the Taliban in contrast to the hashish trade, which they banned. With heroin traders now contributing substantially to the Taliban via the trans-port mafia, the influence of the Pakistan-based transport mafia became enormous.[112]
— Ahmad Rashid, *The Nation* (Pakistan), 1998

After closely reading the above excerpt, one can start to see the relationship between the Afghan Taliban, transport mafia, and drug alliance. The Quetta Alliance may not simply mirror a Western Hemisphere drug cartel. Instead, it must be a loose consortium of smugglers who work for international traffickers based in Kara-chi.[113]

Where the Drugs Go from Karachi

By all accounts, most of the drugs go west by boat from Karachi.

As late as 2003, U.S. spy satellites were watching ships leaving Pakistani shores laden with Afghan heroin and returning with ordnance for the insurgency.[114] Haji Juma Khan had his own fleet of cargo ships that ran to the Sharjah Emirate in the UAE.[115] *Al-Qaeda* is also supposed to have purchased a fleet of freighters, but many may have been intended for other purposes (like military resupply or suicide attacks).[116]

Considering Dawood Ibrahim's Mumbai roots and continuing influence on that city, there is a good chance that some of the drugs go east through India, just like the natural gas will. Then, the U.S. market might be reached through Myanmar or the Malay Peninsula. Dawood's empire extends to 14 countries. He has agents all across South Asia, to include Thailand and Malaysia. Up to 150 of those agents work in Bangladesh alone.[117] Former U.S. counternarcotics officials easily envision the drugs easily entering the venerable "Golden Triangle" conduit and then reaching America through Mexico. That would almost certainly mean Chinese triad assistance. With it comes the possibility of PLA oversight. Dawood visited Hong Kong in July 2001.[118]

Of course, Dawood also has connections in Dubai and Africa. The former is known to play host to "transnational syndicates."[119] While Europe is the most-often-mentioned destination for his westward-bound product, some has to be diverted to America. It must move across Africa to Brazil or Venezuela, then along the Central American causeway into south Texas. Initially, its most probable route would be from one or more of the Emirates, to *al-Qaeda*-controlled portions of Yemen and Somalia, and then across the rebellion-wracked lower Sahara to West Africa. From there, the same *Hezbollah* conduit that brings Colombian cocaine up from Venezuela to Guinea-Bissau could just as easily take Afghan heroin south. On 21 June 2010, BBC News as much as confirmed that route.[120]

> He [the head of the U.N. drug agency] said 50 to 60 tons of cocaine were trafficked every year across West Africa while another 30 to 35 tons of Afghan heroin was being trafficked into East Africa every year.[121]
> — BBC News Online, 9 December 2009

For smuggling, one normally thinks of nighttime boat rides and secretive trucking. More likely, the drugs just find refuge amongst all the air freight that deluges Dubai. There are many flights from Dubai into Karachi daily, and not all are carrying many passengers.[122]

Dawood is More Than Just a Drug Peddler

Most disturbing are Dawood's politics. According to the U.S. Treasury Department, Dawood has "found common cause with *al-Qaeda*."[123] Unfortunately, that cause may involve more than just supporting *LET's* attacks on India.

> Ibrahim's syndicate is involved in large-scale shipments of narcotics in the U.K. and Western Europe. The syndicate's smuggling routes from South Asia, the Middle East, and Africa are shared with Usama bin Laden and his terrorist network.[124]
> — U.S. Treasury Department Fact Sheet, n.d.

Counternarcotics Failures in Afghanistan

In 2003, the British offered cash to any poppy farmer who would agree to grow something else. Thousands of impromptu entrepreneurs promptly planted a few poppies just to get their hands on the easy money.[125]

Clearly, the former U.S. Secretary of Defense made a mistake by being "opposed to targeting drug barons because it would anger war lords he wanted as allies [like Dostum]." His decision to accept help from the Iranian Revolutionary Guards during the Afghan invasion was not that well advised either.[126] Yet, the latter decision was not made in any vacuum. Ever since the hostage rescue negotiations of the early 1980's, the U.S. has been chronically soft on the Iranian revolution.

Which International Syndicate Makes Distribution?

There is little chance that Ibrahim or *al-Qaeda* could get any of their Afghan heroin to the Mexican cartels, much less the U.S. market. There has to be another international syndicate involved.

It may openly purchase the product for resale, or just help with its transport. Depending on its parent government, it may even be helping to further some anti-Western strategy. The most likely suspect is a Hong Kong triad.

Media reports often describe the Taliban as profiting off the drug trade, but it's more accurate to say they service it, working for opium smugglers and the mammoth international organized crime rings behind them.[127]
— Associated Press/ABC News reporter, 2009

A Glaring Need to Refocus the War

As late as 2006, the Pentagon was refusing to help the DEA shut down the Afghan drug mill.[128] U.S. military leaders apparently failed to see how criminal activity could contribute to 4GW. Well funded and politically entrenched themselves, they weren't at all worried about what 90% of the world's heroin might buy in the way of arms, tactical instruction, and political protection. This was despite ample evidence from the Iraq War that Islamic radicals like to set up their own shadow governments, complete with criminal justice systems. As of October 2009 (after eight years of war), 70% of Afghanistan remains outside of government control with the Taliban continuing to expand its own court and security networks.[129] The Afghan Constitution need not be a mirror image of that in America. Within Afghanistan, troops should be allowed to work on law enforcement problems—just as they do in any number of other democratic nations.

Afghanistan's poppy crop now brings in $3 billion a year (or a whopping 25% to 30% of that country's GDP). Some 12% of its population farm that crop for their living.[130] Still, the heroin business involves much more than just the growing of poppies. Next comes processing, warehousing, transportation, security, and any number of other steps. Perhaps that's why the BBC's normally reliable *Country Profile* claims that "Afghanistan's drug industry makes up around 60% of the economy . . . and the country provides 93% of the world's opium."[131]

Any long-term solution to Afghanistan's unpleasantries would necessarily entail diverting all this drug-harvesting to some other endeavor. Concurrently, the flow of heroin to the West has to be stopped. One does that by going after the opium-block-making operations, heroin labs, two to three dozen chemists (with enough knowledge to turn block opium into heroin),[132] stashes, and convoys. In southern Afghanistan, many of the latter do not follow existing roadways, so there is little risk of collateral damage during their seizure.[133] Yet, that seizure must look like a chance discovery during a routine check, or the Global Positioning System (GPS) equipped smugglers will simply alter their routes across the trackless desert.

With these kinds of statistics in hand, it's easier to see how the insurgents now support the drug traffickers, instead of the other way around. According the United Nations Office on Drugs and Crime (UNODC), 98% of 2008's poppy output occurred in Afghan-insurgent-held areas, and more than 3,000 tons of opium were also stockpiled there.[134] The war is no longer about who will run the Kabul government, but whether the West can withstand a gigantic infusion of heroin.

Thus, the U.S. administration's strategy should be more about counternarcotics than counterinsurgency. Going after the drug traffickers will automatically lead to Taliban attrition. Yet, to the people of Afghanistan, the effort will look more like foreign aid than military occupation. It would take the war out of the religious arena, and into the public-service arena. No Afghan citizen wants the danger and uncertainty of living in a narco-state. Only a limited number of Taliban fighters are hard-core extremists anyway. Many are just trying to support their families with the only jobs available. According to Marvin Weinbaum, a former State Department intelligence analyst, drug armies now control large sectors of Afghan territory.[135] Many of the battles are being fought as diversions to protect big drug shipments.[136] To override this cycle of deception, NATO and American forces must primarily focus on the Taliban's main source of funding. Then, the Taliban won't be able to pay its fighters, and those fighters will be more easily brought into the government fold.

All this will help, but a few very important questions have yet to be answered. Does the Baluchistan drug conduit still provide more than half of all U.S. heroin? Is any of that heroin again being carried out on the same trucks, ships, and planes that bring war supplies in? And why isn't there more talk about such things in

Washington? While contemporary pressures on the region have now been explored, the past may hold the most insightful clues to a comprehensive solution.

Part Two

Lessons from History

"Nonviolence is a weapon of the strong." — Mahatma Gandhi

6 Foreign Destabilization of Afghanistan

● Where do the loyalties of the various Afghan tribes lie?

● Do any nations intentionally destabilize Afghanistan?

Afghanistan's rural living standard hasn't changed much.

(Sources: DA PAM 550-21 [January, 1985], p. 337; FM 90-5 [1982], p. 1-6)

Sorting Out the Players

To make any sense out of Afghanistan's current array of factional alliances, one must first review its political history. With U.S. assistance, the Northern Alliance evicted the Taliban in late 2001 and became the nucleus of the new government. The Northern Alliance had been an Iranian proxy, whereas the ruling Taliban was a Pakistani proxy. The two proxies had been mostly feuding over what type of Muslim theocracy Afghanistan would become. Thus, there are Pakistani officials who still do not want President Karzai or any of his northern confederates in charge. And there are

Afghan officials who will always view their eastern neighbor as a threat. That being said, one must remember that Afghanistan has never had a strong central administration. It is a tribal society that resents uninvited guests (particularly those who are non-Muslim). Because of its geo-strategic location, that society has long suffered from Communist interference.

Afghanistan's last monarch, Zahir Shah, ascended to power in 1933. He had come from a long line of Pashtun rulers. His social reforms of the early 1950's (like allowing women out in public) were met with considerable resistance from the more conservative elements of his population. In 1964, Zahir Shah agreed to a constitutional monarchy. This led to even more political polarization and various power struggles. Nine years later, Mohammed Daud dethroned the old king and declared Afghanistan a republic. While playing the Soviet Union off against Western powers, he managed to alienate certain left-wing factions that then consolidated against him. In 1978, Daud was overthrown by the leftist People's Democratic Party. Soon, the same conservative Islamic and ethnic leaders who had objected to social changes began an armed revolt in the countryside. That revolt widened, and the Afghan army was not able to handle it. The rest is common knowledge. The Soviets sent in troops in 1979 to replace the ruling leftist leader (Amin) with one of their own. Soon, the Islamic and ethnic leaders united as *mujahideen* to evict the atheistic occupier.[1] As the monarchy and succeeding governments dissolved, tribal warlords assumed more and more control over the outlying regions. Those regions still had provincial governors, but those governors and warlords were often one and the same (e.g., Ismail Khan and Dostum). That should help to explain why it is now so difficult to install conventional governmental controls over certain areas.

Many familial bonds extend across the Afghan-Pakistani border. Any attempt to categorize tribal loyalties must therefore address their religious orientations. In the most general of terms, the southern half of Afghanistan is Sunni Pashtun, whereas the northern half is not. This Pashtun thread extends well into the FATA and NWFP regions of Pakistan. (See Map 5.6). It just as easily facilitates smuggling as insurgency. Despite an ongoing tradition of blood feuds, dissimilar Afghan tribes more easily ally than one might think. They can be killing each other one day and collaborating the next. This may be due to the precedence of tribal duty over religious nuance. When a tribal chief stands to make some money or political headway, he may enter into an unlikely alliance. This seeming paradox is somewhat unique to the region. It offers both a warning and hope to those who would try to pacify it.

Two Religious Affiliations That Transcend the Border

Inside of Pakistan, *JUI/F* and *JI* both belong to the *Mutahida Majlis Amal (MMA)*—a religious-party coalition that has figured so prominently in the past governance of NWFP and Baluchistan. While *JUI/F* and *JI* are both Sunni, Pashtun, Islamist, and Deobandi-rooted,[2] they widely differ in method. *JI* seeks an Islamic state through the Egyptian Muslim Brotherhood model, whereas *JUI/F* follows the Saudi Wahhabi model.[3] Thus, *JUI/F* and *JI* are rivals, and each has its own set of associates. *JUI/F* indirectly supports Mullah Omar's Taliban. Its military wing—*HUM*—has links to the more radical *LET* (from *JuD*), *LeJ* (from *SSP*), *HUJI*, and *JEM* (an offshoot of the *HUM/HUJI* merger). Meanwhile, *JI* indirectly supports both of Hekmatyar's militias *(HIG* and *Hezb)*. *TNSM* is an offshoot of *JI*.

Which Religious Affiliation Do the Troublemakers Prefer?

Whereas some of *JUI/F's* partners are decidedly anti-Shiite *(SSP* in particular), *JI* is not. As such, *JI* more easily works with the Afghan Northern Alliance, to include Dostum's Uzbeks. Iran would also be more comfortable with a *JI*-associated proxy.

Strictly Wahhabi *al-Qaeda* is more likely to interact with the *JUI/F* crowd, but it can at times exercise considerable degrees of Salafist tolerance. It has close ties to the IMU (which cooperates in the drug trade with Dostum's Uzbeks and in the Swat Valley with the *JI*-linked *TNSM)*. In fact, the *TNSM* may now be part of Osama bin Laden's IIF.[4] According to a U.S. Congressional research study, even Hekmatyar's *JI*-affiliated *HIG* is now an *al-Qaeda* "affiliate."[5]

The Pakistani ISI has used members from both camps as surrogates. In Afghanistan, it started out with Hekmatyar's *JI*-supported army and then switched to the *JUI/F*-generated Taliban.[6]

The drug traffickers are also comfortable with either camp. While Haqqani comes from the Khalis offshoot of the Hekmatyar-controlled and *JI*-affiliated *Hizb-i-Islami,* he cooperates easily with the Taliban.[7] In fact, Haqqani and Mullah Omar both served under *mujahideen* leader Yunis Khalis during the Soviet-Afghan War. To the extent that Baitullah Mehsud worked for, or with Haqqani, the same can be said of him. In February 2009, Mehsud signed a formal declaration of allegiance to both Mullah Omar and Osama bin Laden.[8] While Dawood Ibrahim has supported *LET* during its various Indian forays, he also accepts FATA drug shipments from both *JEM* and *Hezb.* Of course, some of the Afghan heroin goes west into Iran.

Iran's Continuing Designs on Afghanistan

Iran and Pakistan have long fought over Afghanistan. While the point of contention may have been their theocratic preference, it may also have been badly needed income. Of late, Shiite Iranians have been noticed in Sunni Taliban territory.[9] This worries U.S. war planners, because the Iranian Revolutionary Guards *(Sepah)* is known to have provided weapons, training, and volunteers to Sunni guerrillas in Iraq.[10] Just as Sunni *Hamas* is for all practical purposes a Shiite *Hezbollah* proxy, so too might *Sepah* be now trying to employ the Taliban. It has been smuggling state-of-the-art IEDs into Afghanistan to help someone. Yet, *Sepah's* purpose is far from clear, because it was the pro-Iranian Northern Alliance that first initiated the new Afghan government. Additionally, pro-Iranian elements still hold considerable sway over that government. When Ahmadinejad visited Kabul in March 2010, President Karzai "called the Iranian president 'brother' and said Afghans were lucky he had come." Two months earlier, the Afghan Parliament had objected when President Karzai tried to keep former Herat warlord Ismail Khan in his cabinet. Ismail Khan is has been long associated with *Sepah.*[11]

So why would Iran help the Taliban to fight its own political ally? Only two explanations come immediately to mind: (1) *Sepah* has representatives throughout the Pashtun Corridor to more easily smuggle drugs; or (2) *Sepah* is drawing the war out long enough for the U.S. Congress to tire of it. There is evidence that Iranian intelligence agents have been helping to move drugs out of Afghanistan. Some of those agents have also been helping to coordinate Taliban attacks against NATO forces.[12] Those attacks could be to divert attention from the Afghan drug convoys, or they could be to lessen interest in another theater of war (like Iraq, Lebanon, or Yemen). According a major U.S. think-tank, it's the latter:

> [I]ran favors the maintenance of a low level insurgency as long as U.S. troops remain in Afghanistan. Such a low intensity conflict would tie down the U.S. military and alleviate U.S. and international pressure on Tehran over its nuclear program and other controversies.[13]
> — Inst. for the Study of War (Washington, D.C.)

Still, the drug option is possible. Iran's involvement with the Afghan opium trade is far from new. Toward the end of the Soviet-Afghan War, Helmand drug warlord Akhundzada maintained an office in Zaidan, Iran. That office was openly dedicated to his smuggling operation.[14] According to the U.N. Office on Drugs and Crime, between a third and a half of all Afghan heroin was still being smuggled through Iran at the end of 2008.[15]

The Revelation of June 2007

On 7 June 2007, America's former Anti-Terrorism Czar asserted that Iran's war by proxy had shifted from Iraq to Afghanistan.[16] He said the sophisticated EFPs (explosively formed projectiles) recently found in Afghanistan,[17] were associated with arms convoys from Iran.[18] Two of those convoys had just been intercepted by NATO forces and confirmed to be from the Iranian Revolutionary Guards. They were carrying explosives and Rocket-Propelled Grenade (RPG) rounds.[19] The EFPs in Iraq are also of Iranian origin.[20]

This report came as no surprise to students of the region. Even in the absence of a foreign occupier, Iran and Pakistan have still vied—through proxies—over Afghanistan. Iran's most obvious surrogate was the Northern Alliance (formerly the United Front),[21] whereas Pakistan's player was the Taliban. Even during the Soviet-Afghan War, there was only limited cooperation between the two countries' respective *mujahideen* factions. Yet, evidence that Iran is now supporting the Taliban is growing more conclusive every day. While counter-intuitive to a Western thinker, this syndrome is not new to South Asia. Despite helping President al-Maliki to get elected (with counterfeit ballots and voters) in Iraq,[22] Iran has

95

continued to stir up trouble in that country. It must realize that even a pro-Iranian regime will not be free to do what it wants until the U.S. Congress deems the chaos so endemic as to bring home the troops. Whatever the level of *Sepah* involvement in Afghanistan, the U.S. has only itself to blame. That's because *Sepah* was allowed to take part in the 2001 invasion.

Iran's Formerly Welcomed Presence in Afghanistan

Iran's affiliation with the Northern Alliance of non-Pashtun minorities is well documented. The Northern Alliance had Iranian arms and sent its important prisoners to Tehran for questioning.[23] According to Center for Strategic International Studies, *Sepah's* Quds Force still runs camps in Iran that are specifically dedicated to the training of international extremists and terrorists. The one near Mashhad is for Afghan and Tajik revolutionaries.[24]

Past *Sepah* leader and Iranian presidential candidate, Mohsen Rezaie, claims that *Sepah* members fought alongside and advised the same Northern Alliance troops who helped the U.S. to overthrow the Taliban. According to *USA Today* of June 2005, the CIA knew during the invasion that there were *Sepah* advisors and agents attached to the Northern Alliance. U.S. Army commanders encountered Iranian intelligence agents in Kunduz and Herat. Defense Secretary Donald Rumsfeld told Columbia Broadcasting System's (CBS's) *Face the Nation* on 11 November 2001 that there were places in Afghanistan "where there are some Iranian liaison people, as well as some American liaison people," working with the same Afghan elements. A former U.S. State Department official went so far as to say that the Iranians "were equipping and paying the Northern Alliance."[25] A *Radio Free Europe* excerpt confirms that claim.

[A]n aide to Kandahar Province Governor Gul Agha Shirazi, claimed that senior Iranian military officers have been operating in Farah, Nimruz, and Helmand provinces. He said that Iranian generals using the names "Baqbani" and "Dehqan" were offering cash and other incentives in an effort to lure local warlords from their commitments to the administration in Kabul, according to reports in the 24 January issues of "The New York Times" and "The Los Angeles Times."

Iran has sent about 20 trucks filled with money for Ismail Khan [Herat warlord] to pay his troops. . . . [T]he approximately 12 trucks a day that come from Iran carry weapons, uniforms, and other war materiel. . . . Kandahar intelligence chief Haji Gulali said that Ismail Khan was working with the Islamic Revolution Guards Corps (IRGC) and allies of Gulbuddin Hekmatyar, the mujahideen commander who has been based in Iran for the last few years, to arm and fund opponents of the interim administration.[26]
— *Radio Free Europe/Radio Liberty,* January 2002

Of late, whole depots of Iranian mines, rockets, and EFPs have been found in Farah and Herat Provinces.[27] Thus, Iran has more than adequately demonstrated its continuing designs on Afghanistan. These designs do not likely include a secular democracy. Unfortunately, NATO leaders appear either unwilling or unable to counter this Iranian interference. Why, for instance, do their efforts focus almost entirely on the eastern and southern parts of the country?

If Iran were trying to complete its takeover of Afghan society, it would not limit its intelligence and advisory activity to Herat, Farah, Nimroz, and Helmand provinces. The first three lie along its border with Afghanistan, but the fourth is well inland and the primary source of heroin. Either the Iranians are attempting to stop that heroin, or facilitate its flow.

Additional Detail on the Iranian Support

The most logical explanation is that the Iranian arms are going to Hekmatyar. Though Sunni and ostensibly allied with the Taliban,[28] he has strong ties to Iran.[29] He is therefore, their most likely hidden proxy. Still, high-level U.S. sources insist the aid is going to the Taliban. Besides arms, that aid includes more foreign fighters.

"The Iranian Quds Force is reportedly training fighters for certain Taliban groups and providing other forms of military assistance to insurgents," [Gen.] McChrystal said in the report.[30]
— *Los Angeles Times Online,* 22 September 2009

97

Gen. McChrystal reaffirmed on 31 May 2010 that some of the Afghan Taliban his troops were facing had been trained in Iran.[31] A few Afghan War veterans also readily report Iranians amongst their Sunni foes. U.S. commanders should take note of how those Iranians are trying to influence the action, and then do the same kinds of things themselves.

[O]n October 2, 2006, *The Guardian* [UK] published an article stating that "military and diplomatic sources said they had received numerous reports of Iranians meeting tribal elders in Taliban-influenced areas, bringing offers of military or more often financial support for the fight against foreign forces."[32]
— Jamestown Foundation, 21 February 2007

[A] former governor of the western Farah Province, claimed that Iran was training "a large number of political opponents of the [Afghan] government" in a refugee camp in Iran called Shamsabad.[33]
— *Radio Free Europe / Radio Liberty,* 17 March 2007

Other Explanations for the Taliban's Iranian Assistance

Besides drug running and governmental destabilization, there are only two other reasons why a radical Shiite regime would resupply and reinforce radical Sunni guerrillas: (1) both factions have set a new precedent in Salafist cooperation; or (2) an aspiring superpower has directed barely compatible minions to cooperate. In September 2009, there was a clue to that riddle. Iran had been sending Chinese munitions to Afghanistan.[34]

China's Political Meddling in Pakistan

With regard to political manipulation, one normally thinks of diplomatic intrigue or governmental deal-making. With the Chinese, this is not necessarily the case. Just as China has for years had separate diplomatic relations with the Palestinian Authority inside Israel, it has now made an agreement with one of the most radical of Pakistan's religious parties. In February 2009, there was a very interesting CBS News posting from one of its reporters in Pakistan. It began as follows:

> Pakistan's Jamaat-i-Islami (JI), the country's main Islamic political party, and the Chinese communist party have signed a formal agreement to respect mutual interests.[35]
> — CBS News "World Watch," February 2009

This report was allegedly confirmed by a senior *JI* leader from Mansoora, the party's headquarters in Pakistan's Punjab Province. The article went on to say that the Chinese were moving in the direction of holding their own negotiations with Taliban affiliates. It also indicated that, since 9/11, Pakistani intelligence officials had "reported the participation of Chinese Muslim separatists in operations carried out by *al-Qaeda* and the Taliban in the Pak-Afghan region."[36] This came as no surprise to those aware of China's blatant support for Afghanistan's ruling Taliban prior to the 2001 invasion.[37] Now, it seems clearly possible that *JI* and its associated militias have replaced *JUI/F* and the Taliban as the PRC's dog in the fight. *JI* is the party that spawned the *HIG, Hezb,* and *TNSM.* That puts the Chinese squarely in the camp of those who tried to envelop Islamabad through the Swat Valley, and not nearly as opposed to *al-Qaeda* as they would like the West to believe.

China's Economic Manipulation of Afghanistan

Despite ample evidence of Chinese weapons in the hands of Taliban soldiers, most U.S. leaders still consider China to be an ally in Afghanistan. China, in turn, welcomes the chance to remove Afghan copper and more easily bring Iranian oil home. Only inveterate PRC watchers suspect anything amiss. They are all too well aware of China's knack for removing natural resources from nations too unstable to support Western competition. Just in Africa alone, the PRC has so far done so in Sudan, the Democratic Republic of the Congo (DRC), Nigeria, and most recently Guinea.[38] While there is no direct evidence of it destabilizing those countries to more easily extract their resources, that is a very real possibility for a revolutionary government. When NPR reported in October 2009 that the U.S. was to help China open its narrow border with Afghanistan, those suspicions deepened. By building a rail link to one of the biggest copper mines in the world through the Wahkan Corridor,[39] China will have accomplished a "hat trick." Previously it arranged for a Manta-Manaus rail link into the Ecuadorian Andes in 2007;[40] and a Benguela Railroad extension into the northeastern DRC in 2008.[41] (Refer back to Map 1.6.) Yes, that's the same Wahkan Corridor reported to be Osama bin Laden's lair by two highly respected periodicals right after 9/11. It contains a Silk Road detour traveled by Marco Polo.[42] As of October 2009, American troops were providing security for a PRC-owned company that has been exploiting the Aynak copper reserves. Those reserves are reportedly worth tens of billions of dollars and located in Logar Province just south of Kabul.[43]

Farther north, the Chinese have been helping to build not only the Herat to Bamian road, but also the Bamian to Peshawar Road.[44] PRC roads are often the precursors to parallel rail lines. When the Wahkan Corridor tracks intersect the Bamian tracks, they will permit the direct import of Iranian oil, without having to pass through increasingly pro-Western Pakistan.

7 Unresolved Issues within Pakistan

- Is there any connection between the ISI and drug lords?
- Has Pakistan done all it can to evict *al-Qaeda?*

Radical fundamentalism abounds in Punjab.

(Source: DA PAM 550-175 [September, 1988], p. 97)

No Easy Task

Pakistan's central government (like that of Afghanistan) has never held much sway over some of its provinces, much less its tribal agencies. Evidence of the former goes far beyond the *MMA's* (religious parties') recent election victories in NWFP and Baluchistan.[1] As late as 2003, the citizens of Sindh Province (the nation's southernmost) were still feeling dominated by "Zia-ul-Haq's Punjabis."[2] It was President Zia-ul-Haq who in the 1980's tried to "Islamize" the entire Pakistani government, to include its main intelligence agency—the ISI.

Thus, now assessing all "unresolved issues within Pakistan" is a fairly prodigious undertaking. It will require more reiteration and detail than most readers like. Still, that's the only way to arrive at a valid conclusion.

"Big-Picture" Issues

According to one Western analyst, Pakistan's nuclear facilities have already come under attack. Between August 2007 and August 2009, it happened three times. While none of these attacks were particularly concerted, they are still worrisome. They were launched against the following targets: (1) a nuclear missile storage facility at Sargodha on 1 November 2007; (2) Pakistan's nuclear airbase at Kamra on 10 December 2007; and (3) several entry points to the nuclear weapons assembly plant at Wah Cantonment in August 2008. The last two incursions were by suicide bombers. Most of Pakistan's nuclear sites are in the general vicinity of Islamabad. They are at Wah Cantonment, Fatehjang, Golra, Sharif, Kahuta, Sihala, Isa Khel Charma, Tarwanah, and Taxila.[3] As Sargodha is known *SSP* stronghold,[4] it might not have been the best place to store nuclear missiles.

Recent governmental policy within Pakistan was evident from videotaped interviews of top Pakistani officials on PBS's *Frontline* in October 2009. Those officials did not believe that Mullah Omar or Haqqani were anywhere on Pakistani soil. Nor did they acknowledge that Pakistan had authorized the missile attack on Baitullah Mehsud. Nor did they think the ISI was still using armed wings of religious parties as proxies.[5] In essence, they were unwilling to admit to their central government's chronic lack of control over FATA, NWFP, and Baluchistan. Nor would they consider the possibility that their once heavily Islamized ISI might still be fairly autonomous. After factoring in these last two commonly accepted truths, there is no way to be sure of those officials' other conclusions. More likely, the answer to peace in Afghanistan lies somewhere within the borders of its eastern neighbor.

Pakistan's Most Recent Attempts to Fix Its Own Mess

Finally, the Pakistani government rebanned *LET* in early August 2009, after allowing it marginally to operate for many years on its "watch list." Also banned were 24 other militant organizations, to include *JuD (MDI), JEM, TTP, TNSM,* and *LeJ.* It is unclear whether *SSP* or *Hezb* were among the 24.[6] On 13 August 2009, Islamabad also retired 32 senior military officers from its maverick ISI. That was undoubtedly to discourage any more clandestine support for the Taliban.[7]

Even in the best-informed of Western circles, the above actions would seem to be sufficient evidence of good faith. Unfortunately, Pakistan still lies in South Asia. Through the influence of Sun Tzu and others, its level of wartime intrigue is therefore considerably higher than that of Western nations. Yet to be adequately addressed is Pakistan's level of corruption, or more precisely its degree of involvement in the worldwide drug trade. That and somebody's apparent attempt to topple the current Pakistani administration seem to be the only possible explanations for so much internal chaos. Succeeding paragraphs will necessarily move back and forth between various aspects of these two potentially interrelated possibilities. Being doggedly hunted in the process will be the none-too-obvious culprit.

Another Way of Looking at the Pakistani *Tehrik-i-Taliban*

There are now reports that Baitullah Mehsud may have worked for (or with) Afghan resistance leader Jalaluddin Haqqani.[8] Though closely allied with Mullah Omar, Haqqani does have his rear-area headquarters in North Waziristan.[9] In October 2007, a Pakistani newspaper reported that five militant groups had united to form the *TTP* in FATA's Mohmand Agency.[10] Most of Baitullah Mehsud's money is said to have been raised through drug trafficking.[11] And Haqqani is known to be running a big drug conduit from Afghanistan's Paktiya Province to the Waziristans.[12]

The Mehsud's Sometimes Allies

If Baitullah was cooperating with Haqqani on drugs, then some of his allies and counterparts may have been also. Even before Baitullah's death, Haikimullah Mehsud had been in control of Orakzai, Kurram, and Khyber agencies.[13] His militia was undoubtedly part of the "five-group merger" that formed the *TTP* in Mohmand Agency in October 2007. The *TTP* is not alone in southern FATA. Hafiz Gul Bahadur's militia controls North Waziristan and thereby hosts Haqqani's headquarters. (Bahadur's tribe is the Madakhel Wazir.[14]) Maulvi Nazir's militia is based south of Wana in the other Waziristan.[15] It was the Yargul Keil subgroup of the Zalikhel clan of Nazir's "Ahmed Zair Wazir" tribe that led the resistance to the Pakistani Army's search for *al-Qaeda* headquarters in 2004.[16] (Nazir is a member of the Kakakhel sub-clan of the Ahmedzai Waziris.) The villages encircled in that operation were Shin Warzak, Daza Gundai, Kallu Shad, Ghaw Khawa, and Khari Kot.[17] When the Pakistani troops further raided the village of Kosha, some 15-20 "foreigners" escaped (probably through a tunnel).[18] According to one Pakistani newspaper, it is Nazir who now controls Wana.[19]

Bahadur and Nazir agreed with Baitullah Mehsud in February 2009 to form the *SIM* to help Mullah Omar and Osama bin Laden defeat all Western occupiers.[20] Then eight months later, both Waziris switched sides and struck deals with the Pakistani forces about to enter the Waziristans to go after *al-Qaeda*-affiliated Uzbeks and *TTP* headquarters.[21] If either man were also involved with Haqqani, then how the Pakistani offensive played out might give a clue as to the real source of the destabilizing influence. However, before that can be investigated, the extremist offensive against the central government must take center stage. Islamabad was under attack from two different directions.

Both Islamabad Pincers Had *al-Qaeda* Operatives

In 2008 and 2009, there was an extremist push through the Swat Valley (north of Islamabad), and a number of government targets hit in Rawalpindi (15 miles to its south).

Al-Qaeda's influence in the Swat Valley was most apparent through the presence of *TNSM, JEM,* and the IMU.[22] *TNSM* and *JEM* are both part of Osama bin Laden's IIF (along with the *LeJ*).[23] In 2004, the IMU supposedly provided security to *al-Qaeda's* headquarters in South Waziristan.[24]

Then, the piecemeal attack on Islamabad from the south was largely conducted by the *LeJ*. Not only did the *LeJ* attack Pakistani

Army Headquarters in next-door Rawalpindi, but it also truck-bombed Islamabad's Marriott Hotel in September 2008 [with the possible help of *JEM]*.[25] *LeJ* is now undeniably an *al-Qaeda* partner. In fact, it is believed to be *al-Qaeda's* suicide-oriented "delta force."[26] Thus, not only some drug syndicate, but also *al-Qaeda* was playing a significant role in this mixture of South Asian intrigue. Unfortunately, those were not the only players.

Telling Connections from FATA

In Part One of this book, a couple of very interesting trends surfaced: (1) two *JI*-affiliates have been operating out of Bajaur tribal agency (drug-trading Hekmatyar and the *TNSM*);[27] and (2) two *JUI/F*-affiliates have been operating out of the Waziristans (drug-running Haqqani and the *TTP*).[28] Though Haqqani is head-quartered in Bahadur-controlled North Waziristan, many of his Afghan smuggling routes must lead into *TTP*-controlled portions of South Waziristan.[29] That makes the following facts too much of a coincidence. *JI*-affiliated *Hezb* has been carrying drugs south to Karachi from Bajaur,[30] and *JUI/F*-affiliated *JEM* has been bringing drugs south to Karachi from the Waziristans.[31] It then seems that both *JI* and *JUI/F* are peripherally involved with separate drug conduits. That both are still legal political parties within Pakistan does little to quell one's fears of narco-state development.[32]

Unseemly ISI Activity

Everyone within Pakistan, including its new president, is now hoping that the previously Islamized ISI is no longer pursuing national policy through surrogate armies. Among its known proxies have been the following: (1) Hekmatyar's *JI*-supported Afghan militia; (2) *Hezb;*[33] (3) the *JUI/F*-born Afghan Taliban; (4) *LET;*[34] and (5) *JEM*.[35] As an offshoot of the merger between *HUM* and *HUJI*, *JEM* is closely aligned with *JUI/F* and the Afghan Taliban.[36] *Hezb,* on the other hand, was created by *JI* and Hekmatyar in Azad Kashmir.[37] In essence, the ISI has alternately relied on *JUI/F* and *JI* for its surrogate forces.

In 1996, the Pakistani ISI further encouraged thousands of

armed cadres from *SSP, LEJ, LET,* and *HUM* to augment Mullah Omar's forces. It did so to help its new proxy (the Afghan Taliban) to complete its conquest of what was now Soviet-free Afghanistan. *Hezb* did not become part of this "cadre contingent" (now called the "Army of Islam") until it was shifted back to the Kashmir theater by the ISI. Though cadre detachments were to form the backbone of bin Laden's IIF in 1998,[38] they were subsequently driven back into Pakistan during the U.S. invasion of 2001. Their participation in the recent upswing of radical activity within Pakistan may have as its goal the downfall of their own government.

Disturbing Parallels

There were also contingents from *HUM, LET,* and *JEM,* in *al-Qaeda's* Brigade 055. That brigade is now thought to be reforming.[39] *Al-Qaeda's* Brigade 313 had similar representation: (1) *HUJI* (a Deobandi affiliate of *HUM);* (2) *HMA* (another offshoot of the merger between *HUM and HUJI); (3) LET;* (4) *JEM;*[40] and (5) *LeJ.*[41] And *al-Qaeda's* IIF had units from *HUM, LET, JEM, LeJ, and HUJI.*[42] That ISI endorsed the birth of *al-Qaeda* in 1987 is of little consolation.[43] It was also the ISI that orchestrated the Soviet defeat, and then in 1994 launched the Taliban to take over Afghanistan.[44]

Is Islamabad Now More Serious about Evicting *al-Qaeda?*

During Musharraf's presidency, the Pakistani military made several unsuccessful attempts to rid the Waziristans of *al-Qaeda* members. Whether those tries were half-hearted to appease the West, no one really knows. All they know is that *al-Qaeda's* influence has persisted in both tribal agencies.

In the first full-blown incursion into semi-autonomous South Waziristan since 1947,[45] around 10,000 Pakistani troops entered to evict *al-Qaeda* elements, most notably IMU's Uzbeks, in March 2004. Contesting the Pakistani Army's presence southwest of Wana were 400-500 *al-Qaeda* militants and some 2,500 local tribesmen that they had recruited/trained. Local citizens referred to these tribesmen as "The Men of *al-Qaida.*"[46] A subgroup of Maulvi Nazir's tribe is known to have led the resistance, so it most probably constituted "The Men of *al-Qaeda.*"

[T]he Yar Gul Khel, a subgroup of the Zali Khel clan of Ahmed Zai Wazir tribe . . . is believed to be leading the resistance to the Pakistani military onslaught.[47]
— *Christian Science Monitor,* 22 March 2004

After struggling for a week to cordon off several villages, Pakistani forces agreed to a temporary cease-fire to allow a 22-member tribal council to negotiate the hand-over of surrounded fighters. Among them was supposedly the IMU founder who had allied his organization with *al-Qaeda.* Lengthy negotiations ensued about ending the fighting and turning over the foreigners.[48] In Wana, Pakistani officials attempted to force the cooperation of the Zali Khel clan by bulldozing the homes of tribal leaders.[49] That may have given the militant leaders (and *al-Qaeda* members) a chance to escape the army cordons. Pakistani troops later discovered two excavations: (1) a mile-long tunnel under fortress-like compounds in the town of Tellu Shah; and (2) "a 2-kilometer-long tunnel running between houses of two wanted tribesmen and leading to a stream."[50] Under increasing pressure, the tribal chieftains soon formed a force of 600 armed tribesmen to catch militants and wayward clansmen. The subgroups of the Zalikhel clan that formed this tribal posse were forced to pay a $870 daily fine and face house demolitions if they failed to apprehend "foreign terrorists."[51] After a while, the Pakistani government "cut a deal with tribal leaders in South Waziristan." As a result of that deal, "the area became a power vacuum that quickly filled with Taliban."[52]

After all of that Pakistani military pressure in the Spring of 2004, tribal sources say around 600 *al-Qaeda* guerrillas—mostly Arabs, Chechens, and Uzbeks—managed to remain in and around South Waziristan. Like the wanted tribesmen, some of the *al-Qaeda* personnel converged on the forest-covered mountain regions of Shikai, Bush, and Khamran.[53] Others went north. Some of the Uzbeks simply shifted into Mehsud territory, while others traveled all the way to North Waziristan.[54]

In the fall of 2006, Pakistani authorities signed another peace pact—this time, with the tribal leaders of North Waziristan (undoubtedly including Bahadur). After that truce, U.S. commanders saw the number of cross-border attacks triple.[55] Clearly, the unenforceable "deals" were aiding the foe.

Then, starting in late March 2007, Pakistan's President

Musharraf "renewed the peace accord[s] with Waziristan's tribal leaders."[56] By 15 April 2007, Wana-area tribal elders, clerics, and local militants (including Nazir) had all signed an accord.[57] Soon, the Pakistani army and allied tribesmen—to include Nazir's militia[58]—were driving the "*al-Qaeda*-affiliated" Uzbeks out of South Waziristan (and killing 300 of them in the process according to Musharraf).[59] In essence, the Pakistani army had exploited the inherent tribal rift between the Mehsuds and Waziris by backing the faction aligned against the Uzbeks.[60] Both tribes live in South Waziristan (and are rivals),[61] but only the Waziris have historically settled on either side of the Pakistan-Afghanistan border. Such an arrangement would make cross-border movement much easier for *al-Qaeda* visitors and drug smugglers alike.

Since then, Islamabad has had little control over South Waziristan, with its Army garrison being largely restricted to Wana.[62] As Wana lies inside of Nazir's zone of influence,[63] these limits to government control mesh well with supposed *TTP* boundaries. Baitullah Mehsud must not have signed those accords.

An Army contingent had to evacuate the Mehsud-dominated part of South Waziristan in 2008 after some 300 troops were taken hostage. This *TTP*-controlled area north of Wana is thought to contain at least seven camps where suicide bombers are trained. Those camps are at Makeen, Shaktoi, Kanigaram, Dela, Kot Kai, Shawwal, and Badar. Maulavi Nazir runs similar training centers at Shikai and Baghar. Those centers, like most of his followers, are probably south of Wana.[64]

In October 2009, Pakistani forces again invaded South Waziristan. After four days of fighting, they captured Kot Kai—Haikimullah Mehsud's hometown. Qari Hussain, organizer of the *TTP* suicide squads, is also from Kot Kai.[65] By 18 November, the Pakistani units had reoccupied the Sararogha Fort—now a *TTP* stronghold and possible headquarters. In that fight, they killed roughly 500 militants after losing 70 men of their own.[66] Sararogha Fort had been overrun in mid-January 2008 by several hundred pro-Taliban militants who subsequently killed or kidnapped many members of its Pakistani garrison.[67]

The 2009 Pakistani offensive had, as its target, the "1,000 to 2,000 *al-Qaeda*-linked Uzbeks" still believed to be in South Waziristan.[68] Of certain interest were the suicide camps (e.g., Kot Kai) and former outposts. Expecting to encounter heavy resistance from the *TTP,* the Pakistani Army made nonaggression pacts with Nazir and Bahadur.[69] That both had pledged allegiance to Baitullah Mehsud, Mullah Omar, and Osama bin Laden in the January 2009 *SIM* agreement didn't seem to matter.[70] Striking deals with *al-Qaeda* supporters might make sense to Sun Tzu, but it didn't do much good last time. Such deals could be construed as appearing to evict *al-Qaeda* while instead protecting key affiliates. The new president of Pakistan must be made to see that *al-Qaeda* poses a far greater threat to his country than India ever could. He should be further reminded of the abject failure of Musharraf's appeasement policy.

Now that the Pakistani Army's sincerity in the Waziristans has been partially assessed, one can return to the drug linkages of one of its new allies.

Nazir's Background As It Relates to Pakistani Intentions

Maulvi Nazir is a dual citizen of Pakistan and Afghanistan. Although presently residing in South Waziristan, he is a frequent traveler to Afghanistan's Paktika Province and Kandahar (where he owns property).[71] Paktiya Province is the portal to Haqqani's cross-border smuggling route.[72] Like Haqqani, Nazir's first association was with Hekmatyar's *Hizb-e-Islami,* a favorite of Pakistan's ISI during the days of the anti-Soviet *jihad.* He later joined the Afghan Taliban and remains politically aligned with *JUI/F.*[73] Nazir leads 3,000 fighters who are mostly Waziris. His militia also has a Punjabi Taliban component made up of members of banned sectarian and Kashmiri militant groups.[74] Some may belong to *JEM* (the transporter of drugs to the south), and that faction's Balakot camp may be in Nazir's area.

Haqqani's headquarters is in North Waziristan, so Bahadur must implicitly endorse his drug smuggling. Baitullah Mehsud is known to have worked for or with Haqqani.[75] After all the breaks that Nazir has gotten from the Pakistani government, any smuggling link between him and Haqqani would tend to impugn that government's resolve in disrupting the drug conduit. Until 90% of the world's heroin stops flowing through southern Pakistan *en route* to the Western World, America will not be able to fully trust that country's government.

During the FATA Offensive, *TTP* Was Chased into Orakzai

After the October 2009 Pakistani Army assault on South Waziristan, much of the *TTP* fled to the Orakzai (or Arakzai) tribal agency. It could not have done so without the cooperation of Bahadur in North Waziristan. Orakzai is just south of the Khyber Pass and Peshawar. It is also where the mysterious *Fedayeen-e-Islam* is based.

> Led by Hakeemullah *[sic]* Mehsud, the *Fedayeen-e-Islam* has taken credit for multiple terror assaults and suicide attacks throughout Pakistan. The group is made up members of the Pakistani Taliban, the *Lashkar-i-Jhangvi [LeJ]*, *Jaishe-Mohammed [JEM]*, and other Islamist terrorists from Pakistan. It is based in Orakzai and South Waziristan. Senior leaders of the *Fedayeen-e-Islam* include Qari Hussain Mehsud, a former senior deputy to Baitullah who trains child suicide bombers; [and] Qari Mohammed Zafar, the operational commander of the September 2008 attack on the Islamabad Marriott.[76]
> — *Long War Journal,* 17 November 2009

Suddenly, all the pieces were starting to fit. Orakzai is just south of the Khyber Agency. If drugs were coming out on the same trucks that bring war supplies in, then whoever controls the Khyber Pass would also control the drug flow. The most prominent warlord in Orakzai is a member of the Afridi clan. It was Haji Ayub Afridi who ran the heroin empire that held dominion over the Khyber Pass.[77]

> [The] Commander Tariq Group . . . is considered the most powerful outfit in Orakzai. Led by Commander Tariq Afridi and based in Darra Adam Khel, the group conducts attacks on Pakistani security forces in Orakzai, Kohat, Peshawar, and Hangu. . . . .
> Hakeemullah *[sic]* Mehsud . . . was the commander of Taliban forces in Orakzai [tribal agency] prior to taking control of the terror alliance after the death of . . . Baitullah Mehsud, in August. Hakeemulah *[sic]* is known to have an operations center in Ghiljo in Orakzai.[78]
> — *Long War Journal,* 17 November 2009

In essence, the *TTP* was taking refuge in the area where its overseer held sway. And that overseer had more interest in drugs than overthrowing the Pakistani government. In mid-January 2010, one of the few American newspapers still having its own foreign correspondents confirmed the suspicion.

> *Nor* (italics added) are they [the Pakistanis during their FATA offensive] moving against the Haqqani network in North Waziristan or . . . Hekmatyar's Hizb-e-Islami around the Khyber Pass.[79]
> — *Christian Science Monitor,* 17 January 2010

As late as 10 March 2010, NPR News was still confirming that the latest Pakistani offensive into FATA had made no attempt to disrupt the "Haqqani Network." Nor had it interfered with certain "Kashmir-based *jihadis.*" This latter remark appears directed at *Hezb,* but its target could have also been *HUM, LET, LeJ,* or *JEM.*[80] Having the same founder, *Hezb* and *HIG* work together well and could easily be misidentified. Thus, the specter of Pakistani government collusion with the drug runners was beginning to grow. However, there was also evidence of a foreign or domestic entity subverting that government.

The Punjabi Taliban

After the Army Headquarters attack in Rawalpindi, somebody calling themselves "the Punjabi Taliban" took credit. These Punjabi Taliban are generally thought to be remnants of the *jihadist* factions that were sent to Afghanistan by the ISI in 1996 to help the Taliban and then to Kashmir and Jammu to fight the Indians. As a part of the ISI's clandestine "Army of Islam," they eventually consisted of the *SSP, LeJ, LET, HUM,* and *Hezb. JI*-affiliated *Hezb* did not mesh well with the others, but was included to prevent enough bonding to pose an internal threat to Pakistan.

As discussed in Chapter 3, the Punjabi Taliban most probably consists of elements from some combination of *Hezb, LET,* and *LeJ* that is coordinated out of Lahore. Sadly, that membership does little to establish any overall sponsor. It could be *JI* (with or without foreign encouragement), *al-Qaeda,* the ISI, or some drug syndicate.

Possible Sponsor for the Punjabi Taliban

During the Taliban regime in Afghanistan, *al-Qaeda's* Brigade 055 helped to fight the Iranian-sponsored Northern Alliance. Among Arab, Chechen, Uighur, Bosnian, and Uzbek contingents, Brigade 055 contained elements of *HUM, JEM,* and *LET.*[81] *Hezb* had already been "penetrated" by *al-Qaeda's* Salafists, but its non-Wahhabi orientation would have probably precluded its membership in Brigade 055.[82]

There are now reports of a reconstituted Brigade 055 in the *al-Qaeda*-generated "Shadow Army."[83] Historically, Iran and Pakistan have vied for Afghanistan through proxies, so it stands to reason that *al-Qaeda* might do the same. Yet, any of Afghanistan's neighbors are perfectly capable of having more than one surrogate in the fight.

This re-formed Brigade 055 is supposed to be just one of an estimated three to four brigades of mostly "foreign" volunteers. Inside Pakistan, the Shadow Army has reportedly been active in successful Taliban campaigns in both Waziristans, Bajaur, Peshawar, Khyber, and Swat. In Afghanistan, it has conducted operations against NATO and Afghan forces in Kunar, Nuristan, Nangahar, Kabul, Logar, Wardak, Khost, Paktika, Paktia, Zabul, Ghazni, and Kandahar Provinces. By operating along the Pastun corridor (refer back to Map 5.6), it has been apparently able to ignore most of the border restrictions. Thus, it was probably this Shadow Army that conducted the envelopment of Islamabad from the north. That would put the *JI*-affiliated *TNSM* and its IMU advisors into one of the other brigades. The *TTP* and Haqqani Network (more of a drug operation than anything else) have supposedly also provided troops to the Shadow Army. *"Hizb-i-Islami"* (Hekmatyar's *HIG)* has been noticed in joint operations with the *TTP,* Haqqani militia, *LET,* and *HUJI,* so it may also contribute to one of the brigades.[84] If all this were true, one would wonder about this mysterious army's true sponsor. Not only would the Shadow Army then look like an ISI expeditionary force, but it could easily be the brainchild of the Iranian Revolutionary Guards *(Sepah)* or an international drug syndicate.

Haqqani does after all wear two hats. He not only runs much of Afghanistan's resistance, but also much of its narcotics. According to the *Christian Science Monitor,* the three main resistance groups as of mid-December 2009 were the Afghan Taliban, Haqqani Network, and *HIG.*[85] That means two out of those three have been traditionally as much about drug removal as political change. The ISI, *Sepah,* or drug syndicate would be more likely than strictly Wahhabi *al-Qaeda* to tolerate pro-Shiite elements in their midst. *Hezb* was an ISI proxy in Kashmir.[86] While there is no hard evidence of anyone but *al-Qaeda* coordinating things, Western logic often fails in this part of the world. A multi-tour veteran of Afghanistan reports Afghan Taliban, Punjabi Taliban, and Iranians all working in the same geographical areas. Those Iranians are no doubt from the same *Sepah*-generated Quds forces that helped to destabilize Iraq.[87] The so-called Shadow Army appears to be cadred in that it easily interchanges composite elements. It could be working for any kind of international entity.

With all of the above background, the answer to the original question seems no closer. Who or what is behind the Punjabi Taliban? It could be made up of radical elements that simply like to fight, but more probably they are being organized and somehow reimbursed. Like the ISI's Army of Islam in Kashmir, the Punjabi Taliban contains elements of *SSP, LeJ, JEM, LET,* and *Hezb.*[88] That means it is more than just an extension of the *TTP* or *JUI/F* sponsored Afghan Taliban. If the Punjabi Taliban were strictly an *al-Qaeda* creation, it would probably not have *Hezb* mixed in with the others. However, its activity might still be a joint venture with a separate Shadow Army.

The warlord Nazir—who so easily switches allegiance between *al-Qaeda* and the Pakistani Army—has a Punjabi-Taliban-like contingent in his militia.[89] One wonders if his North Waziristan counterpart—Bahadur—does also. He too just switched sides to gain immunity during the Pakistani Army's 2009 FATA offensive. That federal force was ostensibly after *al-Qaeda's* IMU partners and the *TTP.* Haqqani, who is deeply involved with both drug smuggling and the Shadow Army, has his headquarters in Bahadur-controlled territory.[90] As previously mentioned, his "network" escaped damage during that intervention. In October 2008, the U.S. killed Khalid Habib al-Shami, the leader of the Shadow Army, in North Waziristan.[91] Thus, narcotics and the Shadow Army seem to be undeniably inter-twined. Whoever is controlling the drugs may be trying to so destabilize both regimes as to create side-by-side narco-states. While Colombia and Mexico are not immediate neighbors, they still constitute a rather unpleasant example of this same syndrome (needless to say, it is not *al-Qaeda* generating that marriage). Or some foreign power may be so destabilizing the entire region as to achieve its own misguided expansion. The attacks on the Indian Parliament and Mumbai hotels were obviously to draw Pakistani troops away from FATA and the NWFP. Such things might help to establish a caliphate, but they would definitely keep the main conduit open for 90% of the world's heroin. Thus, *al-Qaeda* is not the only possible coordinator of the Punjabi Taliban. Its marching orders could come from a drug syndicate or governmental agency (not necessarily Pakistani).

As an Agency, the ISI Appears Not behind the Chaos

While having used many of these radical factions as proxies, the ISI is not—as an organization—directly behind the assault on its own government. A few rogue ISI agents may be involved, but so may a few Chinese or Iranian agents. The government of Pakistan has never had much control over FATA, NWFP, or Baluchistan. Of late, that same syndrome has simply spread to Punjab. If the ISI were behind the trouble, it would not be attacking its own headquarters

Twenty-three people, including police and officials from the Inter-Service Intelligence agency, were killed after an assault team opened fire on security personnel and stormed the ISI headquarters [on 27 May 2009 in Lahore].[92]
— *Long War Journal,* 10 October 2009

The Taliban have pounded Peshawar with suicide attacks against police, the military, and civilians. One such attack leveled the headquarters of the Inter-Services Intelligence agency.[93]
— *Long War Journal,* 17 November 2009

On 7 December 2009, a Pakistani intelligence center in Multan came under concerted ground assault.[94] Multan is in Punjab Province, about half way down the highway from Islamabad to Karachi. *LET* has training center in Multan.[95]

Depending on the source, Abdul Ghani Baradar was Mullah

Omar's head financier, chief of staff, or top military commander before being arrested in Karachi on 15 February 2010.[96] His arrest has been confirmed to be a joint effort between the ISI and CIA.[97]

Still-Unanswered Questions

It is now widely acknowledged that the ISI launched the Taliban into Afghanistan, reinforced it with religious party militias, and then shifted those militias to its proxy army in Jammu and Kashmir. Since that time, many of the ISI's top leaders have been summarily fired. In a Western-style government, that would have tended to fix the problem. However, Pakistan's government is only Western in appearance. While now a federal republic, it still must come to terms with its most potent political force—the military according to the CIA's *World Factbook*. That *Factbook* goes on to say that political alliances shift frequently among its 13 or so legal political parties (to include *JUI/F* and *JI*). Pakistan's constitution has been suspended and restored three separate times since 1973, with the last time being in 2007.[98] Since 9/11, the Pakistani ISI has been linked by prestigious news sources to the following events: (1) the escape of bin Laden from Tora Bora;[99] (2) the death of Daniel Pearl in Karachi;[100] and (3) the protection of Dawood Ibrahim in Karachi.[101]

Best referenced is the ISI's alleged connection to narcotics trafficking. It dates all the way back to 1993, when that Pakistani intelligence agency was apparently interested in extending its Jammu/Kashmir activities into India. The similarities to more recent events are chilling.

> Before March 1993, the Dawood Ibrahim group, which indulges in large-scale smuggling . . . was operating from Dubai. In March 1993, this group organized at the instance of the Inter-Services Intelligence (ISI) of Pakistan a series of explosions directed at important economic targets in Mumbai. . . .
>
> . . . [T]he perpetrators of these acts of terrorism, all Indian nationals, had been recruited, at the insistance of the ISI, by Dawood Ibrahim in Mumbai, taken to Pakistan via Dubai for training . . . and then sent back to Mumbai via Dubai. . . . After they returned to Mumbai . . . , the explosives

115

and other arms and ammunition required by them . . . were sent by the ISI by boat with the help of Dawood Ibrahim and clandestinely landed on the Western coast of India.[102]
— South Asia Analysis Group, 19 October 2003

A slightly different version of this allegation appeared two years later in a prestigious U.S. news magazine. Here, the ISI had given explosives to Dawood without knowing their precise purpose.

The shift from gangster to terrorist came in 1993, after rioting targeted Bombay's Muslims. Bent on revenge, Dawood engineered the smuggling into India of tons of explosives provided by Pakistan's spy agency, the Inter-Services Intelligence.[103]
— *U.S. News & World Report,* 5 December 2005

Pakistan is known to have had a cash flow problem at various times in its recent history. Perhaps, its nearly autonomous spy agency opted for a supplementary source of income. In 1999, a prestigious Indian newspaper had accused the ISI of paying for its Jammu/Kashmir war with drug money.

That the Inter Services Intelligence (ISI) Directorate of Pakistan has been pumping in crores [tens of millions] of rupees to sustain the proxy war unleashed on India is a well-known fact. But how is the huge fund generated? How does it reach the militants fighting the undeclared war in the Kashmir valley?

According to information collected by The Tribune from various agencies and individuals, the ISI is working in collaboration with *Jamaat-e-Islami [JI]* of Jammu and Kashmir . . . and the *Markaz al-Dawah al-Irshad [MDI* or *JuD]* for raising funds to keep up militancy in the valley. . . .

. . . The Markaz al-Dawah has its headquarters at Lahore and collects huge sums to fight the so-called "holy war" in Kashmir. . . .

. . . However, donations are not enough to lubricate the proxy war. There are certain other ways also to ensure an uninterrupted supply of money. These include: (1) sale of narcotics on a large scale (the United Nations Drug Control Program has it that the ISI annually makes around $ 2.5

billion through this source and it must be spending anything between Rs 537.5 crore and Rs 1,075 crore on fuelling militancy every year.[104]
— *The Tribune* (India), 28 November 1999

Unfortunately, that same American news magazine also confirms the ISI's drug smuggling involvement.

The [1993 Mumbai] bombings . . . made Dawood India's most wanted man. The ISI then made Dawood an offer: If he relocated to Pakistan's port city of Karachi and kept working with the ISI, it would guarantee him control of the nation's coastal smuggling routes.[105]
— *U.S. News & World Report*, 5 December 2005

What Is Not Being Said about Daniel Pearl

As America's heroic investigative reporter Daniel Pearl was killed shortly after 9/11, most of the research into his death has revolved around Karachi's *al-Qaeda*-affiliated militant factions. However, it is now widely acknowledged that something of a symbiotic relationship has existed between many of those factions, the ISI, and a Karachi-based drug-trafficking syndicate.[106] Thus, one can't delve too hard into one of the three without discovering something unpleasant about another. Because of the massive amounts of money involved, questions about drug smuggling could have gotten Pearl killed in Karachi just as easily as any about airplane bombing. That much money can buy any number of connections (that wouldn't stop at Dubai). Add to that, Pakistan's rather strange affinity for expeditionary extremists and smuggling revenue,[107] and one has all the makings of world-class nightmare. Several researchers go so far as to claim that Dawood and the ISI were both involved in the selling of Pakistan's nuclear secrets.[108] If true, that country's internal problems may be more severe, and have more strategic import on the world stage, than anyone dared to imagine.

Not much has been said about claims that Daniel Pearl went on 23 January 2002 from Karachi's Sheraton to the Village (or Village Garden) Restaurant to conduct an interview about organized crime.[109] (Refer back to Map 2.1.) Then, someone by the name of Saud Memon drove him to a personally owned compound where

117

others did the killing.[110] Memon was supposedly just a textile manufacturer who had helped to finance *HUM* or some other militant faction.[111] But, a well-respected Pakistani researcher claims he was much more than that. He was a garment exporter with close ties to local smugglers. That researcher calls Memon "one of Dawood's shadowy henchmen."[112] Then, he confirms that Pearl was murdered because he had been asking too many questions about Dawood Ibrahim.[113]

Such detailed assertions are not very easy to corroborate. It is Yakub and Tiger Memon who are usually associated with Dawood Ibrahim. The now deceased Saud was not part of the same family,[114] and hundreds, if not thousands, of other Karachi residents bear the same surname. Still, big money is just as probable a motive for high-stakes murder as extremist hatred. As late as 2000, the ISI was still financing its foreign adventures by radical proxies with drug money.[115] Pearl may have gotten too close to this unfortunate truth.

If nothing else, this line of reasoning will help to reveal the multi-headed *Hydra* that the West now faces in the region. To define it only as "*al-Qaeda*" is to underestimate its capabilities. The real "bull in the china shop" is drug trafficking. When that has been controlled, much of the ideological controversy will simply fade away. Any number of reactionary elements may be behind it (to include the biggest remaining Communist nation). If organized crime did have something to do with Daniel Pearl's murder, then who's to say it didn't help with other obscene acts? According to one author, "[Dawood's] power and capability in the underworld remain undiminished; he can still do what he wants."[116] Thus, it is far more likely that rogue elements of the ISI worked for Ibrahim's syndicate than the other way around. Still, the ISI does hold far too much sway over its parent regime and Pakistani society as a whole.

The State within a State

Whether any segment of the ISI is still associated with drug trafficking is anyone's guess. Even more worrisome is that some portion may still consider itself a "state within a state." That is classic *jihadist* methodology. It is what *Hezbollah* did in Lebanon, and what al-Sadr's followers are still attempting in Iraq.

"It [the ISI] is a state within a state," says Wajid
Shamsul Hasan, a former Pakistani High Commissioner in
Britain. . . .
"Pakistan's foreign policy has been run by the ISI rather
than the foreign office," he said.[117]
— BBC News Online, 9 January 2002

In late May of 2005, an American tourist was confronted one
night in the lobby of his Islamabad hotel by someone who had to be
a leader in both the Taliban and Pakistani government. That tourist had just returned to the hotel after being closely followed by a
bearded man in a black turban (the distinguishing characteristics of
a Taliban). As he sat in the lobby near the front entrance, the door
guard(s) and five or six other lobby guests suddenly left. Then, a
well-dressed and clean-shaven man entered the hotel and sat down
facing the tourist. Supremely confident, he said the tourist looked
worried. When the man then started talking about harm coming
to the U.S. president, the tourist decided to remind him about the
"hospitality to strangers" tradition that is so prevalent in the tribal
regions. Clearly enraged, the stranger jumped up, said he would
be hospitable to the tourist but not to his leaders, and stormed into
the hotel. To this day, that tourist is convinced that he had been
talking to a high-level ISI official about whether he would be allowed
by the Taliban to leave Islamabad in one piece.[118]
    If the ISI has not now been purged of all wrongdoers, its possible
degree of complicity in the chaos and drug running is mind-boggling.
It is known to be deeply involved in Pakistan's internal politics.[118]
Supposedly comprised of armed forces personnel on three-year
tours, no one can figure out how it still manages to wield so much
power. Its director-general is appointed by the prime minister,[120]
so any chronic problems may be inherited from a wayward clique
inside the Pakistani Army. After all, it was a Pakistani-Army-run
trucking company—the NLC—that was bringing the drugs out of
Afghanistan during the Soviet-Afghan War.[121] Perhaps, that's where
the real problem lies.

What All This May Mean to the Future of the Region

That anti-Western Iran seized 71 times more opiates in 2007
than pro-Western Pakistan does little to assuage one's concerns

about the latter becoming a narco-state.[122] Additionally, some nation, organization, or movement is clearly trying to so destabilize Pakistan as to topple its current government.

> In the wake of the four well-orchestrated commando-style attacks . . . by different terrorist groups against security establishments on October 15, 2009, . . . Rehman Mallick, Pakistan's Interior Minister, is reported to have aptly described the increasingly uncontrollable situation faced by Pakistan in the Pashtun tribal belt and in Punjab as a guerrilla warfare launched against the State of Pakistan.[123]
> — South Asia Analysis Group, 15 October 2009

The hidden culprit may be *al-Qaeda,* part of the Pakistani bureaucracy (Zia and Musharaff both came to power via military coups), or just a political party. A well-respected local researcher thinks it's *JI*. He claims that *JI*'s stated agenda is to take over the State from within. Constantly trying to infiltrate Pakistan's power structure,[124] it already has considerable influence inside the Pakistani military.[125] (Almost 70% of the officers and men in the Pakistani Army are Punjabis, and the majority have attended Lahore schools.[126]) With the Swat offensive by *JI*-affiliates and China with its own *JI* alliance,[127] that researcher may be right. However, it is also possible that an expansionist neighbor has been using *JI* as its unsuspecting instrument. While Iran and China are both capable of such things, the latter is more likely to be interfering with Pakistan's internal affairs. Nepal finally succumbed to 20 years of that nation's subversive activity in 2008.[128] Now both India and Afghanistan seem to be under the same type of duress. For the second time in five years, the Indian government announced on 18 February 2010 that its Maoist rebellion constituted its "single biggest internal security threat."[129] In mid-April 2010, 76 Indian policemen were killed by Maoist rebels in a single incident.[130] Whereas 55 districts in nine states were beset by Maoists in 2004, a full third of the 636 districts in 20 of India's 28 states were by May 2010.[131]

Did not another Communist neighbor try to add Afghanistan to its sphere of influence in the 1980's? Because its armed forces conducted counterinsurgency operations in much the same way as those from America, the reasons for its defeat must be remembered.

8   Reasons behind the Soviet Failure

- What was the Soviet's strategic priority in Afghanistan?
- Why didn't it work?

The Soviets tried to kill every Afghan rival.

(Sources: FM 21-76 [1957], p. 89; Orion Books, from *World Army Uniforms since 1939* © 1975, 1980, 1981 by Blandford Press, Ltd., Part II, Plate 2)

The Overall Scheme of Soviet Maneuver

As American forces had done in Vietnam, the Russian Army attempted many "sweep" operations in Afghanistan—with limited effect.

> When the Soviets entered Afghanistan, their combat manuals did not consider the cordon and search (block and sweep) as a form of combat. Therefore Soviet forces considered this a new tactic.[1]
> — After-Action Report from Russian General Staff

The Soviets' large-scale, high-tempo operations mostly failed to meet their own expectations. They would block off one end of a valley, and then—after artillery and air strikes—come charging in the other with all guns blazing, fully intending to beat someone. In addition, they sent special operators against enemy resupply routes, established outposts to protect their own lines of communication, and built up the Afghan Army. In essence, they tried to win their war at the operational level with overwhelming might. Their force structure, weapons, and tactics were all tied to this operational and "ordnance-heavy" vision.[2] Unfortunately, Afghan guerrillas too easily went to ground to be badly hurt by this much strategic drama.[3] With an overall mission of "death by a thousand razor cuts,"[4] they needed no orders, routinely swarmed to each other's assistance, and easily made do with whatever they could steal or smuggle. As a result, the Soviet force structure, tactics, and weapons were all quite inappropriate for the job at hand. During enemy engagements, their long chain of command made timely instructions as unlikely as bottom-echelon initiative. Their tactics were decidedly 2nd Generation (based more on firepower than surprise). Additionally, their weapons were far too large for what often amounted to a policing exercise against a minority criminal element. In fact, they frequently bombarded whole villages.[5] As a result, the civilian population became less and less enchanted with their puppet regime.

Counterinsurgency takes small-unit proficiency—enough to sneak up on an enemy camp, outmaneuver enemy ambushers, or single-handedly defend an isolated outpost. On all three counts, the Soviets were deficient. Their infantry was so unfamiliar with surprise-oriented missions as to defer to *Spetsnaz* on all raids.[6] Ambushed columns seldom, if ever, used their security platoons to outflank the enemy. Instead, cargo-laden vehicles had to endure RPG fire and looting while everyone waited for air support. For defense, Soviet outposts also depended on supporting arms. In deep, narrow valleys, even "smart" artillery shells have too low a trajectory to hit many targets. Every outpost would have needed its own aircraft "on station" to repel a ground assault. Those same Soviet-era outposts depended for all sustenance on passable roads. In Afghanistan's highly precipitous terrain, the *mujahideen* soon made an art form out of blocking those roads. That's how they acquired much of their ordnance.

Despite the improbability of future large-scale, theater-level, conventional war, the Russian Army has been unable to change since its Afghan lesson.[7] That most likely means that a "bottom-echelon" deficiency has been perpetuated by its "top-down" structure. Other Westernized armies suffer from the same problem.

How the Soviets Conducted Reconnaissance

The Soviets had trouble figuring out what the *mujahideen* were up to in Afghanistan. Their problem was twofold: (1) not knowing what to look for; and (2) amassing intelligence the wrong way. The parallels to Vietnam are striking, and some may still apply to U.S. expeditionary forces.

Looking for structure where it didn't exist, the Soviets viewed the principal *mujahideen* factions within Pakistan as military commands that planned, coordinated, and conducted operations. In reality, those factions were religious/political parties that served only as logistics conduits and haphazard relays for operational advice.[8] The Pakistani ISI was only able to control the action by giving more Western aid to those factions that most closely followed its strategy.[9] The ISI accepted this reality, whereas the Russians could not. In Vietnam, U.S. intelligence also appeared oblivious to the Asians' "bottom-up" way of doing things, heritage of deception, and more advanced small-unit tactics. As such, it seldom came up with anything of use to a U.S. rifle company commander.[10] That particular shortfall is less true today, but far from gone.

The Soviets relied heavily on radio intercepts, overhead photography, and Afghan spy networks. Unfortunately, the latter were heavily infiltrated by *mujahideen*. The Soviets also had experienced scouts, but they were unwisely channeled into active combat. After quadrupling their reconnaissance force to a full fifth of the 40th Army, the Soviets still could not get the better of the *mujahideen*. Part of the problem was that most raids and ambushes were being conducted by reconnaissance instead of infantry forces. The two brigades of world-famous *Spetsnaz* were dedicated to interdicting enemy logistics conduits along the Pakistani border. Instead of mapping and discreetly sabotaging caravans or depots, those *Spetsnaz* ambushed and raided them. This left the *mujahideen* heartland relatively free of ground observation.[11]

While deep-reconnaissance personnel were used as aerial observers (to call in airstrikes) in Vietnam, there is a more contemporary parallel to the Soviet mistake. Hasn't the Pentagon been recently increasing its special-operations capabilities? U.S. Army Special Forces personnel have traditionally been used for ground reconnaissance.[12] Now that they are doing more training of indigenous troops, who will fill that vital reconnaissance role? The answer to that question must lie in the grossly overrated and economy-stimulating field of technology. When one can see every part of a battlefield from satellites, why have any ground reconnaissance at all? Those who routinely close with the enemy know why, but their highest-level commanders have apparently forgotten. One still needs continuous ground assessment for two reasons: (1) wood gathers can look like combatants from 50 miles up; and (2) satellite imagery is almost as easy to deceive as aerial photography. The only difference is in the movement and heat signatures. If enemy activity is carefully enough choreographed and mostly below ground, today's electronic surveillance devices still cannot decipher its true intent. Would Iwo Jima have been any easier to take if under surveillance by satellite? Probably not, because only within the last 10 years have Western tacticians fully realized its defensive genius.[13]

Even along repeatedly ambushed stretches of road, the Soviets seldom reconnoitered with dismounted infantry.[14] As the *mujahideen* dug more and more positions at the best ambush sites, they were able to use those sites over and over. Now able to shift between bombardment resistant holes,[15] they grew bold enough to bait armored columns.[16] All the while, they took few precautions with exposed flanks, because the Russians had shown so little interest in their ambush pattern or ground pursuit.[17]

How the Soviets Viewed the Rest of the Security Mission

During the Soviet-Afghan War, the *mujahideen* forces preferred to attack governmental/manufacturing installations, military garrisons, and lines of communication (LoCs). Many of the Soviet troops were thus allocated to safeguarding "security zones" and "LoCs" (roads). Their security duties mostly consisted of manning "picket" or "guard" posts. The Soviet 40th Army established 862 picket posts in which 20,200 personnel served (or a fifth of the total force).[18]

The mujahideen launched never-ending attacks on the Soviets' long, vulnerable lines of communication, both back to the U.S.S.R. and within Afghanistan. Security of the open, western LoC[s] required only three battalions, but the difficult eastern part needed 26 battalions manning 199 outposts and constantly patrolling or escorting convoys. Generally, at any given time, over three quarters of the [Soviet's] Limited Contingent was tied down in essential security missions of various sorts, drastically reducing the numbers available for offensive action.[19]

— Sandhurst (British Military Academy) Research

As for the Puppet Regime's Army

The DRA (Democratic Republic of Afghanistan) Army had many of the same problems as its current sequel. The *mujahideen* had so heavily infiltrated the DRA that they enjoyed help from inside many of their attack objectives. Here's what happened during a weapons raid on the DRA's 15th Infantry Division garrison at Kandahar in the fall of 1987.

We crept to the building and saw that our contacts had placed a ladder against the wall for us. Some 50 of our group took up positions outside the compound while our raiding group of 50 climbed the ladder up onto the roof of the building. Then we climbed down from the roof inside the compound walls.[20]

— Akhtarjhan, *mujahideen* commander

The *Mujahideen's* Proficiency at 4GW

The *mujahideen* were not as brutal as the Taliban. Though fully capable of political assassination and prisoner abuse, they never singled out groups of Soviet or Afghan citizens for destruction.[21] Instead of rocketing downtown Kabul, they preferred to raid its bussing authority,[22] radio station,[23] and electricity grid.[24] In short, they attacked infrastructure and then sidestepped response. By so doing, they discredited the puppet regime, segmented/isolated its forces, and nurtured popular support.

125

From the *mujahideen,* there is no evidence of the alternative legal and governance system that *Hezbollah* started in Lebanon, al-Sadr instituted in Iraq,[25] and the Taliban has adopted in Afghanistan.[26] Still, something similar may already exist in any tribal society. Nor is there any evidence of *Hezbollah-*like basic services or humanitarian aid being provided to the local citizenry by either the *mujahideen* or their modern equivalent. The Taliban takes over each village's leadership, terrorizes its inhabitants, and then provides the only job in town.

If the Drug Trade Harmed the Soviets

Not much has been written about the extent to which drugs funded the *mujahideen,* or if the Soviets tried to stop those drugs. In the 1980's, most of the region's opium was being grown/produced in Pakistani FATA.[27] However, some came from Afghanistan's Helmand Province. At the time, Mullah Nasim Akhundzada was Helmand's most powerful warlord and already harvesting opium to help fight the Russians.[28] Then, for control of Helmand's poppy fields, Hekmatyar launched a two-year internal war against Akhundzada.[29] Toward the end of the Soviet occupation, Hekmatyar had a series of heroin labs along the Afghan border and was tied in with Pakistani smuggling networks.[30] Already the ISI's favorite of seven *mujahideen* leaders, he would soon become its instrument for determining the future of post-Soviet Afghanistan. By the late 1980's, Stinger-protected convoys were regularly driving from Helmand, through Pakistani Baluchistan, into Iran, and ultimately to Turkey. They did so under the joint auspices of Iranian Revolutionary Guards and rogue Pakistani officials.[31]

Another top *mujahideen* leader, Yunis Khalis also smuggled drugs from Afghanistan to FATA during the Soviet-Afghan War. Along the Pakistani border, he operated several of his own heroin labs and smuggling conduits.[32] It was Khalis who was to sell Stinger missiles to the Iranian Revolutionary Guards.[33] One of Khalis' subordinates—Haqqani—probably ran his principal smuggling route. While fighting the Russians, Haqqani's area of operations was just south of the Parrot's Beak around Khost—right where *al-Qaeda* had many of its training camps.[34] He also frequented North Waziristan's capital of Miram Shah—the entrance to one of the main supply routes.[35]

During the Soviets' struggle for Afghanistan, a Pakistani-Army-run trucking company (the NLC) took Western arms for the guerrillas from Karachi to Quetta or Peshawar and then returned with heroin for export.[36] Many of those same trucks may have entered Afghanistan. Instead of a civilian trucking conglomerate, Haji Ayub Afridi—the Afghan drug lord whose empire straddled the Khyber Pass—used NLC trucks to move his opiates into Pakistan.[37]

U.S. Stinger missiles are generally credited with beating the Soviets, so few analysts assign much meaning to the financial and other benefits of drug smuggling. It was Stingers that stopped the Soviet resupply of outposts by helicopter, but it was established smuggling conduits that made possible the *mujahideen's* infusion with Western arms. That's why *Spetsnaz* had so much trouble interdicting the supply routes. The Pakistani border crossings alone must have resembled modern-day, Mexican cartel "plazas"—replete with corrupt customs officials, freight forwarders, and police chiefs.[38] Just as U.S. guns are now smuggled south through those plazas, so too did Western arms then more easily flow into Afghanistan. Many may have been completely dismantled and then transported one part at a time, as is still often the practice.[39]

Other Problems the Soviets Did Not Have

There were no suicide bombers in Afghanistan during the Soviet era. Only after 9/11, did they start to appear.[40] Haqqani has since been credited with introducing them to the resistance,[41] so *al-Qaeda* is most likely responsible.

While the *mujahideen* lacked the sophisticated IEDs of the modern era, they did fairly well with old-fashioned land mines. Most of their mines were of the pressure-release variety, but not all. During the earliest stages of the Soviet-Afghan War, remotely controlled "shartaki" mines were already in use.[42]

The mujahideen were also enthusiastic proponents of mine warfare (during the war, the Soviets lost 1,191 vehicles and 1,995 men to mines). They mostly employed anti-vehicle mines (often piling three on top of each other for a catastrophic kill) and delighted in improvising huge homemade mines. Mines, sometime[s] command detonated, were usually covered by fire and dug up for reuse if not set off by enemy vehicles.[43]

— Sandhurst (British Military Academy) Research

The *mujahideen* of the 1980's were no more tactically sophisticated than the Taliban are today. The difference is in their relative potential. The *mujahideen* were given whatever quality of training and weaponry their handlers dared to share. Today's Taliban can afford the best training and weaponry that the world has to offer. One can only pray that U.S. leaders discover a viable strategy to oppose them before that occurs. To have any chance of quickly working, that strategy must widely differ from that of the Soviet Union.

Still Probable
Conduits and Depots

- Where were *mujahideen* conduits in Soviet-Afghan War?
- Does the Taliban still use the same routes and depots?

View of the terrain between North Waziristan and Paktiya.

(Source: DA PAM 550-35 [September, 1991], cover)

The *Mujahideen* Resupply Effort

The Afghan *mujahideen* were resupplied in much the same way as the Viet Cong had been 20 years before. Whatever they couldn't salvage or capture from their oversupplied foe, they received from outside the country over well-disguised resupply conduits. More of the Afghan routes were visible from the air, but their contraband was so well mixed in with legitimate civilian traffic as virtually to disappear (like it had at Hue City [1]). The end result was an extensive smuggling network with its mostly Pakistani entrance channels eventually branching off into a myriad of micro-filament ends.

Without much fear of ground or aerial interdiction, its designers made full use of traditional caravan routes, roads, and trails. In largely barren Afghanistan, that was more possible through smuggling tricks than camouflage. Either the number of resupply runs was high enough to compensate for any brush with airstrike, raid, and checkpoint, or the routes and depots were randomly rotated.

In order to cross the border, the Mujahideen used over 50 routes, which split into a large number of roads and trails suitable for the movement of mechanical, animal-drawn, or pedestrian traffic. In all, there were 99 caravan routes in Afghanistan, of which 69 were vehicular and 30 were for pack animals.[2]

—After-Action Report from Russian General Staff

The guerrillas took much of their ordnance from the Soviet or Afghan Army and much of their food from their own population. Everything else they got from Pakistan or Iran along cleverly designed resupply conduits.[3] From the ISI's Ojhiri Camp in Rawalpindi, supplies went to forward ISI depots in Peshawar and Quetta, and then into religious party warehouses for transshipment along the various routes into Afghanistan.[4] (Notice the party border base areas on Map 5.5.) One resupply route originated at Miram Shah, the capital of North Waziristan.[5] Its first waystations inside Afghanistan were elaborate and below ground.[6] Due to the region's scarcity of vegetation, conduits followed tunnels, narrow gorges, or irrigation ditches whenever possible.[7] Then, they branched off into thousands of feeder routes, each leading to its own terminal cache.[8] Those caches were often hidden below ground, just outside of an Afghan town or village.[9]

The Major Resupply Conduits and Depots

Along the major entrance channels into Afghanistan from Pakistan (as depicted in Map 5.5), there were strings of relatively inaccessible and well-hidden (mostly underground) supply depots. The *mujahideen* chieftains to whom the supplies were eventually delivered then shifted them into smaller caches near the fighting, just as the North Koreans had done in the early 1950's. That way, the supplies only went to the units in most immediate need.

The only real indicators of many depots' whereabouts were security garrisons in places that local tribesmen did not ordinarily inhabit.

The mujahideen were forced to bring in food and medical supplies, mainly from Pakistan, as well as the weapons and ammunition being provided in increasing quantities from abroad. These had to be stockpiled in a series of dispersed base depots, sited in inaccessible areas. Such bases were also needed for training and rest and the treatment of wounded. Still valuable, but less critical because they were smaller, were forward supply points established to support current operations. The latter could be moved relatively quickly and frequently to avoid attack. The former, on the other hand, required defending. In defense, the guerrillas exploited rugged or otherwise difficult terrain and their detailed knowledge of it. They also put immense efforts into preparing their bases for defense, as for instance in the Zhawar cave and tunnel complex in Paktiya province or the green zone of Baraki Barak district between Kabul and Gardez.[10]
    — Sandhurst (British Military Academy) Research

The North Waziristan to Paktiya Supply Channel

The resupply channel that originated at Miram Shah below the Parrot's Beak in Map 5.5 is the one on which there is the most information. Its history will be reviewed and then any evidence of continuing use. To establish its location and method, one must work eastward from its Afghan exit depots.

Toward the end of the Soviet-Afghan War, *al-Qaeda's* first training site inside Afghanistan ("al-Ansar") was near the Afghan village of Jaji in Paktiya Province.[11] "Zhawar" was only one of two *al-Qaeda* camps over the "Zawwhar Kili al-Badr" complex 30 kilometers southwest of Khost astride the Pakistani border (the other being "al-Badr").[12] Formerly run by *HIK* (the Khalis faction of *Hizb-i-Islami),* the two camps sat just inside Afghanistan on a hillside atop an expansive network of caves and tunnels. When the Soviets attempted to attack that complex in 1986, its defenders escaped at the end of a three-week battle through subterranean passageways into Pakistan.[13] The Zawwhar Kili complex covers nine square miles and contains at least 50 caves.[14] Somewhere else in the Zazi mountains of Paktiya, Osama bin Laden blasted enough roads, tunnels, and subterranean rooms to accommodate field hospitals, arms depots, and a training facility for hundreds of fighters. That complex stretched over several kilometers as well.[15] Other al-Qaeda underground facilities existed at Kabul, Khost, Mahavia, Jalalabad, Kunar, and Kandahar. Al-Qaeda "depots" (presumably supply) were reported at Tora Bora and Liza.[16] After the U.S. invasion, al-Qaeda tried secretly to regroup near Gardez.[17]

Whether North Waziristan to Paktiya Route Still Operates

When fighting the Russians, Jalaluddin Haqqani's area of operations was just south of the Parrot's Beak around Khost.[18] (Refer back to Map 1.7.) For whatever reason, he also frequented Miram Shah in North Waziristan.[19]

Originally from JI-affiliated HIK,[20] Haqqani now professes his allegiance to the Afghan Taliban and operates a series of camps in the border districts of Paktiya Province.[21] His Paktiya Province camps now include "Jaji" (al-Qaeda's first camp) and neighboring "Dand Wa Patan." In addition to Paktiya Province, Haqqani currently operates in Khost and Paktika provinces.[22] He has been directed by Mullah Omar to control the southeastern border region from a forward headquarters in North Waziristan.[23]

By some accounts, Haqqani has since become the Taliban's director of operations against U.S. and NATO forces.[24] More likely, he runs one of their biggest fund-raising and resupply efforts—drugs out and ordnance in. As late as June 2010, the U.N. was still showing his old route operational. (See Map 9.1.) Haqqani's relationship with the "Shadow Army" also suggests an affiliation with al-Qaeda.[25]

The Other Afghan Conduits

There were six major supply channels from Pakistan into Afghanistan during the Soviet-Afghan War. (Look back at Map 5.5.) According to the following account, Zwadar lay at the start of the route from Miram Shah. Then, near Gardez, its northern branch led into Logar Province, while its southern branch headed for Ghazni. The Haqqani Network must still use them. (See Map 9.2.)

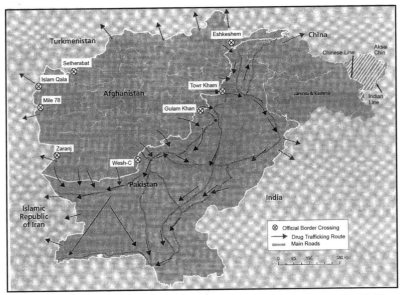

Map 9.1: U.N. Depiction of Regional Drug Movement in 2010
(Source: Courtesy of U.N. Cartographic Section and UNODC, © 2010, based Maps 3, 4, and 5 of *World Drug Report 2010*, and China_India_Pakistan_map_tmp.pdf
[the boundaries and names shown and the designations used on this map do not imply official endorsement or acceptance by the United Nations])

There were six main routes leading into Afghanistan. Starting in the north, from Chitral a high route led to the Panjsher valley, Faizabad and the northern provinces. This was the shortest, cheapest and safest passage to these regions, but it was closed by the snow for up to eight months every year. We could only use it from June to October. Next came the busiest route. From Parachinar (the Parrot's Beak) via Ali Khel into Logar Province was the gateway to the Jihad, through which some 40 per cent of our supplies passed. This was the shortest route to Kabul, only a week's journey away. We also used it for journeys north over the mountains to the plains around Mazar-i-Sharif, although this could take a month or more. The disadvantage lay in the strong enemy [pro-Soviet] opposition that tried to bar

133

Map 9.2: A Closer Examination of Haqqani's Old Conduit
(Source: Courtesy of General Libraries, University of Texas at Austin, from their website, for map designator "txu-oclc-300481561-afghan_paki_admin_2008.jpg")

the way. When the Soviets wanted to decrease pressure on Kabul it was in the eastern provinces that they launched their largest search and destroy missions.

A little further *[sic]* south, the third route started around Miram Shah via Zhawar, again into Logar Province. Supply trains could either swing south near Gardez or Ghazni, or north to join the second route over the mountains. This was another busy route, but enemy interference was relatively light.

The fourth route started in Quetta, crossed the frontier at Chaman, before leading towards Kandahar and nearby provinces. There was much open country which meant vehicles were required to shift the bulk of the supplies quickly. We aimed to get trucks to their destination in one day's or night's fast driving. Suspicious vehicles were subjected to enemy ground or air attacks.

Over 400 kilometers further *[sic]* west, on the southern border of Helmand Province, was the smaller and unpopular base at Girzi-Jungle [Girdi-Jungle]. It was used to replenish Helmand, Nimroz, Farah, and Herat Provinces. It was unpopular as vehicles were so vulnerable to attack. Seldom did we send in a convoy without incident. It was an arid, open area, sparsely populated, with little possibility of early warning of attack. Trucks travelling north were easily spotted from the air and were often shot up by gunships or ambushed by heliborne troops prepositioned ahead of them. To reach Herat by vehicle took a week.

Finally, the sixth route was via Iran. A glance at Map 9 [5.5 in this book] will show that to get supplies quickly and safely to Farah and Herat Provinces a long drive west along the Baluchistan border to Iran, then another 600 kilometers north from Zahedan in Iran to the Iran-Afghanistan frontier opposite Herat, a three-day journey, was the answer—in theory. In practice it was very different. Although we did use this route it took up to six months for the Iranians to grant a special permit, then only small arms could be carried, while every convoy was checked, inspected and escorted by Revolutionary Guards. It was the same when our empty vehicles reentered Iran.[26]

— Brigadier Yousaf, Afghan Service Bureau Chief

That the "militants" were still disrupting all road travel into Kurram tribal agency as late as May 2010 speaks volumes about the current status of the Parrot's Beak resupply route.[27] Another Soviet-era route may be back in service as well—this time for export. Haji Kuma Khan was recently found to have underground drug storage facilities at Girdi Jungle.[28] (Refer back to Map 5.5.)

The Taliban's Major Resupply Bases

Now that U.S. and other NATO troops are pulling back into populated areas, much of the former resupply network may again

135

become operational. While its number of depots is known, their specific locations are still largely a mystery. Yet, the very fact that all would still be heavily defended should give satellite imagery interpreters a clue as to their whereabouts in uninhabited space. But beware, trying militarily to destroy them may not help to win the war. The Russians dedicated all of their *Spetsnaz* capability to this task and still lost.[29] That may be because smuggling waystations are too easy to rotate. Perhaps, the Soviet special operators should have covertly sabotaged them instead.

> The Mujahideen would establish temporary bases for weapons, ammunition, and other combat material. Along the borders with Pakistan and Iran, they would establish transfer bases on caravan routes in the mountain passes. They would establish supply groups and detachments at intervals [along those routes] where they would distribute and sell weapons [at supply points]. These supply points were controlled by an identity card and pass system and had an observer organization, an early warning system, an air defense system, and a guard system. Sometimes transfer bases were combined with regional supply bases. In the territory of Afghanistan, there were eighteen major supply bases, which included nine regional bases, two supply transfer bases, and seven supply transfer points.[30]
> —After-Action Report from Russian General Staff

The Watershed Realization

As first suggested in Chapter 5, more closely watching the bottlenecks in Afghanistan's limited road system may now be the best way to interdict the Taliban's flow of wherewithal in and drugs out. Despite wholly dedicating *Spetsnaz* to interdicting the *mujahideen's* inward flow of supplies, the Soviets were never able to do it. Like the outbound drugs, most of the inbound *mujahideen* ordnance must have been smuggled "in pieces" by vehicle along public roadways instead of carried "in tact" by mules over obscure trails.

Fully aware of the regional pressures and historical failures, one can now begin to formulate some other ways of doing things. Without commensurate technique, the new U.S. strategy will stand little chance.

Part Three

The Martial Part of a 4GW Equation

"There is no such thing as 'tough.' There's 'trained,'
and there's 'untrained.' So which are you?"
— Denzel Washington in *Man on Fire*

(Source: Attributed to the screen writers of "Man on Fire")

10 Changes in How the Taliban Fights

● What do the Afghan Taliban now do differently?
● Where do they get their wherewithal?

The Taliban have their own criminal justice system.

(Source: DA PAM 550-65 [January, 1986], p. 139)

The Afghan Taliban May Now Have a New Strategy

As the U.S. Surge began to reach Afghanistan, there was a noticeable increase in the sophistication of suicide attacks within that nation. Just as the Indian Parliament had been in late 2001,[1] Afghanistan's presidential palace and several of its ministries came under ground attack on 18 January 2010. Some 20 enemy fighters participated (many wearing suicide vests). At one point, an Afghan Army ambulance showed up carrying a large quantity of explosives. They were immediately detonated.[2] Suicide bombers had targeted Kabul's governmental complex before, but this attack was

139

substantially different. In October 2008, a lone suicide bomber had penetrated the Ministry of Information and Culture.[3] Four months later, six suicide bombers had split up to hit the Justice Ministry and Department of Prison Affairs. All were carrying "machineguns," so they most likely shot their way in before self-detonating.[4] In a similar attack on 28 October 2009, gunmen with automatic weapons and suicide vests stormed a U.N. guest house.[5] After all three episodes, Taliban "militants" were given the credit. Yet, the 2010 attack on downtown Kabul was unique in that it encompassed not only governmental headquarters, but also civilian gathering places. Two shopping malls and a cinema had been involved.[6] That brings back unpleasant memories of the Mumbai attack of November 2008. There, several hotels, a train station, two hospitals, a police station, a Jewish community center, a restaurant, and a cinema all came under duress.[7]

The precise details of the 2010 Kabul event are sketchy. After a series of blasts and more than three hours of ensuing gunfights outside several ministries and inside a shopping mall, President Karzai declared security had been restored. Some seven militants had died, including several who had detonated explosive vests. The first blast was heard shortly before 10:00 A.M. in an area where important buildings are concentrated—among them, the Presidential Palace, Central Bank, and luxury Serena Hotel frequented by Westerners.[8] One suicide bomber had blown himself up near the Bank's main gate,[9] but none of his accomplices had gained entry.[10] Five minutes later, three intruders penetrated the five-story Foreshgah Buzerg Afghan shopping complex near the Presidential Palace throwing grenades. After taking up fighting positions in its upper stories, they began firing at the Finance and Justice Ministries, Serena Hotel, and National Palace. While this firing was still in progress, another militant detonated the ambulance bomb in front of stores near the Foreign Ministry.[11] Before long, the first shopping complex was engulfed in flames as government forces pressed their attack.[12] Then, two of the intruders detonated their vests, and Afghan security forces killed two others. Elsewhere in the city, Afghan troops surrounded a cinema and opened fire on the terrorists inside. That fighting ended when the last suicide attacker blew himself up.[13] Any others may have escaped.

Later, Afghan officials claimed that only two civilian structures had been actually occupied by the attackers.[14] However, one reputable Indian news source claims a suicide bomber detonated his explosives-filled vest inside the Ministry of Information and Culture. Its security guards had opened small-arms fire at the bomber, but he still managed to enter the building and blow himself up.[15] In addition, the luxury Serena Hotel may have been hit by a rocket of some kind. A Taliban website claimed that a few of its foreign occupants had been killed, but there was no confirmation of that claim.[16]

Having fought several wars with Pakistan, India has become very good at identifying the Islamist factions that periodically raid its territory. Its intelligence service and news media are both quite thorough in their investigations. *LET* and *JEM* are thought to have run the 2001 raid on India's Parliament,[17] whereas *LET* alone is known to have run the 2008 raid on Mumbai.[18] As this latest assault on Kabul is an amalgam (in method) of both forays, criminal investigators would say that *modus operandi* evidence makes *LET* the most likely perpetrator. Shortly after the attack, the Afghan Interior Minister did tell a press conference that the bombers were trained outside of Afghanistan.[19]

As the armed wing of *JuD (MDI)*, *LET is* a sizeable faction. Still, it is only one of several that provide suicide assault squads to *al-Qaeda*. *LeJ, JEM,* and *LET* are all part of Osama bin Laden's IIF. As discussed in Chapter 3, *LeJ (SSP's* armed wing) is the one that ran many of the recent attacks against Pakistani government installations. It has been called *al-Qaeda's* "delta force."[20] Both it and *LET* have adolescent and female suicide bombers.[21] Add to that *JEM*—a radical offshoot of *HUM* that is still aligned with the Taliban-supporting *JUI/F* [22]—and one has quite a ground assault "stable." None of its suicide assault squads are very sophisticated tactically, but all (through drugs or indoctrination) are quite fearless.[23] Together, they could greatly influence the outcome of the war, just as naked sappers did in Vietnam. All the operational strategy in the world won't be enough to stop them.

The Glaring Need for a Change in Perspective

Both the Islamists and Communists are "bottom-up" thinkers and doers. In essence, they more easily achieve strategic objectives through grassroots efforts than their Western counterparts. That's how the war in Afghanistan must now be viewed, if NATO and America are to have much chance of winning it. A multi-tour veteran says his talks with village elders have revealed a type of game going on. Lecturing them on their responsibilities to the central government is not likely to win that game. Only someone with a little cultural insight and his Afghan interpreter (or indigenous CAP platoon partner) has much chance of uncovering this game's rather basic parameters. To do so, he must first learn of all terrorist acts (like night letters) and blood feuds within his general vicinity. Then, pointed questions in a relaxed tea-drinking environment may reveal which men from nearby villages are locally hated for committing those acts.[24] Those are just the types of "tips" U.S. village contingents would need to disrupt the local Taliban effort. Any "top-down" approach to the same problem (except with the overall tribal chieftain) is likely to create more ill will than progress.

The Situation at the Village Level

To truly fathom what is going on in Afghanistan, one must talk to those who have personally experienced village life many times. The U.S. military now groups all resistance fighters into what it calls the Anti-Afghan Forces (AAF). They include Taliban, *HIG*, and any criminal element (mostly drug smugglers). The resistance is following a method very similar to that of Mao Tse-Tung. It creates an AAF subcommander in each village, forms a small militia of three to five fighters, replaces the village mullah, and then replaces the village leader. By so doing, the AAF cell creates an alternative governance system—complete with its own police force, religious cleric, and political representative. With the help of all the other cells, its long-term goal is to take over the Afghan government through the electionary process. So subverted, the villages in each geographical area form a type of defense matrix. They swarm to each other's aid, generally attack from standoff range with RPGs or IEDs (with an occasional, heavy machinegun or recoilless rifle), and then withdraw under pressure. When actively pursued, they break down all crew-served weapons and then smuggle their various parts to a less dangerous place.[25]

Those who watched while southern Africa came under Communist control through U.N. elections will recognize the similarities between agendas of Islamist subcommander and Communist commissar. The U.S. military has become so enamoured with "force protection," there is little chance it will risk enough tiny village detachments to reverse this process. Still, one can hope because of a very interesting paradox. The Afghan population has become so disenchanted with violence that it will turn against whichever side uses it most. Thus, a Gandhian strategy emerges. If NATO were to outpost hundreds of villages and never resort to supporting arms in their defense, the local populace would turn against the inherently brutal Taliban. As previously intimated, the key to this whole process is the blood feud tradition. Whenever anyone is killed for no apparent reason, a blood feud with that person's tribal subgroup automatically ensues. That's why Taliban fighters are deployed to regions far from their homes. What if the NATO contingent consisted of a U.S. squad, Afghan police squad, and Afghan army squad—namely, a CAP platoon. Then, it could legitimately help with local law enforcement. To counteract the AAF subcommander, at least two of that platoon's indigenous personnel would have to speak English. Then, by fully understanding the local situation and blood feud tradition, the U.S. squad leader could find out whatever he wanted from the local citizenry about the raiding Taliban. If a local Taliban fighter can be shown that a neighboring tribe killed someone in his village during an attack on the Americans, he would readily divulge what he knows about Taliban perpetrators. In Afghanistan, the local citizens group foreign AAF fighters into three general categories—Punjabis (Pakistanis), Arabs (possibly Middle Eastern *al-Qaeda* affiliates), and Chechens (possibly Chechen *al-Qaeda* affiliates). (See Figure 10.1.) The Taliban are further broken down into "fighters" and "students."[26] The latter must be just graduated from *madrasas* or still undergoing "on-the-job" military training.

The Advent of the IED

Throughout the Soviet-Afghan War and its immediate aftermath, there was no suicide and very little remotely controlled bombing by the *mujahideen*. The first suicide bombing was of Northern Alliance leader Massoud right before 9/11. Then, in January 2004, a man with artillery and mortar rounds strapped to his chest self-detonated next to a NATO convoy,[27] and a taxi bomb interrupted the subsequent funeral.[28] Not until August 2005 were sophisticated IEDs introduced to Afghanistan.[29] As in Iraq, all Afghan IEDs—to include the more lethal EFPs—are from Iran.[30]

Figure 10.1: Middle-Eastern *al-Qaeda* Advisor
(Source: Courtesy of Michael Leahy, © 2005)

Both changes in strategy are probably due to *al-Qaeda's* closer working relationship with Lebanese *Hezbollah*. One is fundamentalist Sunni, and the other fundamentalist Shiite, but both are Salafist—namely, they both wish to return to the purest roots of Islam.[31]

During the Marjah offensive of February 2010, U.S. Marines discovered that the sites of the foe's pressure-detonated anti-personnel mines were often marked so that civilians could avoid them. That mark was a small stone atop a slightly larger stone.[32] Few of those Marines realized how many more mines had been encountered in Vietnam. In that war, the enemy liked closely to ring his buried caches and subterranean hideouts with mines—to discourage any closer approach. Where there was something of great strategic value, they would add in a little long-distance sniper fire to draw away the intruding unit.[33]

A More Formidable, But Still Flawed, Ground Assault

The early Afghan guerrilla seldom followed through on ground assaults. The average attack involved firing at an objective from several different sides after a half-hearted attempt to infiltrate it through a gate left open by a turncoat.[34]

Throughout the Soviet-Afghan War, the *mujahideen* reused this same maneuver to bring pressure on enemy outposts. They surrounded them and then brought fire to bear from every side. In this way, they were able to disguise the side from which the main assault was planned. Now, the Taliban still operate about the same way. Only a few variations to its general theme have been noted. One is that various Taliban contingents alternately cover each other's movement forward as in the U.S. Army's "bounding overwatch" maneuver.[35]

With any luck, Taliban soldiers still suffer from the same bad habits their predecessors had, like lack of flank security and tending to ambush the same places over and over. Those predecessors disliked crawling and secrecy in general—something to do with their masculinity or afterlife.[36] Below is one of the few summaries of the *mujahideen* fighter's personal shortcomings in existence.

[W]hat was wrong with my method was that it lacked noise and excitement. It was not their [the *mujahideen's]*

145

way to fight, with no firing, no chance of inflicting casual-ties, no opportunity for personal glory and no booty. Their method was to bombard the posts with heavy weapons by night at long range, move closer to fire mortars, get 30-40 men to surround them, and at short range open up with machineguns, RPGs and RLs (rocket launchers). If the garrison withdrew, the posts were captured and the muja-hideen secured their loot in the form of rations, arms and ammunition, all of which could be used or sold. Then, only then, was the charge laid on the fuel pipeline. If the garrison stuck it out, the pipeline remained untouched.

It often took a serious setback, with quite severe casu-alties, to force a [mujahideen] Commander to review his methods. Like most soldiers the Mujahid hated digging. He was decidedly unhappy in a static defensive role; it was alien to his temperament; it restricted his freedom to move, and he could seldom be convinced of the need to construct overhead cover. Similarly, his fieldcraft was often poor as he was disinclined to crawl, even when close to an enemy position. The hard stony ground, or the possibility of mines, may have had something to do with it, but I had the impres-sion that it was a bit beneath his dignity. Walk, or crouch perhaps, but crawling was seldom acceptable.[37]

— Brigadier Yousaf, Afghan Service Bureau Chief

As evidenced by the January 2010 raid on downtown Kabul, NATO forces should now expect vehicular bombs to precede any ground assault on an urban target, just as they have for years in Iraq. If those rolling bombs can be made to look like Afghan Army ambulances, they may in the future imitate anything. Without a vehicular breaching device, the al-Qaeda assault squads will simply send a suicide bomber into the first security station. Sadly, that suicide bomber could now be a child or woman.

More About *al-Qaeda's* Supposed "Shadow Army"

Because the reconstituted Brigade 055 of *al-Qaeda's* new "Shadow Army" no longer enjoys a protected garrison environment as it did at Rishikor during the Taliban regime,[38] it may not be a fully fleshed-out brigade. Instead, it is a cadred brigade that can quickly add structure to a varied assortment of resistance forces. Or, it may seldom fight as a brigade and send contingents to help the Mullah Omar's Taliban inside Afghanistan or various resistance groups inside Pakistan. The *Long War Journal* article claims that "Afghan and Pakistan-based Taliban forces have integrated elements of their forces into the Shadow Army."[39] Instead, it may be the other way around. That Shadow Army may routinely integrate small elements of its own into the Afghan Taliban, *TTP,* Haqqani Network, and others. Nazir already appears to have one.[40] And the IMU did help the *TNSM* during its advance through the Swat Valley on Islamabad.[41] During the Soviet-Afghan War, *al-Qaeda* routinely put tiny contingents of instructors into religious faction training camps inside Pakistan.[42] They did so instead of establishing their own camps. Thus, under increasing pressure from Western forces, there is now a greater chance that *al-Qaeda* is simply providing advisors or special assault elements to other resistance forces. On 24 February 2010, PBS's *Frontline World* confirmed that Arab *al-Qaeda* advisors were embedded within *HIG* forces in Baghlan Province. Their job was to help those forces interdict the NATO supply road from Tajikistan to Kabul.[43] One would hope that they are not also there to help the drugs flow north.

11 The Drug Runners' *Modus Operandi*

- Who besides the Taliban are fighting for Afghanistan?
- What do they hope to gain?

Best armed are the drug smugglers.

(Source: DA PAM 550-65 [1986], p. 209)

Stranger Things Have Happened

"Corruption" is a word that is seldom associated with the U.S. government, but illicit drugs do produce monumental profits. Wherever there is enough money, there is always the possibility of corruption. At the end of the Soviet-Afghan War, over half of all heroin on U.S. streets was coming from southern Afghanistan.[1] Several researchers agree that a Pakistani-army-run trucking company (the NLC) was bringing heroin back down to Karachi after delivering Western war supplies to the *mujahideen*.[2] Then, some of the ships that had carried Western supplies in must have returned to their

149

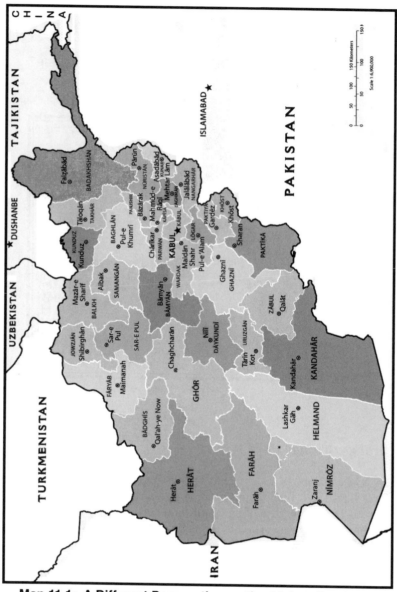

Map 11.1: A Different Perspective on the Afghan Provinces
(Source: Courtesy of General Libraries, Univ. of Texas at Austin, for map designator "txu-oclc-309296021-afghanistan_admin_2008.jpg")

home ports with hidden heroin on board. Plus, there is the distinct possibility of a similar game now being played. A respected local journalist says the same "pipeline" that carried arms in and drugs out for the *mujahideen* during the Soviet-Afghan War continued to do so for the Taliban regime until 2001. He also confides that this conduit involved trucks and Pakistani-government contracts.[3] As Pakistan and America are now allied in the War on Terror, it stands to reason that some of the same trucking companies may now be carrying NATO supplies to Kabul and Kandahar. Most researchers agree that trucks are still the most likely means of conveyance for Afghan heroin from FATA and NWFP to Karachi.[4] Their only contractor may now be a religious party militia—like *Hezb* or *JEM*.[5] However, both have previously worked as ISI proxies.[6] As late as 2003, U.S. spy satellites were watching ships leaving Pakistani ports with Afghan heroin and then returning with ordnance for the insurgency.[7] That may have given someone the idea to hide heroin aboard ships that had just delivered NATO supplies. Neither are all drug "mules" aware of their loads. With sufficient "payoffs" along the way home for those Western vessels, less concealment of the heroin would be necessary. In this age of jet travel, air-freighting of drugs is also an option.

More about Those Who Smuggle Afghan Drugs into FATA

While fighting the Russians, Haqqani's area of operations was just south of the Parrot's Beak around Khost—right where *al-Qaeda* had many of its training camps.[8] Haqqani has since been credited with introducing suicide bombers to the resistance,[9] so he must still have *al-Qaeda* ties. A reconstituted version of *al-Qaeda's* Brigade 055 is now thought to form the nucleus of the "Shadow Army" with which Haqqani is associated.[10]

As confirmed by both the *Washington Times* and *Christian Science Monitor,* Haqqani is also the person who, during the last days of the Taliban regime, clearly stated that "China was secretly assisting the Islamic militia."[11] While no details were divulged during his interview, that Chinese aid may have taken many forms. Haqqani primarily operates out of Paktiya Province, but he gets much of his refined product from labs in Nangarhar Province.[12] It is from Nangarhar that the Khyber Pass enters Pakistani FATA.

Thus, Haqqani would have undoubtedly known about the Chinese chemists who have been refining heroin for years in the Khyber Agency.[13]

It has been said that Haqqani and Hekmatyar both prefer to be thought of as military commanders. As such, they do not personally take part in the drug smuggling.[14] That means they may be using an intermediary at the border. (See Map 11.1.)

It was Haji Ayub Afridi who ran the massive heroin empire that controlled the Khyber Pass during the late 1980's. Instead of a civilian trucking conglomerate, he is known to have used NLC trucks.[15] While Afridi was then sent to jail, he was prematurely released by the Pakistanis in December 2001. Subsequent research shows his Khyber Pass smuggling operation to be still active. It also reveals some very interesting details on how Afghan drugs reach the U.S. (After being found guilty of drug trafficking again in 2005, Ayub Afridi failed to appear before the court and disappeared from view.)[16]

> U.S. authorities in Maryland this week announced indictments against 11 men targeted in a two-year investigation into a drug-smuggling and money-laundering operation with ties to Afghanistan and Pakistan.
>
> U.S. court records describe a sophisticated, large-scale heroin-smuggling and money-laundering group with operatives in Pakistan, Thailand, and Canada, as well as in the U.S. states of California, Maryland, and Virginia. . . .
>
> Those indicted in the case include two members of the ethnic Pashtun Afridi clan in Pakistan, which has a decades-long history of trafficking opium and heroin from Afghanistan. The Afridi clan and its allies control key customs posts and local administrative offices on both sides of the Afghan-Pakistani border crossing at Torkham, near the Khyber Pass.
>
> Bill Samii is an RFE/RL regional analyst for Southwest Asia who specializes in counternarcotics issues. He said the indictments highlight a new trend involving heroin smuggled from the Afghan province of Nangarhar through Pakistan's North West Frontier Province (NWFP).
>
> . . . "The interesting thing is that until now, most of the Afghan opium has headed for Europe. Now, it is going

the other direction—through Southeast Asia to the United States. I think that is the new trend and that is a very worrisome sign," Samii said.

. . . "Up until now, most of the heroin and opiates that were abused in the United States originated [either in Latin America] or in the 'Golden Triangle' of Southeast Asia," he said. "So now, what we are seeing is the 'Golden Crescent' of Southwest Asia possibly taking over from that." . . .

. . . He said the Afridis are well entrenched along the area on the Afghan side of the Torkham border crossing, as well as in Peshawar, Pakistan, and along the North West Frontier Province. "They've also got good connections with some of the Afghan so-called warlords who operated along the eastern side of Afghanistan," Samii said. "Even before current events—i.e., during the Taliban period—they had some connections with them. And then, especially back in the 1980's and into the early 1990's, they had connections with some of these people smuggling opium and opium products across the border."

Pierre-Arnaud Chouvy analyzed Afghan drug-smuggling routes in March for the London-based defense-industry publication "Jane's Intelligence Review." He said the opium trade around the Torkham border crossing tends to be monopolized by the Shinwari tribe on the Afghan side and the Afridi clan in the NWFP. Chouvy believes that heroin is easily trafficked in the NWFP from Afghanistan across Afridi territory and the Khyber Pass through what has been termed a "drug pipeline." . . .

Thomas M. DiBiagio, the U.S. prosecuting attorney involved with issuing this week's indictments, said the ties to Afghanistan and Pakistan have led investigators to explore the possibility of links to terrorist organizations. But DiBiagio said no such links have been found.[17]

— Radio Free Europe (RFE), September 2003

By saying that Affridi has had dealings with the same border warlords since the 1980's, this reporter all but names Hekmatyar and Haqqani. From the Radio Free Europe/Radio Liberty (RFE/RL) article, it can be further inferred that most Afghan heroin to reach America in 1989 did so through Europe. Then, in 2003, it started going eastward (possibly still via Dubai) into the Southeast Asian pipeline. In 2009, the U.N. Office of Drugs and Crime arrived at this same conclusion.

[A]lternative [drug] routes are emerging from South-West Asia to South-East Asia and the Oceania region. . . .
. . . [T]here have been reports of shipments of heroin from Afghanistan via Pakistan to China. The heroin is being shipped either directly (mainly by air) from Pakistan to various Chinese destinations as well as indirectly, via Dubai (United Arab Emirates). The amounts involved are still modest, but may represent emerging trafficking patterns. In 2007, Pakistan reported an additional new route to Malaysia, both direct and via Dubai. Until recently, heroin in Malaysia originated exclusively in Myanmar. This new route shows that Afghan opiates may now reach other destinations since Malaysia has been mentioned among the key embarkation points for heroin shipments into Australia (Australian Crime Commission, Illicit Drug Data Report 2006-07, Canberra, March 2009) . . .
. . . New trafficking routes from South-West Asia to North America are emerging. Canada reported that 98% of the heroin found on their market in 2007 originated in South-West Asia. The heroin was mainly trafficked by air via India and Pakistan into Canada. Organized crime groups in Ontario and British Columbia are involved in heroin imports (Criminal Intelligence Service Canada, Report on Organized Crime, Ottawa, 2008).[18]
— *United Nations World Drug Report (for) 2009*

Vancouver has been identified as the trans-shipment point into the "Lower Forty-Eight" by both the U.S.-government-sponsored RFE/RL and U.N. Those "organized-crime groups" mentioned by Canadian authorities are none other than the Hong Kong triads. The most likely candidates for funneling Afghan heroin into the world's biggest drug market are Sun Yee On and 14-K.[19]

[FBI] Agents determined that large quantities of heroin were regularly being shipped from Southeast Asia to Vancouver, Canada, then on to Toronto, Canada before being smuggled into the United States. New York FBI agents identified

four distinct trafficking organizations directing the operations from Southeast Asia. . . . [E]vidence was uncovered showing that several of the leaders of these organizations were members of the 14-K Triad criminal enterprise based in Hong Kong.[20]
— FBI Case Study, 1998

Heroin moves from the source in Southeast Asia through China's Guangdong Province to Vancouver, which is a central distribution point for North American sales. Big Circle [Boys] and Hong Kong-based triads regularly have used commercial transport to move large shipments of heroin into Canada (Criminal Intelligence Service of Canada, "Annual Report 1998").[21]
— Library of Congress Research Paper, April 2003

Instead of transiting Vancouver, that Afghan product now more probably lands in Panama City or one of the other Hutchison Whampoa ports along Central America's Pacific Coast. Then, it is transported by truck across the Mexican border as a well-hidden iota of the North American Free Trade Agreement (NAFTA) deluge.[22]

Hutchison Port Holdings, part of the Hong Kong conglomerate Cheung Kong Group, has announced plans to invest $1.2 billion in the Port of Ensenada, Mexico so that that port can handle 1.5 million containers per year, up from the current 100,000.[23]
— U.S.F. Center for the Pacific Rim, June 2005

How the Drugs Get through the Khyber Pass

Because the RFE/RL article describes the Afghan drugs traveling from Nangarhar Province, through the Khyber Pass, and into NWFP, one can be fairly sure they are moving by truck into Peshawar. NWFP does not abut the Afghan border at this location; only the Khyber tribal agency does. (Refer back to Maps 1.5, 2.2, and 3.1.) Before reaching Peshawar District, the road from the Khyber Pass runs through the FATA town of Landi Kotal. Torkham is the little town on the Afghan side of the pass. The most likely carriers are the trucks having just delivered NATO supplies to Kabul.

An estimated 70 percent of NATO supplies move through Khyber to resupply troops fighting against the Taliban in Afghanistan. The bulk of NATO's supplies arrive in the port city of Karachi, move north to Peshawar, and head west to the Torkham crossing into Afghanistan and the final destination in Kabul.[24]
— *Long War Journal,* 6 September 2008

More than 70 percent of NATO supplies and 40 percent of its fuel moves through Peshawar.[25]
— *Long War Journal,* 27 August 2009

It is within hidden compartments on tanker trucks that many of the drugs may be hidden.[26] Of course, more important that the actual hiding place is the illicit cooperation of border officials. In August 2009, someone made an example out of 22 Khyber Pass Pakistani border guards with a suicide bomber.[27]

Who Protects Drug Loads Passing through Khyber Agency?

The Khyber Agency Afridi tribe is large, and not all Afridis are supportive of Ayub's smuggling activities. Still, it may be no coincidence that Mangal Bagh Afridi now heads up a rather large group of fundamentalist "volunteers"—the *Lashkar-e-Islam (LI)*—who claim to guard against all gambling and crime. This would make the perfect cover for seeing that no harm came to any drug-laden vehicle. Some 10,000 cargo trucks transit the Khyber Pass *en route* to Peshawar every month. Some are undoubtedly carrying Afghan heroin. *LI* is by all indications an offshoot or affiliate of the *TTP.*[28]

Who Then Transports the Drugs South from Peshawar?

That *Hezb* and *JEM* are carrying drugs from FATA to Karachi does not necessarily mean that they also handle the majority of Afghan product from Peshawar.[29] Peshawar is not in FATA; it's in the NWFP. Finally to succeed, the U.S. strategy for Afghanistan must take this and the northern drug conduits seriously.

12

Present U.S. Strategy

- Would occupying every town better protect a population?
- How does drug trafficking affect counterinsurgency?

Law-enforcement-savy Marines protect an urban center.

(Sources: DA PAM 550-175 [1989], p. xxxvii; DA PAM 550-24 [1989], p. 39; Orion Books, from *Uniforms of the Elite Forces* © 1982 by Blandford Press, Ltd., Plate 5, No. 15)

Success Will Hinge on the New Strategy's Particulars

This research was done to alert the U.S. security establishment to several obscure variables within South Asia. The ultimate success of its new Afghan strategy may well depend on whether all have been considered. Warnings of the "overlooked" must be accompanied by commensurate solutions. Unfortunately, so many experts have already helped to shape this strategy, that any generalized proposal now would appear naive. To be taken seriously, one must be very specific about easy-to-integrate modifications to what has already been decided. That takes total familiarity with ongoing policy.

157

U.S. State Department Policy As of March 2009

According to NPR News, Hillary Clinton prefers a more "regional approach" to the problems in Afghanistan and Pakistan than did her predecessor. Such an approach might more greatly involve their neighbors—like India, Iran,[1] and China[2]—in the overall solution. Unfortunately, China has already demonstrated its expansionary nature in Tibet, northern India, and Nepal; and the Iranian Revolutionary Guards have subverted every Afghan regime since 1979. That those Guards helped with the U.S. invasion of 2001 is clear proof of that.[3] Because Iran, Pakistan, and the Communists have traditionally vied (through proxies) for Afghanistan's political future,[4] such an "open-ended" diplomatic policy could further undermine the country.

Pentagon Policy As of June 2009

There are almost certainly U.S. military "white papers" that detail all changes to Afghan strategy, but news media articles are more accessible. On the surface, that strategy looked very promising in the Spring of 2009.

The United States will change the way its forces are arrayed in Afghanistan . . . , a senior defense official said Friday.
. . . [I]t would call for new garrisons in far-flung Afghan communities.[5]
— Associated Press, 21 March 2009

The approach seemed to provide much wider coverage of the country than had been possible through the previous operational plan.

That [new garrisons] would help the U.S. to hold ground against a resurgent Taliban-led insurgency, the official said. Under today's hub-and-spoke system, U.S. forces leave protected bases to conduct anti-insurgent operations. When they leave, insurgents come back.[6]
— Associated Press, 21 March 2009

However, the projected number of American "garrisons in far-flung communities" might have been far fewer than minimally required to counter local corruption. Most of the pro-government outposts would be manned only by indigenous institutions with a veritable heritage of bribery and brutality.

The emerging plan contemplates a large buildup of Afghan armed forces, to as many as 400,000.[7]
— Associated Press, 21 March 2009

The new plan made more sense than the old, but its success would still depend on how heavily the Afghan force was infiltrated by the Taliban and drug lords. On 29 May 2009, Gen. Petraeus provided a few more of its details. On NPR News, he confided that most U.S. troops would not be stationed inside Afghan villages, but rather on their outskirts. He explained that the villages lacked the vacant buildings of Baghdad, and that Afghans did not want U.S. troops in their midst.[8] Village centers were thus spared from Taliban attack, but they also masked U.S. defensive fires. GIs (government issue troops) would not be able to shoot in that direction to save themselves. The new Rules of Engagement did not seem to adequately address this problem.

[Gen.] McChrystal is expected to formally announce new combat rules within days that will order troops to break away from fights—if they can do so safely—if militants are firing from civilian homes. . . . "[T]roops may have to wait out insurgents instead of using force to oust them," he said.[9]
— Associated Press, 25 June 2009

"Protecting the weak" is a noble goal, but the U.S. military is more used to "overpowering the strong." Anything less tends to demoralize its "rank and file." Morale at those lower levels has more to do with local victories than lofty expectations. The "weak" normally inhabit a much larger geographical area than the strong. Adequately protecting them involves widely deploying a myriad of tiny contingents. Each such contingent runs the risk of surprise attack from a much larger force. That's where any deficiency in its tactical training becomes a liability. American troops have been shown how to get maximum stand-off effect from their weapons, not how best to survive many times their number at close range.

159

To operate most effectively under those conditions, they would have finally had to embrace the same advanced squad maneuvers that their German, Japanese, and North Vietnamese counterparts did. At close quarters, he who first finds cover lives to tell the tale. Until Stateside training focuses more on squad, fire team, buddy team, and rifleman movement than shooting, U.S. troops will have a hard time meeting either general's expectations. Nor are those troops as well prepared for more "conventional" forms of combat as most top U.S. military leaders seem to think.

> "Traditionally American forces are designed for conventional, high-intensity combat," McChrystal said.[10]
> — Associated Press, 25 June 2009

Other Problems Associated with Breaking Contact

Not only is breaking contact hard on morale, but it generally requires a follow-up. In Vietnam, that follow-up was all too often an artillery barrage. Even the shells that missed occupied homes did collateral damage. Stand-off warfare is like that. As such, it is little respected in the Muslim community. If U.S. troops knew more about small-unit maneuver, they wouldn't have to break contact to avoid harming civilians. In either mountains or village, all one has to do is climb to where the enemy isn't and place well-directed small-arms fire downwards. Even in the village outskirts,[11] U.S. troops will most probably continue to occupy little prison-like forts from which they bombard or snipe at whatever threatens from any non-inhabited direction.

Should NATO then attempt to copy the Russian takeover of Chechnya, it can't possibly arrive at Western-style peace and prosperity in Afghanistan. Islamic extremists thrive on violence. One must defuse their misguided logic with a widespread and order-oriented blanket, and then growing public pressure. That takes staying in nonviolent contact with enemy and community alike.

The McChrystal Strategy As of November 2009

In late August 2009, Gen. McChrystal announced it would take a completely new strategy to win in Afghanistan. That strategy would be to protect the Afghan population rather than hunt down insurgents.[12] Soon, the *Philadelphia Inquirer* revealed some of the new plan's specifics. Gen. McChrystal wanted widely to change how U.S. troops interact with civilians—everything from how or if they travel to when they fight. The focus would shift from going after Taliban strongholds to clearing and holding populated areas. Instead of hunting down insurgents, the troops would attempt to understand local, tribal, and social power structures. Then, they would try to lessen the corruption (and possibly the Taliban-supporting drug trade).[13] Implicit in the General's plan was to eliminate most of the need for supporting arms.

Late in September, after Gen. McChrystal's request for more troops was shelved for further study by the White House, U.S. troops started to move into populated areas from rural outposts.[14] If by "populated area," the General meant "city," then the majority of Afghan territory will be forfeited. If he meant "town," then there may still be a wide enough NATO presence.

Two weeks later, *Newsweek* did a report on Gen. McChrystal's credentials and perspectives. Something of a maverick who much prefers the field over a desk, he seems a perfect choice for the Afghan dilemma. A long-time student of history and counterinsurgency,[15] he knows the latter cannot succeed without the help of the civilian population. As such, he frequently chides his subordinates on driving too fast through Afghan villages while pointing their weapons at inhabitants. One of his favorite sayings is "that shot you don't fire is more important than the one you do."[16]

"If you encounter 10 Taliban and kill two," he says, "you don't have eight remaining enemies. You have more like 20: the friends and relatives of the two you killed."[17]
    — Gen. McChrystal, as quoted by *Newsweek*

More importantly, Gen. McChrystal appears fully to realize the adverse effect of supporting arms. He doesn't think there are big enough targets in Afghanistan to justify massive munitions. He even issued a directive "instructing troops not to call in airstrikes or supporting fire unless necessary for self-defense." Of course, such an open-ended directive leaves far too much to the discretion of each local commander. "Absolutely necessary" with some hard and fast rules might better prevent collateral damage. Still, the General's disdain for the "force protection" mentality that so permeates the U.S. military establishment is well appreciated. He "wants his troops to get . . . away from the . . . forward operating bases and into the street[s]." Of course, that would be more likely to happen if U.S. infantry squads became more self-sufficient. Still, the aggressive spirit that comes from five years as head of U.S. hunter-killer operations could help the necessary paradigm shift finally to take hold.[18] The method of a tiny village contingent would be similar to that of a hunter-killer team—except that the former might hide after the enemy showed up. During each village-occupied night, that contingent would then locally neutralize enough "high-value targets" to maintain its own credibility. Having never encountered a U.S. squad that talented and fearing a blood feud instead, most Taliban units would soon leave.

Further Input from the CENTCOM Commander

About this same time in *Parade Magazine,* Gen. Petraeus outlined the greatest differences between Iraq and Afghanistan. Among other things, he warned that the latter has never had a strong central government. That makes its villages more important strategically.

> His [Commander of U.S. Central Command] view on power in Afghanistan—namely, that village and tribal traditions are what matter—results in a strategy far less dependent on massive force and more on helping local leaders provide for, and protect, their people.[19]
> — *Parade Magazine,* 29 November 2009

Gen. Petraeus is further quoted as saying, "There are few true *[jihadist]* believers, but . . . many others who support the enemy only because they feel threatened or intimidated."[20] He sees the need for "small, nimble, clandestine forces to eliminate pockets of terrorism and train local militias to defend themselves."[21] It is unclear whether he also envisions widely dispersed teams trained in police procedure and Unconventional Warfare (UW—how to alternately hide or fight like a guerrilla).

Preliminary Speculation as to the Final Strategy

As the U.S. President worked out the final strategy for Afghanistan, the media professed to know its direction. ABC News reported it being fourfold: (1) protect the big cities so as to deprive the militants of popular support; (2) continue to train Pakistani military and police forces; (3) try to reconcile with the least radical factions of the Taliban; and (4) continue to use drones against the Taliban's most radical factions.[22]

The Commander-in-Chief's Actual Directive

On 1 December 2009, President Obama appeared on national television to announce his decision. He had decided to send 30,000 more U.S. troops to Afghanistan. If Kabul and the southern cities were to be protected, most of those troops would be needed for that purpose alone. However, the President didn't say that. Instead, he briefly mentioned the drug trade hampering the surge, and then the overall strategy. The American objective would be to deny safe haven to *al-Qaeda* and momentarily reverse its capacity to overthrow the Afghan regime. The reinforced U.S. contingent would become a "security force." Its initial goal would be to break the Taliban's hold, and then to secure key population centers. To make sure the Afghan government realized its ultimate responsibility for the war, U.S. troops would start leaving in 2011. In the meantime, those troops would support all who combat corruption. They would also hold the door open for negotiations with "good Taliban."[23] The president's final comment reveals considerable insight into the only hope for this region. Here, inter-factional fighting has become so prevalent as to be the norm. Only by deviating from this norm can NATO have any real chance at peace. That being said, it's also important to realize that all the leaders of major "Taliban" factions are closely allied with *al-Qaeda* and/or the various drug syndicates. It's hard to see how Karzai's attempts at negotiation with Hekmatyar and Baradar (Mullah Omar's chief of staff) in March 2010 accomplished anything.[24] The only "good Taliban" with whom one might constructively negotiate are distant subordinates who have become disenchanted with the program. Thus, the president's guidance more aptly applies to local "Taliban" representatives.

A few days after the President's speech, Gen. McChrystal gave a few hints as to how the surge would be implemented. He wanted to partner with Afghan police and military throughout the country (presumably in population centers).[25] Thus, the U.S. plan appeared far more viable than what the Soviets had tried, but—against an equally determined enemy—much would depend on its final particulars.

Early Indications of the Outposting Procedure's Chances

On 11 January 2010, ABC News carried a story about a day in the life of a U.S. Army company that had been operating from an outpost just outside a "pro-Taliban" village. This outpost was heavily fortified. Its occupants routinely sallied forth from their fully bunkered movie theater to go on patrol. On the day that was videotaped, they did a nighttime helicopter lift to the top of a nearby peak and then at dawn worked their way back to their camp. While trying to surprise Taliban snipers, they ended up looking for their positions and caches. Each opening in the rock was subsequently marked with orange paint to facilitate future airstrikes. On this particular patrol, they were taken under fire from the high ground as they entered the valley bottom and then (in lesser amount) from the village. They only responded in kind to the first attack, and then briefly entered the village. This earned the heartfelt thanks of one elderly inhabitant. Then, a U.S. drone sent a 500 pound bomb onto the suspected source of the high-country fire. The reported result of that airstrike was "one Taliban leader and four of his subordinates killed," though no film footage was ever presented confirming the claim.[26]

It's difficult objectively to assess this patrol without sounding condescending. The brave lads who conducted it were only doing what their organization had implicitly directed. From a numbers standpoint, the patrol was a success. Five enemy were killed without any U.S. losses. Moving downward against suspected enemy positions is known from the Vietnam years to be much more productive than moving upward. The officer-led patrol's soft entry into the village was also very well advised. It created a vital presence and reinforced at least one "heart and mind."[27] Still the only strategic ground in the whole area seems to have been mostly ceded to the enemy—namely, the village as a whole. Its elders were still under Taliban control.

The airstrike was probably made possible by U.S. satellite surveillance of the patrol. By keeping the follow-up attack away from the village, that satellite may have prevented blatant collateral damage. Still, "eyes in the sky" have their limitations. This particular airstrike may have killed five *jihadists,* but what of the hundreds of thousands of replacements available from Pakistan alone. As proof of their Taliban affiliation was never produced, many of their relatives may now be bent on revenge. In the Afghan hinterlands, most men walk around armed. In the minds of the villagers, the unlucky five may have been rabbit hunting, watching for raiding tribes, or heading off on their own blood feud. Or, as in a thankfully aborted bombing run in another part of Afghanistan, that same five may have been women and children collecting firewood.[28] Either way, the villagers are now effectively confined to their homes and quite possibly terrified during any U.S. outing. Assuming the five were fully radicalized Taliban, the bomb's long-term influence on their paradise-seeking replacements would be minimal anyway. Many senior U.S. commanders are known to dislike the use of heavy ordnance, so one wonders if the drone strikes had been politically perpetuated to give the Air Force something to do. While the above-mentioned outposting method shows some signs of imagination, it is not that different from what failed in Vietnam. Soldiers who spend their off hours watching movies are not in the right frame of mind to outmaneuver anyone. They must be better trained and then—by squad—allowed to work with equal numbers of police and soldiers inside a village. Otherwise the depletion of Taliban influence across the vast expanse of Afghanistan will almost certainly take too long for Congress to be willing to fund it. Even with troops only partially versed in UW, this is not as dangerous as it sounds. All it takes is allowing lower-ranking Americans to reach their full potential. Without their common sense and courage, World War II (WWII) would have almost certainly been lost.

As for the Counternarcotics Aspect of the Strategy

Until well into 2006, U.S. military leaders had made little, if any, attempt to slow the flow of drugs out of Afghanistan.[29] Possibly because of the Posse Comitatus provision of the U.S. Constitution, they were hesitant to assign any law enforcement role to their subordinates.

As late as May 2009, the new U.S. Secretary of Defense stipulated that counternarcotics would remain an Afghan responsibility, and that U.S. troops would only be given "greater freedom to track down the networks of those who are funding the Taliban." During operations to "provide security and build stability," U.S. troops would only have the authority to destroy any drug-production facilities and supplies that they happened to encounter.[30]

Then, in late October 2009, Associated Press reported that the U.S. had "decided to go after the drug production and distribution networks after eradication programs had done little more than alienate the farmers."[31] That prodigious announcement may have looked like a situationally driven improvement in policy. However, it is completely possible that those same networks had been providing over half of the heroin on U.S. streets since the end of the Soviet-Afghan War.[32] So why has this chronic conduit been virtually ignored by the latest U.S. government drug assessments? [33]

Thankfully, the Pentagon has since gotten more involved with the Afghan drug war. In August 2009, someone in Washington published a list of 50 Karachi drug smugglers "to be either arrested or killed."[34] On 24 February 2010, NPR News reported that "Haqqani's brother" had just been killed by drone missile attack.[35] (More likely, it was Sirajuddin's brother, or another of Jalaluddin's sons.) Jalaluddin Haqqani is the long-reigning drug lord who was so little pressured during the Pakistani Army's recent Waziristan incursion. The massive U.S. Marine encirclement of Marjah in February also had more to do with narcotics than Taliban. Marjah had long been the "hub of drug processing . . . in Helmand Province."[36] While these things were encouraging, a comprehensive defense strategy for Afghanistan would address all drug conduits.

Still, the situation at home is dire. As predicted by *Homeland Siege* in July 2009, Afghan heroin may have started to deluge the U.S. market in March 2010. On the 29th, ABC's Nightly News reported that there had been a fivefold increase in the amount of heroin for sale on the streets of suburban middle America. This was not the heavily diluted heroin of old, but rather a 70% pure variety that was instantly addictive. Though packets were on sale for $5 each, some were given to school children for free—just to get them hooked.[37]

13 Drug Interdiction Tactics

● How can the drug flow from Afghanistan be slowed?
● Where are the transitional stashes of drugs?

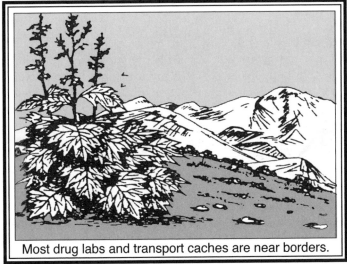

Most drug labs and transport caches are near borders.

(Source: FM 21-76 [1957], p. 88)

The Real Difference between Afghanistan and Iraq

Through dogged determination and a new willingness to seek outside advice, the U.S. military was able to turn the tide in Iraq. If it now believes the same strategies will be enough for Afghanistan, it has another "think" coming. Iraq had only rabble rousers (of indeterminate origin) playing Sunnis off against Shiites to advance their own misguided agenda. Thus, many of the Iraqi tribes could be "cajoled" back into the nationalistic fold. While Afghanistan is also tribal, it has only a ceremonial tradition of central government. Additionally, it and its eastern neighbor already constitute a fully functioning narco-alliance. Until, the U.S. government puts as much emphasis on disrupting the flow of drugs as in fighting the Taliban, it will experience no more success in Afghanistan than it has in Colombia. In that latter country, not all drugs come from, or leave, its southern confines either. Minimally, deployed Americans must slow the export of society-sabotaging heroin from every Afghan exit. If the more peaceful northern and western borders are ignored, then the main sources of enemy funding and government corruption will simply shift location.

It's truly encouraging that the new U.S. strategy involves helping all Afghan governmental departments, but those departments don't just suffer from Taliban infiltration. They have been chronically corrupt as long as they have existed. This is not the type of corruption that grows out of political or monetary ambition. It's the type that happens after death threats, top-echelon payoffs, and expert blackmailing. To do this much business, the various drug conglomerates must capture the allegiance of some very important people. Among the Afghans already suspected of drug trade involvement are cabinet members,[1] provincial governors, security agents, police chiefs, judges, and regional military commanders.[2] Unless all exit conduits and "plazas" are at least partially interdicted, the ineffective governance will continue. And the democratic process will not weed out enough of the dead wood.

Additionally, one can't too quickly wean the farmers from their current livelihood. Until new ways are developed to get winter wheat to market in India, the poppies may have to be tolerated. Luckily, there are alternatives to crop eradication: (1) inner dissension among drug lords; (2) buffer zones along borders; (3) reduction of caches and drug labs; and (4) impediments to motorized "transpo." To provide over 90% of the world's heroin, regional drug barons have been using more than "mules." (See Figure 13.1.)

A Much More Dangerous Opponent

Most policemen recognize drug dealers as the most violent of all criminals. Of course, their suppliers, "transpo" contractors, and parent organizations are not all that patient either. An infiltration attempt, product loss, or payment shortage at any stage of a drug deal is routinely met with sudden and unceremonious death. Like a casino owner, the drug smuggler needs only a certain percentage

Figure 13.1: Most Afghan Drugs Are Not "Man-Packed" Out
(Source: DA Pam 550-35 [September, 1991], p. 105)

of his effort to succeed. As long as some lesser fraction of his cumulative load is seized, he still makes a profit. Whether or not that drug smuggler will remain in the good graces of his supplier and boss will depend on seizure circumstances. Within most organized crime circles, there are always people willing to "skim a little off the top."

Most drug cartels are loose confederations of factions, so that

169

the loss of any particular person or linkage does not endanger the overall operation. In essence, those cartels can't be disrupted by assassination or seizure. Both have been applied to the Afghan drug smugglers for years with very little overall effect. The intent of this chapter is to show deployed U.S. military units how better to help the DEA.

A Multi-Sided Monster

Afghanistan's drug-trafficking problem isn't just limited to Hekmatyar's *HIG* and the Haqqani Network. Along its eastern border alone, there are also the Khyber Pass Affridis and Quetta Alliance, as well as separate "transport mafias" in each place. Another drug conduit runs from Helmand Province to Pakistan's Makran Coast.[3] Just to the west of it, Haji Kuma Khan's nephew probably still runs the convoys to Iran via Baluchistan that used to carry drugs out and IEDs in.[4] Along Afghanistan's western side, there are more direct smuggling routes to Iran from Nimroz and Farah Provinces.[5] Finally at its northern border, the *al-Qaeda*-affiliated IMU may get the help of Dostum's Uzbeks while "deeply involved" with the smuggling of drugs into Turkmenistan and Tajikistan.[6]

All these drug corridors must be continuously monitored/disrupted by NATO representatives. Occasional convoy seizures will not be enough. Within the haphazard world of international drug trafficking, a single dope theft can cause more internal chaos than any amount of assassination, arrest, or seizure.

The Best Way to Disrupt a Drug Alliance

Even if fake drug gangs were possible in Afghanistan, they could not—through turf takeovers—spread enough distrust to damage its export apparatus. So, the role of "cohesion destroyer" falls to whoever happens to stumble upon the next hidden drug stash. A handful of DEA agents have far less chance of doing that than the current surge of ground troops.

As this next drug cache is spirited away, a little U.S. deception could do a lot of good. In the late 1980's, Hekmatyar fought a two-year war with Akhundzada over Helmand's poppy crop.[7] Some major Taliban dissension could thus be generated by spreading a little *HIG* "sign" around subsequent narcotics confiscations south of Kandahar.

As the succeeding paragraphs will demonstrate, most of the Afghan drug caches and laboratories are near the Pakistani border. Haji Bashir Noorzai and Mullah Omar are rumored to have huge hidden reserves near Kandahar,[8] but they and other war lords also maintain production and warehousing facilities closer to the frontier. As late as 2004, Noorzai had 18 drug refineries in the Registan District of southern Kandahar Province.[9] Haji Kuma Khan also possessed a massive opium refinery and underground storage depots at Baramacha. (Baramacha is the dusty smugglers' town that straddles the border between the Dishu District of southern Helmand and Baluchistan.[10]) When Baramacha was attacked, Khan created other refineries and stashes in the remote Chahar Burjak District of southern Nimroz and along the mountainous border with Iran. Then, he developed mobile labs that could either function from Toyota trucks or private homes. (See Map 13.1.) At the Girdi Jungle refugee camp (just inside Baluchistan opposite the boundary between Dishu and Reg-e Khan Neshin Districts of southern Helmand), Khan is said to have had more underground bunkers for the storage of opium.[11] (Look back at Map 9.1.)

Along Afghanistan's eastern frontier, Haqqani operates a series of narcotics smuggling camps in the border districts of Paktiya Province. Much of that heroin comes to him from Hekmatyar to his north and laboratories in Nangarhar Province.[12] As Haqqani and Hekmatyar both date back to the Soviet-Afghan War, other intelligence from that era may still be valid.

By the end of the Russian occupation, Hekmatyar had a series of heroin labs along the Afghan border that were tied in directly to the Pakistani smuggling network.[13] At other places on that same border, Yunis Khalis operated heroin labs (at least seven at Ribat al Ali) and his own smuggling conduits.[14] By 1988, according to the CIA, more than a hundred such labs were operating just inside Afghanistan, across from Pakistani FATA.[15] A year later, raw opium was also being refined into low-grade heroin in the "hilly Chaghi region" of Helmand Province (possibly just across the border from the Chagai District of Baluchistan). Hekmatyar's factories (at least six) were in Koh-i-Soltan.[16] As the Soviet-Afghan War came to an end, the labs producing more than half of all heroin sold on U.S.

streets were located along Afghanistan's southern border (according to the head of the DEA).[17] There has been no hint as to the preferred storage place for recently refined drugs, but the *mujahideen* used to place their supply caches below ground and just outside villages.[18] In Iraqi courtyards, weapons were sometimes buried near solitary accent plants. (See Figure 13.2.) The narcotics caches must also be marked in a way that would only subtly clash with the natural background.

During the Taliban regime in Afghanistan, massive drug bazaars were permitted at the following locations: (1) Ghani Khel in Nangahar Province (possibly between Jalalabad and the Khyber Pass); (2) Sangin in Helmand Province; and (3) Maiwand in Kandahar Province (between Kandahar City and Lashkar Gah).[19] Additionally, former Northern Alliance chieftain Abdul Rashid Dostum is rumored to have had his own fields and labs in the northern part of the country. Until 2004, he controlled Balkh, Jowzjan, Sar-e Pul, Samangan, and Faryab Provinces with a large Uzbek militia.[20] During this same period, most of the Pakistani drug-processing facilities moved a short way into Afghanistan for greater security. Of late, some may have returned to FATA. Today, "criminal syndicates"

Figure 13.2: An Unusual Plant May Mark the Spot
(Source: FM 21-76 [1957]; FM 90-3 [1977]. p. 4-2)

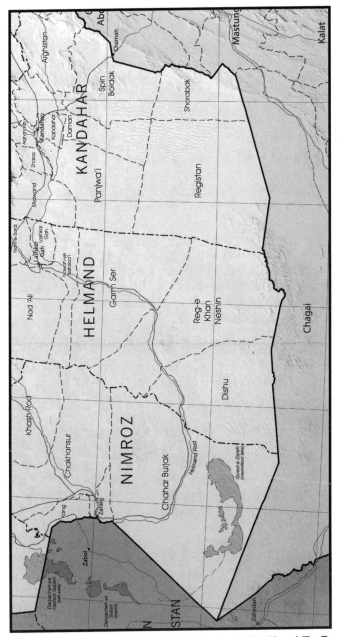

Map 13.1: Where Most of the Drug Activity Used To Be
(Source: Courtesy of General Libraries, University of Texas at Austin, from their website, for map designator "txu-oclc-300481561-afghan_paki_admin_2008.jpg")

173

reportedly run the trucking companies that transport opium to labs in the frontier regions of Pakistan (like the Khyber Agency where Chinese chemists are available).[21]

From the above history, one can see that most labs and caches are probably still near the Afghan-Pakistani border. Stealing their dope would cause the most dissension, but sufficient losses (of any variety) would undermine the drug lords and Taliban.

Finding Those Drug Caches and Labs

Instead of sweeping the trackless deserts of Nimroz, Helmand, and Kandahar Provinces for Taliban strongpoints and supply dumps, why not start piecemeal patrolling of the southern boundary? Wherever those patrols "cut the trail" of a mysterious convoy, they could backtrack along it to find the drug labs and stashes. The same thing holds true for the mountainous border with FATA, with the only difference being mule instead of vehicle tracks. Seldom, if ever in Vietnam, did any U.S. infantry unit attempt to backtrack up the coastal outlets to the Ho Chi Minh Trail. Such an undertaking was never deemed too dangerous, just not in keeping with procedural habit. This would be a good time for that particular habit to be broken. Unlike those forces in Vietnam, deployed U.S. units now have a growing number of mantrackers.

Lessening the Amount of Motorized "Transpo"

As with the drugs crossing the Mexican border, most of the Afghan drug exports are by vehicle. While uninspected shipping containers carry most of them into Laredo, secret compartments aboard fuel, passenger, and commodity conveyances most probably bring them into Quetta and Peshawar. The best way to slow this flow of narcotics in Afghanistan is more closely to watch its limited supply of roads. Local officials may be corrupt, so NATO troops will have to do it. Once a drug load is spotted, any subsequent interdiction must be by accident, or the smugglers will simply alter their method and route. If there were more NATO troops stationed in a town farther down the same road, they could help to arrange an appropriate reception.

A Tremendous Opportunity for Buffer Zones

The term "buffer zone" denotes an area that has been somehow occupied to separate a drug producer from his trans-shipment point. In this regard, Afghanistan's precipitous terrain favors that occupier over the drug producer's "transpo" contractor. Afghanistan has very few exit roads. Cross-country convoys are still possible in Nimroz, Helmand, and Kandahar Provinces, but advances in overhead-surveillance technology make them much more risky. As a result, the drug smugglers have had to slip piecemeal loads into the heaviest flows of civilian traffic. Still to provide 90 percent of the world's heroin, that equates to using the major highways. They offer the best access to big-city chemicals for their labs and corrupted "plazas" at the borders. No one notices their use for three reasons: (1) the major LoCs are clogged with Western war supplies; (2) many of the Highway Police are on the take; and (3) the opiates have been widely dispersed and carefully hidden among legitimate cargo. Therefore, the roads are the key to significantly reducing the Afghan drug trade. Collectively, the villages along each major LoC would make a perfect buffer zone. Because they are so few, they wouldn't cause much of a drain on the limited U.S. manpower pool. As of 2008, there were only 14 mapped roads that led out of the country. (See Figure 13.3.)

Afghanistan's borders have just as much strategic value as its cities. Almost every major border crossing has a road running through it and a small built-up area on the Afghan side. Each of these built-up areas must be outposted by a squad of U.S. troops. Those troops would not be there to keep the crossing open, but rather to monitor its traffic. A bus load of Pakistani *madrasa* graduates who over time got picked up by motorcycles would not be doing the Coalition any good. Nor would a produce truck that—upon hitting a bump—started to trail white dust. Yet, none of these things will be apparent from several miles overhead. They will only be noticed by ground observers with very little else to do.

Thus, one can make a good case for narrow buffer zones between the major cities and most heavily used border crossings to limit the flow of enemy reenforcements/supplies in and drugs out. Those buffer zones would be superimposed over the major LoCs. They would be manned by Combined Action Platoons (CAPs)—lone American squads helping Afghan army and police squads—at each village along the way. Besides looking for raw opium, they would watch for the lime necessary to turn it into morphine bricks. They would monitor the sale and movement of the acetic anhydride and hydrochloric acid then required to create heroin base. They would even keep an eye out for the chloroform, sodium carbonate, charcoal filtration devices, and chemists finally needed to produce white heroin.

Kandahar to Quetta, Pakistan, with a built-up area at the border

Khost to Thal, Pakistan

Jalabahad to Peshawar, Pakistan, with Tor Kham at the border

Gardez to Parachinar, Pakistan

Asadabad to the boundary between Upper and Lower Dir, Pakistan

Asadabad up the Kunar River Valley to Chitral, Pakistan

Kunduz to Panji Poyon, Tajikistan

Mazar-e Sharif via Uzbekistan to Dashanbe, Tajikistan, with Hairatan not far from the border

Mazar-e Sharif to Termiz, Uzbekistan

Mazar-e Sharif to Ashkhabad, Turkmenistan, with Keleft at the border

Qul'ah-ye Now to Tagtabazar, Turkmenistan

Herat to Gusgy, Turkmenistan

Herat to Taybad, Iran, with Islam Qal'ah near the border

Farah to Zabol, Iran

Figure 13.3: The Only Roads out of Afghanistan
(Source: Courtesy of General Libraries, University of Texas at Austin, from their website, for map designator "txu-oclc-300481561-afghan_paki_admin_2008.jpg")

By being deployed in series along the roads, the CAP platoons will provide the sequential intelligence so vital to happenstance seizure. With this kind of help, the DEA could more easily arrange a "cohesion-destroying" hijacking.

America's new "inside-out" counterguerrilla strategy may work if applied to enough neighborhoods and villages, but Afghanistan's borders cannot be simply abandoned in the process. Those in the peaceful north and west deserve almost as much attention as the ones in the volatile south and east. That's because only at the borders are the drug shipments sufficiently channelized, and only at the borders are the drug laboratories and stashes sufficiently concentrated.

When Dealing with Possible Drug Smugglers

In the years to come, there will be many meetings between American military leaders, Afghan officials, and village elders. Within the last two categories, anyone suspected of drug trade involvement (albeit peripheral) must be carefully watched. He is much more dangerous than the most zealous of religious fanatics, for he bases every decision on money. Plus, he will have access to enough of that particular commodity to purchase the world's best anti-aircraft missiles, sapper-attack instructors, and assassination operatives.

Within the deadly struggle between narcotics and counternarcotics, both sides routinely "set up" on the other during any "preliminary meet and greet" and some subsequent encounters. Setting-up entails secretly covering the other party from a distance with telescope-mounted .50-caliber sniper rifles. While many of these specialized weapons have already reached the international market from America, U.S. forces may have to settle for their optics-mounted M-16's. (See Figure 13.4.) Still, it is better to be safe than sorry. In conventional battle, people without uniforms are either trying to fight or cooperate. During a drug war, those two possibilities sometimes merge.

Something Must Be Concurrently Done about Karachi

Even if American troops spent most of their time looking for

Figure 13.4: Snipers "Set Up" on Afghan Parley Contingent
(Source: Courtesy of Sorman Information and Media, from Soldf: Soldaten i falt, © 2001 by Försvarsmakten and Wolfgang Bartsch, Stockholm, p. 261)

Afghan heroin, a fair percentage of that unhealthy substance would still reach Karachi. That city is, by far, the most active of the trans-shipment points. Thus, America must put more pressure on Karachi. Part of that pressure could come from the Pentagon's overseas transportation departments. Every civilian ship and plane carrying NATO supplies into that particular seaport must be thoroughly searched by drug-sniffing dogs or their electronic equivalent before being allowed to leave. Every truck returning to Karachi after carrying NATO supplies north should undergo a routine search at a "weigh station," "vehicle registration check," or the like, north of the city. Finally, a concerted (yet secret) effort must be made to find the big heroin bunkers in Karachi's Sohrab Goth neighborhood. With that much support next door, U.S. troops would be chomping at the bit to participate in an Afghan CAP.

14 New Techniques on Offense

- Are most wars won through killing?
- What alternatives would help to reestablish peace?

Taliban fighter automatically snagged through drug bust.

(Source: FM 7-8 [1984], p. N-1)

Surprise Is Not the Only Substitute for Firepower

Maneuver Warfare proponents have come to see that surprise and firepower are often interchangeable in combat. With enough surprise, the attacker need not shoot at all, and the defender shoots far less. Though not a big part of U.S. method since the North African and European campaigns of WWII, forcing one's foe to surrender presents a third alternative. As a fringe benefit, it often makes no noise and thus preserves the element of surprise. From this realization comes one of the most productive axioms of counterinsurgency—"to arrest the most bothersome of one's foes is

179

better than shooting them." That's because host-country laws can then be invoked, thereby preventing the alienation of U.S. troops from the local citizenry.

A Useful Deviation from Standard Exploratory Procedure

U.S. military personnel usually conduct any "detailed" inspection of enemy territory through sweeps or patrols. As their overall goal is enemy contact, they worry most about movement security. If they fail to meet with resistance, they deem that sweep or patrol a success. Unfortunately, both maneuvers have limitations with regard to uncovering whoever or whatever may not be particularly obvious.

Sweeps require all participants to move in unison, while they stay roughly on line. As a result, most lower-ranking riflemen seldom get the chance to investigate an irregularity in the ground. And the average U.S. sweep can walk right over spider holes or the first buried forts in a strongpoint matrix without ever realizing it. They did both on vegetation-devoid Iwo Jima.[1]

Patrols are conducted in column. That means they closely inspect only narrow corridors of the areas they cross. As with a surveyor, that leaves a whole lot of doubt as to what the rest of the area looks like (particularly its microterrain).

While cordons are also within the GIs' repertoire, only their centers are ever thoroughly searched. And that only happens when an encircled foe has made a dramatic last stand.

Thus, one can see why standard operating procedure is of so little help in discovering hidden caches of anything. Only where U.S. troops are allowed to rest for a couple of days in a captured enemy stronghold, do they regularly come up with significant quantities of buried wherewithal. That apparent coincidence will be the foundation for a more productive search technique. But first, U.S. traditionalists must be reminded of the limits to their procedural heritage.

GIs patrol in the few ways established by their manuals and along routes picked by their officers. Where there is the threat of mines or boobytraps, they move along compass headings to avoid "lines of drift." Where there is less chance of mines, they run flankers, follow existing roads or trails, and pass through associated junctions. Only occasionally are they permitted to follow up on a previous sighting, move to a better vantage point, or even deviate from their route more closely to investigate what they have seen. Almost never are they allowed to follow enemy footprints (nor do most have any real mantracking experience). In essence, those U.S. patrol members are neither actively seeking enemy contact, nor actively seeking enemy caches. Apparently, this is good enough for conventional warfare. However, it leaves a lot to be desired for counterinsurgency or counternarcotic operations. Another way of searching an area might prove more useful in Afghanistan. For its inspiration, one must turn to enlisted wisdom, law enforcement procedure, and ancient Chinese maneuver.

A retired Marine Gunnery Sergeant recently pointed out that "the troops could sniff out the drugs in Afghanistan."[2] Most enlisted veterans of foreign wars would agree, with the following qualification: ". . . if they were allowed to." In other words, standard levels of organizational control would generally preclude it. Any military commander who deems drugs the job of some other agency could search for buried munitions instead. As long as all drugs are confiscated, the reason for their discovery matters little. It is on the strictness of that commander's control that the degree of troop initiative and contribution will depend. After certain parameters have been set, U.S. troops don't need much direction or supervision. Those parameters are things like world-class battledrills, fire restrictions, and unit boundaries. American infantry leaders who have yet to discover the vast potential of their entry-level riflemen should seriously consider what Asian riflemen routinely manage. For centuries, Chinese units have been able widely to disperse and then quickly reassemble. This capability is undoubtedly based on the ancient Chinese "Cloud Battle Array" maneuver. (See Figure 14.1.)

> Before engaging in [any] battle one must first train the soldiers. . . . The troops must learn the strategy of how to assemble and disperse. Follow the commands of attack, lying still, advance and retreat.[3]

Implicit to the Cloud Battle Array is every leader's willingness tactically to withdraw and every soldier's ability to evade enemy searchers. Both are inherent parts of the Asian tradition of UW. With a little of the same kind of training, American GIs could do something similar. Widely dispersing poses little problem.

However, quickly reassembling takes knowing where the next higher headquarters and sister units are at all times. With the current proliferation of GPS devices within the American military, that should now be easier than ever. Normally, U.S. infantry units would use a squad patrol pattern to search an area. (See Map 14.1.) Why couldn't newly acquired dispersal/reassembly methods permit a zonal search by self-sufficient fire teams? (See Map 14.2.) When left in an area 400 meters square (roughly four acres) for a couple of days, the average "grunt" fire team could find whatever there was to be found. Plus, they would revel in the opportunity to do so.

How the Drug Variable Changes Things

Where the ultimate objective is drugs, the searchers must be somewhat conversant with counternarcotics procedure. Theirs is a ruthless foe, who is not the least bit hesitant to use children or women for his menial chores. Thus, they must be both ready for trouble and to exercise restraint. They will most likely be working in fire team size, much as a counternarcotics reconnaissance team might. (See Figure 14.2.)

Figure 14.1: Cloud Battle Array

The New Maneuver

Caches (whether they be arms or drugs) don't just lay around begging to be discovered. (See Figure 14.3.) Thus, the challenge becomes blanketing an area with enough inquisitive souls to sniff them out before they get moved. In Vietnam, anyone who even headed toward a cache of enemy war supplies incurred sniper fire from the side or rear. When in the vicinity of an Afghan narcotics stash, today's GIs may summon a much more substantial presence. When that presence arrives, they must be ready to do one of two things: (1) fight (with squad-sized "swarm tactics"); or (2) withdraw (with individual or buddy team exfiltration).

At first, the fire team sectors of the tiny squad zones will seem devoid of human life. (See Map 14.2 and Figure 14.4.) Then, a close watch on the surrounding countryside may reveal a few "Taliban" (or more correctly drug-lord militia) moving in. (See Figure 14.5.) For the sake of discussion, an element of the platoon that has been

Figure 14.2: Counternarcotics-Qualified Recon Team
(Source: Courtesy of Sorman Information and Media, from Soldf: Soldaten i falt, © 2001 by Forsvarsmakten and Wolfgang Bartsch, Stockholm, p. 436)

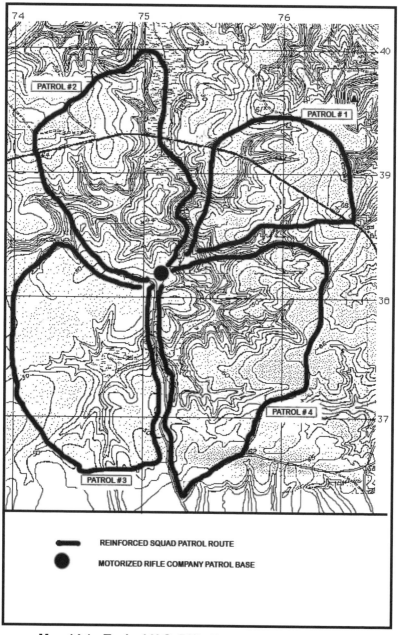

Map 14.1: Typical U.S. Rifle Company Patrol Pattern
(Source: U.S. Dept. of Interior, "Jacksonville South Quadrangle," 1:24,000)

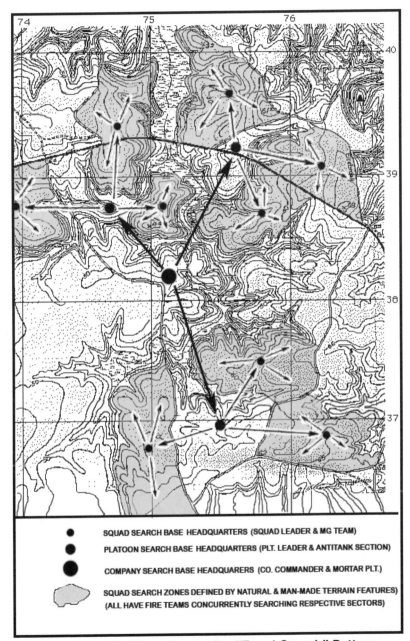

Map 14.2: The More Productive "Zonal-Search" Pattern

(Source: U.S. Dept. of Interior, "Jacksonville South Quadrangle," 1:24,000)

deployed to the southern part of Map 14.2 will be the one making the sighting. Soon one quickly reassembled squad is embroiled in an active fire fight. Using the same method with which Russian squads stopped a whole German Army from reaching the Volga at Stalingrad,[4] sister squads will come to the engaged squad's assistance. One sister squad will attack from the rear of the enemy unit, while the other rolls up its flank. (See Map 14.3.)

On paper, such a maneuver seems relatively easy. In difficult, enemy-infested terrain, it may be a little harder. Unless those GIs are familiar with land navigation by "terrain association,"[5] they

Figure 14.3: Finding What Doesn't Want to Be Found
(Source: FM 7-11B1/2 [1978], p. 2-H-8-3.3)

Figure 14.4: At First, the Zones Are Uninhabited
(Source: FM 7-8 [1984], p. 8-3)

Figure 14.5: Then, the Southern Platoon Has Company
(Sources: FM 7-11B1/2 [1978], p. 2-II-C-4.2; FM 22-100 [1983], p. 113; MCO P1500.44B, p. 12-66)

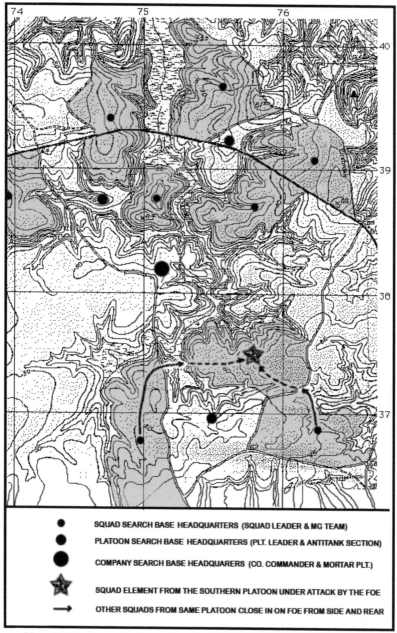

Map 14.3: Squads from the Same Platoon Move In to Help
(Source: U.S. Dept. of Interior, "Jacksonville South Quadrangle," 1:24,000)

may not be able to sneak up on the opposition. Since the American military's widespread adoption of the GPS system, that skill has been largely lost. (Terrain association uses fingers and draws in the country as one would streets in a city.) Fingers and draws provide unobstructed avenues of advance, with the latter being more secretive. (See Figure 14.6.) As long as the squad in contact knows that the other two are coming (and from which direction), it can restrict its small-arms fire accordingly. As the two rescue squads draw closer to the scene of the skirmish, grenades become the weapon of choice for any target that is not clearly visible. (See Figure 14.7).

The final sequence may take any number of forms depending on the nature of the terrain and actions of the enemy. One of the rescue squads may lie in ambush as the other tries to push the foe into it. Or one of the rescue squads may divert the foe's attention, while the other moves into base-of-fire or assault position. While a standup assault would normally be too risky, it may eventually become necessary to clear a "die-hard" enemy force from the area. (See Figure 14.8.) Such things work best when total surprise is possible.

Whenever the enemy feels it necessary to intercede in one place, he often shows up in another. In this case, one of the two northern platoons next spots trouble. (See Figure 14.9.) That trouble comes as no surprise, and this enemy force is bigger than before. Because no enemy cache has yet been discovered, it's clearly time for the GIs to leave. The easiest way is just to tell the deployed fire teams of the affected squad to make their way over to blocking positions established by a sister platoon. With a little prior UW training, they should be able to do so by fire team, buddy team, or individual. (See Map 14.4.)

By exercising a little fire discipline, the blocking squads from the sister platoon should have no trouble receiving their exfiltrating brethren. (See Figure 14.10.) Before the moon gets too high in the sky, everyone should be accounted for. (See Figure 14.11.)

Other Types of Offensive Maneuvers

Without some measure of surprise, no infantry attack should ever be attempted. In a counterguerrilla or counternarcotics environment, that particular axiom goes double. There, without a

Figure 14.6: After Assembling, Each Squad Obscurely Moves
(Source: FM 7-8 [1984], p. 8-2)

FRIENDLY GRENADE

Figure 14.7: One Comes Up behind Foe and Uses Grenades
(Source: FM 7-8 [1984], p. 3-57)

Figure 14.8: The Other Assaults Foe from the Side with Rifles
(Sources: FM 22-100 [1983], p. 185; FM 90-10-1 [1982], pp. B-3, B-4)

Figure 14.9: Up North, Another Enemy Contingent Is Spotted
(Source: FM 7-8 [1984], p. 8-4)

191

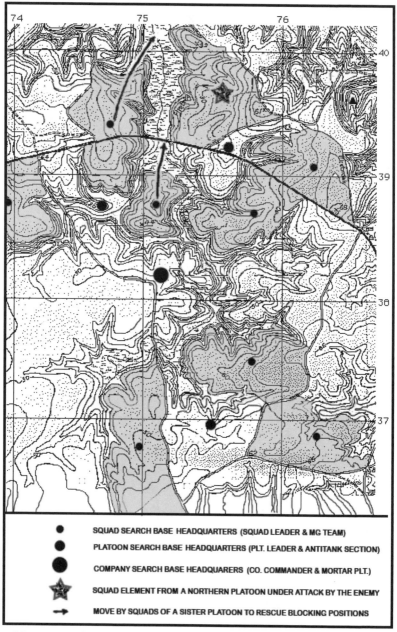

Map 14.4: Other Platoon Sets Up Rescue Blocking Positions
(Source: U.S. Dept. of Interior, "Jacksonville South Quadrangle," 1:24,000)

Figure 14.10: Egressing GI Is Covered from Blocking Position
(Sources: FM 5-103 [1985], p. 4-7; FM 7-8 [1984], p. 3-1; FM 7-11B1/2 [1978], p. 2-II-A-5.2; FM 90-10-1 [1982], p. E-18)

Figure 14.11: As Darkness Falls, Everyone Is Accounted For
(Source: FM 7-11B1/2 [1978], p. 2-II-A-4.2)

well-veiled approach and deceptive assault, the attacker routinely encounters casualty-producing fire and a mysteriously vacant objective. Cordoning off an area by vehicle or helicopter doesn't qualify as a surprise attack. It didn't in Vietnam, and it doesn't now. If the guerrilla or drug lord knows that a search is imminent, he will simply hide his stash or people in ways that the U.S. forces cannot counter.

Third-World militias have become quite skilled at discovering an unwanted presence. For that purpose, they will use everything from community watch networks to dogs and early warning devices. (See Figure 14.12.) If Tora Bora was any indicator, multibattalion cordons expend far too many resources for what they accomplish. To find the Taliban stashes with a limited number of U.S. troops, each company must be allowed to replace squad-sized patrols with fire-team sized zones of responsibility.

Within Afghanistan, most of the supplies, reinforcements, and drugs move along roads and trails. As such, the right kinds of administrative cargo searches could also prove very useful. Each company needs its own drug-sniffing dog. (See Figure 14.13.)

Figure 14.12: Guerrillas Use Old-Fashioned Alarm Systems
(Source: Courtesy of Sorman Information and Media, from Soldf: Soldaten i falt, © 2001 by Forsvarsmakten and Wolfgang Bartsch, Stockholm, p. 370)

Figure 14.13: Every Rifle Company Needs a Drug-Sniffing Dog
(Source: Courtesy of Sorman Information and Media, from Soldf: Soldaten i falt, © 2001 by Forsvarsmakten and Wolfgang Bartsch, Stockholm, p. 436)

15

New Techniques on Defense

- Can isolated squads survive without air/artillery support?
- How else might a tiny outpost deal with a huge attacker?

Diversionary measures are best accomplished after dark.

(Source: Courtesy of Sorman Information and Media, from Soldf: Soldaten i falt, © 2001 by Forsvarsmakten and Wolfgang Bartsch, Stockholm, p. 189)

More Is Possible with a Different Mind-Set

U.S. forces are already fairly good at positional defense. In fact, they can so easily hurt an all-out enemy assault that they routinely try the same things on offense. They helicopter into enemy assembly areas, fight for a while from a static position, and then leave. While "sweeping" through enemy territory, they form impregnable perimeters every evening. And, if their patrols fail to make contact, they assume that the opposition has fled. Though no doubt valid under certain circumstances, this has all the earmarks of "fighting defensively." Against a suicidal opponent, it has its place. However,

197

against a world-class guerrilla or 4GW expert, it will not work. The tactical axiom is "maximize the amount of offensive action during every defense," not "routinely attack defensively." Thus, American troops in Afghanistan should be allowed to turn every mandatory perimeter into a Taliban trap. It will no longer be "the Alamo," "Dodge City at noon," or the "OK Corral." Nor will it operate like a bull's-eye-shaped prison. From now on, it is an insidious ambush through which any number of Muslim extremists may finally reach paradise. And, this ambush will not include any of the artillery or airstrikes that have so disconcerted the Afghan populace. All of its baiting and elimination will be done through enlisted ingenuity and undersized munitions—possibly to include a few claymores and 60-mm mortar rounds.

Pursuant to that end, the first lesson is fire discipline. There will be no more videotaped sequences of GIs firing at an elevated angle into the distance. Without a clearly visible target, they won't shoot at all. Fire superiority on all sides is not that realistic a goal anyway. In the rocky defiles of Afghanistan, most attempts at fire suppression only waste ammunition. First, the attackers must be drawn in closer.

How the Taliban Almost Always Attack

The average Taliban is not as accomplished a tactician as former foes. He doesn't like to crawl, hold his fire, or go after strategic assets. He is more into demonstrating his *"jihadist* fervor," manhood, or sense of paid responsibility. Under ideal circumstances, his commander finds a lone U.S. contingent in a deep valley and then quietly encircles it. After directing heavy fire onto the hapless quarry from all sides, he sends one of his elements forward for the kill. Any walls in the way, that element penetrates with RPG fire or explosives. Like a Communist assault force, its objective is to capture or annihilate all opposition.

With proper preparation, that "hapless quarry" can become a stand-fast avenger. Many the following ideas are already part of U.S. defensive doctrine, but seldom tried to this extent. When applied with gusto, they become almost offensive in nature. The key to their success is first learning how the enemy interprets the battlefield.

Taliban fighters encounter the same difficulties during an assault as American infantrymen do. They have trouble sneaking up on anyone, lack the skill to infiltrate a perimeter, and would be completely unnerved by a modern "strongpoint matrix." So, the avenging GIs must create the impression of a traditional perimeter while secretly building its sequel. Plus, that sequel must be lethal enough during the preliminary ground assault to discourage any others. For all of this to happen, the GIs must first do their homework. Among other things, they will determine the following: (1) most likely enemy approach routes; (2) best kill zones; (3) any channelization opportunities; (4) all hidden-strongpoint possibilities; and (5) a way secretly to abandon their temporary perimeter.

Most Likely Approach Routes

The Taliban assault force will pick a final route to the outpost that cannot be easily seen from that outpost. It might be through a gully, series of boulders, patch of vegetation, deep shadow, or any combination of these things. To the American who is willing thoroughly to traverse the area around his outpost, the foe's most probable routes should become obvious.

Potential Kill Zones

The U.S. contingent won't have the benefit of artillery or air strikes, so it must rely on its own ordnance to discourage the foe. Sadly, that will still take extreme lethality. Two types of kill zones must be identified—the ones along the most probable approach routes to the outpost and the ones inside its temporary perimeter. Where automatic weapons and claymores are to be used, those kill zones must be on level ground, whether sloping or otherwise. For mortars and grenades, they will be in defiladed areas where concussion is concentrated.

Whether each zone is to be attacked by standoff weaponry or ambush is then decided. A cleverly hidden and relieved two-man sentry post can spot for, then set off, multiple "daisy" chains of explosives without ever revealing their presence. Explosives without shrapnel do little damage, so these daisy chains are of claymores connected by "det cord." When properly rigged, they will seem to the Taliban like an old minefield.

Channelizing the Enemy Attack Force

A tangle of old barbed wire, thorny brush, or dead-tree limbs can be so placed as to lead the foe into the most advantageous (for the Americans) of several approach routes to the outpost. So can an unarmed and poorly hidden mine. For the routes chosen, certain side exits may also have to be blocked.

Conversely, an attacking foe can be lured—by weak impediment—into some route or action that favors the defender. At the perimeter wire, a seldom-used gate or poorly built segment might draw him through. Inside the wire, unusually light defensive fire might prompt him to make his final assault.

Hidden-Strongpoint Possibilities

Strongpoint matrices offer two advantages that perimeter defenses do not: (1) firesacks in apparent gaps between successive strings of fighting holes; and (2) each defensive position protected by crisscrossing fire from the two behind it.

The Taliban will place the majority of their fire onto the main building and any U.S. vehicle in view. As such, neither makes a good strongpoint. A distant clump of bushes would better qualify. However, there is no way to create enough overhead cover to protect its occupants without compromising its camouflage. If heavy planking or detachable armor were available, there are better strongpoint candidates. Piles of nonflammable anything can be quickly transformed into tiny fortresses that could withstand plunging fire. Among the most appropriate are trash, compost, and manure. Similarly, the bottoms of livestock watering troughs and feeding cradles can be rapidly reinforced without giving away their new purpose. Each inhabited rural space offers opportunities. They may range from a bushy tree, grape trellis, or water tank, to something closer to the ground—like a burn pit, wellhead, or grinding stone. All that matters is that the secret strongpoints be so arrayed as safely to shoot at whoever attacks another. While this is usually accomplished through carefully marked fields of fire, it is also possible through intermediate obstructions. Where there's a rock, stump, or pile of bricks directly between strongpoints, those manning those strongpoints should be able to shoot in each other's direction without any chance of fratricide.

Fake-Perimeter Abandonment Plan

The initial defensive formation should be roughly circular and as near the edge of the outpost-occupied low land as possible. There, pickets will be less likely to be shot. Others can use existing walls or ditches for cover. When abandoned, those types of positions will offer no additional protection to the assaulting Taliban. If a sand-bagged emplacement is unavoidable, it should be of the open-ended variety that can be quickly kicked over. Then, one or two single strands of barbed wire around the entire perimeter will complete the deception.

The trick is secretly to pull back from this fake perimeter, and then—while the foe celebrates his ease of penetration—decimate him from alternate positions. The source of that decimation would be far less apparent to the enemy's base of fire, if the assault force were allowed initially to pass those alternate positions. One of the best examples in history occurred at Tarawa. During the first night of the U.S. invasion, Japanese machinegunners secretly occupied shipwrecks just offshore from the main landing beaches. The next day, many a Marine in the succeeding-waves died before the true source of the deadly fire could be determined.[1]

At this Afghan outpost, hidden strongpoints will double as the alternate positions. Right after dark, most of the perimeter pickets should be able to sneak into them unobserved. But first (while it is still light), the rest of the pickets must run screaming to the central fortification/structure (in spurts between intermediate objects). After seeing terror-stricken GIs for the first time, the Taliban commander will want to immediately launch 20 or so of his best warriors on a final assault. Though that structure has been the target of his heavy machineguns, rocket launchers, and recoilless rifles all afternoon, it is still the best place for a "safe room." This safe room will be the final refuge for the U.S. squad leader and his reinforcing elements, while they, the strongpoint fire teams, and an ambush team spring their trap. If the once-beaten opposition commander is then foolish enough to try subsequent assaults, the safe room defenders have other tricks ready.

The Safe Room

The average Afghan compound has a tunnel, bomb shelter, or

"potato cellar." Any one could function as a refuge. Once secured from below, its trap door would only succumb to explosives. Any blast would further delay entry—by blocking the way with debris. However, no self-respecting American would enter into such a confined space without a rear exit. He would rather be above ground where he can fight back. Thus, the building's ground floor would be the best for a "safe room." A good bunker could be constructed at the corner of thick exterior walls. It could still have a big hole in the floor to be used as bomb shelter, grenade sump, or escape route. It would also have a heavy wooden cover to deflect grenades

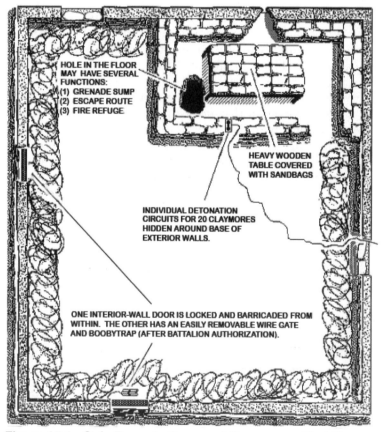

Figure 15.1: Safe Room in Corner of Masonry or Mud House
(Source: FM 90-10 [1979], p. C-5)

or collapsing beams and sandbagged sides to block bullets. The safe room itself would be ringed by concertina barbed wire. At the first sign of a breach to its walls, a U.S. grenade would come flying out of the hole. (See Figures 15.1 and 15.2.)

The extent to which a house can be turned into a living hell for intruders is only limited by one's imagination. Every part of it can be monitored through peep holes and mirror fragments. As long as all explosives are command detonated, they take no authorization from higher headquarters. For this particular dwelling, most of the focus will be on the outer base of its foundation.

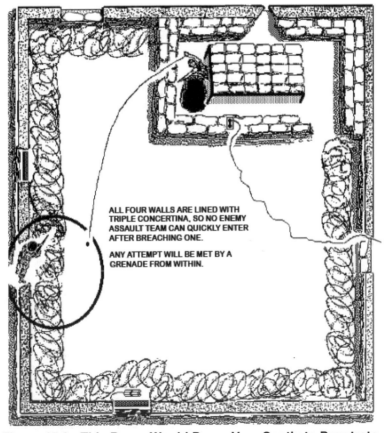

ALL FOUR WALLS ARE LINED WITH TRIPLE CONCERTINA, SO NO ENEMY ASSAULT TEAM CAN QUICKLY ENTER AFTER BREACHING ONE.

ANY ATTEMPT WILL BE MET BY A GRENADE FROM WITHIN.

Figure 15.2: This Room Would Prove Very Costly to Penetrate
(Source: FM 90-10 [1979], p. C-5)

A Full Example of the Procedure

In a narrow Afghan valley lies a mud house, water tank, compost pile, bushy tree, and abandoned well. To protect the road that runs through this valley, a reinforced squad of U.S. Marines (about 20 men) has been assigned to this location. All they have in the way of ordnance are three squad automatic weapons (SAW's), a 60-mm mortar, rifles (some grenade launcher equipped), and a moderate supply of ammunition/peripherals. The narrow confines of this val-

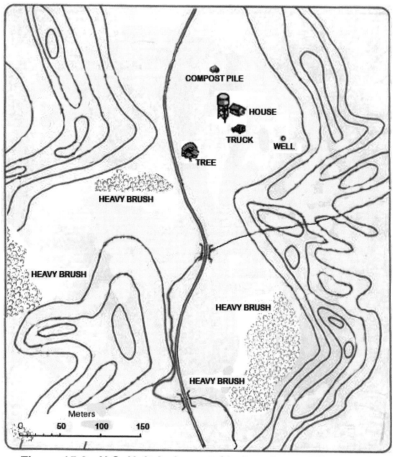

Figure 15.3: U.S. Unit Arrives at Chokepoint on Minor LoC
(Source: FM 90-6 [1980], p. 3-37)

ley make help from supporting arms unlikely. So, the squad leader has wangled 100 claymore mines, enough "det cord" to rig them in series, and a way remotely to explode those series. (See Figure 15.3.) Upon arrival, his men follow established procedure and create a valley-wide perimeter of eight two-man positions. Still, this perimeter is only temporary, and its occupants more like pickets. (See Figure 15.4.) These Marines have no intention of succumbing to any number of local extremists. Should their peaceful mission be interrupted, they have a less traditional plan.

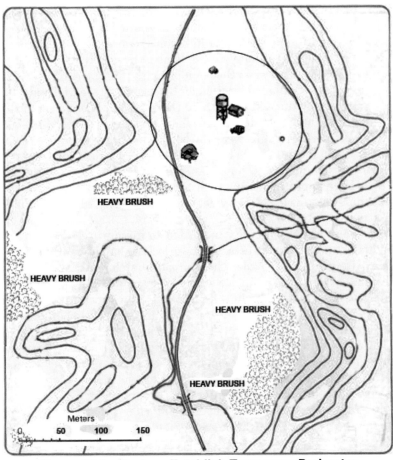

Figure 15.4: Marines Establish Temporary Perimeter
(Source: FM 90-6 [1980], p. 3-37)

The Planning Phase

Upon making friends with the resident tribe, the Marines hear of an impending attack. They decide to implement their "death trap" maneuver. They will first disorient the enemy's assault force and then totally annihilate it. Only after that assault has miserably failed will the majority of Taliban leave. However, this disorientation and annihilation will not happen in the usual way, because these are Marines who would prefer not to resort to artillery and air strikes.

Properly to lay this trap, the Leathernecks must first try to think like the enemy. (Refer back to Figure 15.4 as necessary.) The rear slope is the one closest to the house/building, so they assume his assault will come from that direction. Near the top of the three most likely approach routes to the house, they preregister several large depressions between the boulders with their mortar. (The foe may use such a defiladed location for his assembly area.) Then, two Marines survey the rest of all three routes. They wish to establish a "fighting sentry post" in a place where all three will be visible but enemy soldiers won't go. Near the bottom of the middle route, they find a virgin hard-to-reach crevice at the top of a rock outcropping. Before returning to the house, they do two things: (1) block all alternative approach routes with tangles of thorny brush; and (2) hide daisy chains of remotely detonated claymores along the three routes they have chosen.

When extreme lethality is needed to discourage repeated assaults, it's not enough to establish interlocking bands of machinegun fire. After being disrupted in the approach march, the enemy assault force must be lured to a place where every square yard and fold in the ground is covered by fire. In this case, it will be drawn toward the building by frontline pickets retreating to it and sporadic fire coming from it. Then, they will be cut to shreds by claymore blasts at the base of the house and reverse-angle fire from its detached strongpoints. That fire will be like that of a sniper—by well-aimed single shot, and only when no assault element member is looking. If by silenced M-4, even high-ground observers won't be able to determine its source. Should silenced M-4's not be available, there should be enough shooting from the house to mask the sound of a few backwards M-16 shots from strongpoints. As long as none of these tiny hidden forts are spotted by the Taliban, they will be safe from destruction.

All of a sudden, everyone in the assault element will be dead, and their high-ground commander at a loss as to why. There must have been an accidental explosion or mix-up with supporting fires. With any luck, he will follow the *mujahideen* pattern and depart the area. Attacking by fire is his preference, and any ground assault an afterthought. To him, pulling back for more crew-served-weapons ammunition makes more sense than another look at the destruction.[2]

Final Construction

There are three good strongpoint possibilities in this location: (1) a pile of damp compost; (2) a bushy tree; and (3) an abandoned well. After dark on the first night, they are prepared. The compost position is the easiest. It requires only digging out the pile's center, a few house planks for a roof, and a few more planks or sandbags for interior walls. The tree and well positions take longer. The first must be dug in among the roots and covered with planks and sod. All excavated soil will be spread into mounded rows to resemble a garden plot. At the well, a sub-floor must be built from wood, a few rocks removed from the wellhead for gun slits, and a piece of armored plating used as a well cover.

The Marines will also need a "safe-room" in a corner of the house that faces the rear slope. Any safe-room is only as secure as its host structure is fireproof. Luckily, the walls and roof of this particular house are mostly adobe.

When the Taliban arrive, 12 of the 20 defenders will man the hidden strongpoints, two will go to an ambush site, and six (to include the squad leader) will defend this fortified room. As such, all five locations will need adequate stocks of food, water, and ammunition.

When the Taliban Show Up

One afternoon, the Marines find themselves completely surrounded by hundreds of hillside Taliban. (See Figure 15.5.) Soon, the enemy's softening up process begins. Most of the Taliban fire is directed at the house and truck. (See Figure 15.6.) The pickets at the very edge of the meadow cannot see the enemy crew-served weapons well enough to take them under fire, nor can they themselves be effectively targeted. So, holding their fire to conserve ammunition, those pickets simply maintain their positions and wait for a chance to feign a retreat or secretly man the strongpoints. That chance finally comes as the sun starts to set. First, six frontline defenders abandon their widely separated posts and run screaming for the house. Then, right after dark, two of them and the remaining frontline pickets sneak into the strongpoints—four per location. Finally, two house occupants set out for the ambush site.

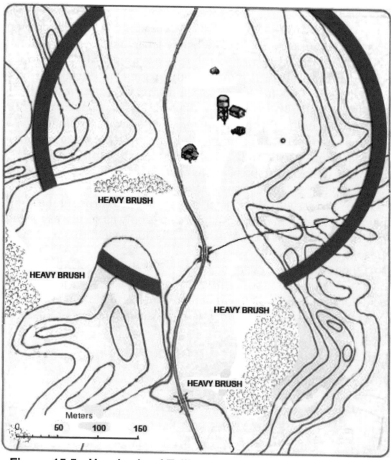

Figure 15.5: Hundreds of Taliban Move Down from the Peaks
(Source: FM 90-6 [1980], p. 3-37)

Several milestones have now been accomplished. The terror-oriented Taliban think the Americans afraid. (The sight of GIs bolting for the house should be enough to precipitate their ground assault.) The outer perimeter has been abandoned, a new inner one (the three strongpoints) secretly occupied, and an ambush team deployed. Only if one of the strongpoints attracts too much enemy attention will the others protect it or the spaces between by fire. (Equipped with night vision scopes, the occupants of any one should be able to shoot overly inquisitive Taliban right off the top of any other.) Otherwise,

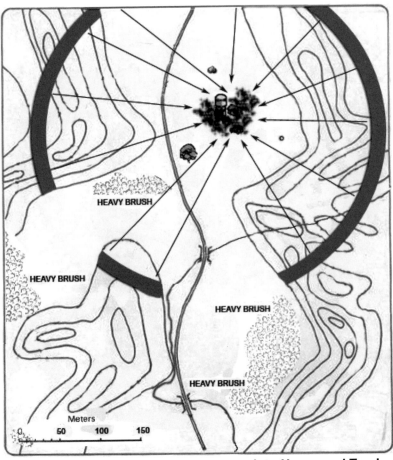

Figure 15.6: Foe Fires Heavy Weapons into House and Truck
(Source: FM 90-6 [1980], p. 3-37)

all three hidden forts let the enemy assault team pass by them *en route* to the house. For it is there, that the demoralizing explosion is about to happen.

The Taliban's Ground Assault

As predicted, the Taliban launch their ground assault from the incline behind the house. Fearful of supporting arms, they do so

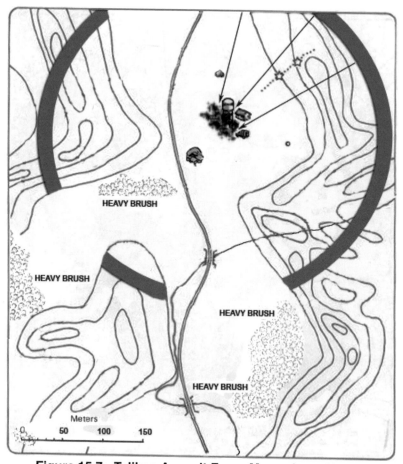

Figure 15.7: Taliban Assault Force Moves In on House
(Source: FM 90-6 [1980], p. 3-37)

early on the first night of the encirclement. Their "unlucky" assault element first encounters a 60-mm mortar concentration and then what appears to be a minefield. (See Figure 15.7.)

Then, those left in the assault force approach the house fairly easily—encountering only light fire from its sandbagged windows. As they prepare to blow a hole in its outer wall, there is an apparent accident. A huge blast occurs all along the base of its foundation. Only four of the attackers live through it. Then, they too are dispatched from the compost pile and well. (See Figure 15.8.)

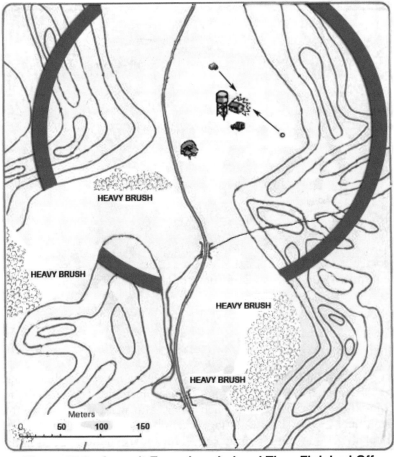

Figure 15.8: Assault Force Leveled and Then Finished Off
(Source: FM 90-6 [1980], p. 3-37)

Figure 15.9: With an Obstruction, Little Chance of Fratricide
_(Source: FM 7-8 [1984], pp. F-27, O-4)

 Though quite logical, this kind of defense is completely foreign to U.S. troops. That's because it violates doctrine. GIs are seldom even allowed to fire close to each other. But what if two are below ground or have a thick wall, log, or sandbags between them? Such an obstruction would reliably deflect any stray rounds. (See Figure 15.9.) Couldn't two U.S. positions then fire in each other's general direction without much chance of an accident?

Strongpoints need not be restricted to firing outboard. They weren't at Iwo Jima, and Iwo Jima may have been the most ingenious defense ever designed.[3]

With such bad luck during the initial assault, the Taliban commander won't chance another. Now, the U.S. strongpoints can assume more of a traditional role. Their location will still be secret, but their final protective fires will be more like that of an inner perimeter. (See Figure 15.10.)

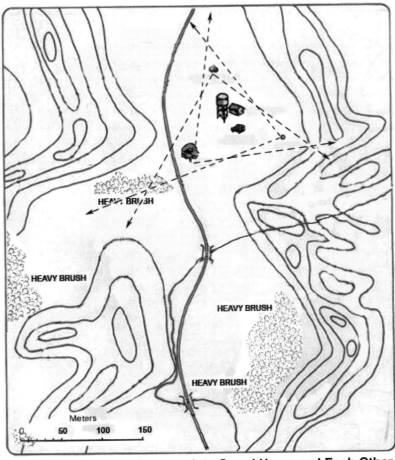

Figure 15.10: Veiled Strongpoints Guard Home and Each Other
(Source: FM 90-6 [1980], p. 3-37)

Not As Dangerous As It Looks

The key to lowering casualties is staying out of the enemy's heaviest line of fire. In the above sequence, the foe's primary target—the house—offers some protection from incoming shells and never contains more than six people. All movement (except the hillside reconnaissance and feint) is done after dark to limit the danger of being shot.

U.S. Doctrine Must Be Relaxed

In deference to all good things at Quantico and TRADOC (the Army's Training and Doctrine Command), doctrine may partially to blame for U.S. squads not keeping pace with tactical innovation worldwide. The best light infantry now comes from East Asia. North Vietnamese, North Korean, and Chinese commanders are allowed encirclements, double envelopments, and firesacks between defensive positions (as were the Japanese and German).[4] Inherent disregard for their soldiers' lives is not the reason. To the contrary, they more heavily train and trust their lowest ranks than do their American counterparts.[5] Such maneuvers are allowed, because they are necessary to defeat a more-numerous or better-supplied foe. In almost every case, Asian soldiers who shoot towards one another are taking well-aimed shots from excellent cover.[6] Often, they are also firing downwards or upwards so that any stray rounds will either hit in front of, or fly over, their juxtaposed buddies.[7] A substantial obstruction between them would also block any errant bullets. Thus, more tactical ingenuity is possible for American infantry organizations that come to value victory over procedural tradition.

In Answer to the Nay-Sayers

How else could this tiny outpost be defended against hundreds of well-armed Taliban? Would bombarding the surrounding hillsides produce a more acceptable result? Even if the encircling Taliban were sent packing, they would eventually be back. At some point, the post would have to be abandoned. This way, the tiny contingent of Americans can continue to perform its important mission. Bombardment has side effects. In terrain this precipitous and close, the most technologically advanced artillery isn't accurate enough to preclude mistakes. Aircraft-applied munitions—however smart—would subject the GIs and LoC to rock slides. Soviet airstrikes and artillery proved ineffective in the narrow Afghan canyons.[8]

To win in Afghanistan, something totally out of the ordinary must be tried, and soon. Its prerequisite may be an experimental modification to U.S. doctrine. God and America should, after all, take precedence over tactical habit.

Decision Time

Though the "Taliban" depends upon *madrasa* graduates and paid villagers for most of its manpower, it still constitutes a major battlefield threat. It does not do so in the sense of being able to stop a multi-battalion sweep, but by endangering tiny outposts. Either the U.S. and NATO must more widely confront the Taliban or find some way to render the whole martial part of the 4GW equation unnecessary. In a place this segmented and corrupt, that may be easier said than done. Either way, the Taliban will have to be beaten at its own game, one village at a time. In counterinsurgency, sweeps do little good unless all the villages they encounter are immediately outposted to rebuild their leadership cadre.

This chapter has shown what it would take to defend a tiny outpost from massive assault. As most U.S. military leaders have yet to appreciate the advances in squad tactics or depth of enlisted potential, they would never allow an outpost this small to be defended in this way. That leaves them with one other option. Through progress in the other three 4GW arenas (economic, political, and psychological), they must eliminate the need for as much success in the martial arena. That will be the subject of the next and final chapter. Its proposals would more fully utilize U.S. infantry squads, without spilling as much Taliban blood.

By having to be more self-sufficient, those squads would automatically arrive at UW technique. That would be quite an accomplishment—win an almost impossible war, and in the process overcome a systemic deficiency. Soon, bottom-up training would take hold, and U.S. squads would also catch up to the state of art on "conventional-warfare" technique.

16

The Village Contingent Option

- How can local Taliban leaders be most easily contacted?
- Do all fight for the same reason?

There will be Taliban leaders among the "village elders."

(Source: DA PAM 550-65 [1986], cover)

The Biggest Crack in the U.S. Plan

In mid-December 2009, there were two widely separated incidents that do not bode well for the current U.S. strategy. Just north of Kabul, troops from Hekmatyar's *HIG* overran a police checkpoint, killing 8 out of 10 occupants. On the same day in Helmand Province, militants overran a police outpost after being assisted by three of its surviving defenders.[1] These are clear indicators of enemy infiltration. Why else would the survivors be spared? The eight-year "effort to create an effective Afghan police force . . . has been a disaster," according to *Newsweek*. Through poor recruiting, improper influence, infiltration, and scant public-service tradition, that police force is still too corrupt and brutal to be trusted by the Afghan populace.[2] To be of much help to the U.S. exit strategy, it will have to be assisted/supervised at the local level.

> Ambassador Richard Holbrooke . . . has publicly called the Afghan police "an inadequate organization, riddled with corruption." . . .
> . . . "We're trying to train them to respect and relate to [the] people [Carabinieri Lt.Col. Massimo Deiana]."[3]
> — *Newsweek,* 29 March 2010

The Afghan Army has been equally susceptible to penetration. According to another *Newsweek* article, it has become so corrupt that the same people can desert, sell their weapons, and rejoin over and over without ever being discovered.[4]

> [E]stablishing an effective Afghan army would be extremely difficult, if not impossible, because the Americans and their NATO allies lacked knowledge and sophistication in distinguishing friend from foe among those being recruited into the army. This problem is compounded by the fact that there are very few written documents in a country like Afghanistan that could corroborate identities. The Taliban would seed the Afghan army with its own operatives and supporters, potentially exposing the army's operations to al-Qaeda.[5]
> — *Stratfor Weekly,* 11 January 2010

So quickly creating hundreds of thousands of illiterate and underpaid Afghan police and soldiers is clearly too unimaginative a way to consolidate this traditionally tribal society. The Russians already tried that. Somehow or other every village contingent of Afghan police or soldiers must be closely enough supervised to counter the effect of corruption, subversion, and infiltration. Periodically patrolling through some of those villages won't provide enough of that kind of supervision.

"Top-Down" Strategies Don't Work Well in Asia

Things are routinely accomplished in a more "bottom up" or

grassroots fashion in Asia than in most Western nations. India still has very few stop signs and street lights. That's because its citizens are so used to working together that they don't require as many instructions. Often, there are so many of those citizens in one place that any attempt at control would be futile anyway. In essence, Asian "group-oriented" culture makes strong central government less necessary in many ways. The same thing holds true for Afghanistan. Because that country has so many competing factions and impediments to travel and learning, each village must be treated as its own separate campaign.[6] Its residents no more follow every dictate of some overall tribal chieftain or provincial governor many miles away than of the president in Kabul. Each village or neighborhood has its own set of local leaders, and it is they who will provide most of its governance.

In counterinsurgency lingo, "helping one village at a time" is called the ink-spot strategy. Small military units deploy across a wide, hostile territory, to establish safe havens in which they bolster local confidence, launch development programs, and improve governance. Slowly extending their influence, those units spread their control just as more drops of ink on a piece of paper. While attributed to the British in Malaya, this more closely resembles what the North Vietnamese were able to accomplish in South Vietnam and again in Cambodia (to defeat the Khmer Rouge). It has yet to work in Afghanistan because of piecemeal attempts. In essence, too few government enclaves have been created to allow for those adjacent to assist one another.

The Dutch Model Better Appreciates the Village

Unlike the Americans and British with their barbed-wire-enclosed forts, the Dutch in Uruzgan have been operating from small, mud-walled compounds. These are "multi-functional" *qalas* (Pashto for house). Each has a traditional guest room where visitors can come for impromptu meetings. The soldiers in each *qala* are expected to make regular house calls to neighbors throughout a 12 to 30 square kilometer zone of action to see how they are doing and monitor their needs. Those needs may range from determining the status of an arrested relative to forwarding a report of government excess.[7] In essence, the Dutch are helping to provide basic services until the local government can better assume that responsibility. However,

219

their real genius lies in the subtle supervision of Afghan police and soldiers. This removes any need for the residents to turn to the Taliban's shadow government for assistance.[8] The insurgents only push back where the Dutch have gotten too near to an established drug route.[9]

Not all armed groups in Afghanistan are opposed to the national government. Yet, there is no way of knowing which are which without talking to them. That's why negotiation is such a key element of 4GW.[10] If so much as a tribal sub-group leader were to show any interest at all in supporting the Kabul government, he and the rest of his sub-group should be immediately hired for guard duty. The Dutch fully understand the strategic value of local inroads. Instead of a more traditional forceful entry, they asked to negotiate with the village elders at the entrance to the volatile Balochi Valley. Then, they spread a rumor up the valley that they wanted to come in without fighting. The scheme worked. Not only were the village elders at the meeting, but also the Taliban.[11] By asking the impromptu assembly's permission to enter, the Dutch automatically invoked the region's "hospitality to strangers" tradition.[12] U.S. forces might be wise to widely copy this method.

> It's a strategy focused on supporting the local government rather than killing its supposed enemies, talking with the Taliban instead of fighting them, and treading carefully with an understanding of how little any foreigner knows about this untamed country.[13]
> — *Globe and Mail* (Toronto), 3 December 2006

How the U.S. President's Policy Might Be Better Applied

Among the more useful paradoxes of guerrilla warfare is that friendly troops are safer without as much force protection.[14] Anyone who has traveled alone through dangerous regions of the world can attest to this.[15] Basically, local residents feel more protective of a somewhat vulnerable visitor. According to a Rand Corporation analyst, there is another counterinsurgency adage—"the best weapons don't shoot." He claims that "soft power" has already worked in certain regions of Afghanistan.[16]

Afghanistan has never had a strong central government. Yet, Washington has assumed that this political tradition can now be altered overnight. According to PBS's *Frontline,* the U.S. must instead work through the various tribal hierarchies.[17] "From the top down" is implicitly suggested. If most tribal heads were not openly allied with the drug lords or Taliban, that would have a far better chance of succeeding. Perhaps, more could be accomplished by approaching the most progressive or geographically isolated of the sub-group leaders to each clan of each tribe.

The "Grassroots" Approach to Victory

The Afghan Taliban have been taking control over areas they believe to be strategically important by subverting key villages. Because they require so few people to do so, they easily influence entire regions. Their method is like that of the Communists in Vietnam in the 1960's and southern Africa in the 1970's. In both places, a political commissar and his tiny armed cadre would take over a village any way they could. That often included executing the village leaders (or bourgeois). In Africa, it also involved citizen networks to spy on government forces, inform on each other, and care for incoming guerrillas. To a generally illiterate populace that was additionally deprived of any news media, cease fires meant Communist victories. Attached to every election announcement was the warning that each person's vote could be later determined.[18] As more Communist enclaves sprang up, the pro-government area grew smaller. Every time government forces tried to seize such an enclave by force, they just drove the villagers further into the Communist camp.

Within Afghanistan, the subversion happens through three separate "chains of command"—political, religious, and providing of security. The three men of each village who oversee these functions are the insurgents' target. Recognizing the need for local cooperation, the Taliban will work through indoctrination before resorting to coercion. Still, all too often, one or more of those village leaders has been recently installed after a predecessor's untimely departure. Below is an excellent description of this strategically important village relationship. It comes from a multi-tour Special Forces veteran of Iraq and Afghanistan. He is additionally an expert mantracker.

[T]o understand how the Taliban can subvert a village,

we can use a simple social structure model. . . . [T]hree areas
. . . most affect how daily life is lived. . . . [They are] political
. . . , religious, and security. . . . The Malik and village elders
represent the political aspects. . . . The Imam represents the
religious node. . . . Security is traditionally conducted by the
men of each individual village. If one of the . . . [three] nodes
of influence is controlled by either the Taliban or the Afghan
government in each village, then they heavily influence . . .
the area. . . .

. . . The Taliban build networks by getting a fighter, religious leader, or village elder to support them. Whichever
. . . are initially used will be exploited by tribal and familial
ties [or coercion] . . . . In villages where the locals say there
is no Malik . . . , it is most likely the Taliban have neutral-
ized the desired representative of that village. . . . [A] person
who has [recently] come to represent the village . . . will also
most likely . . . support . . . the Taliban. . . .

A "sub-commander" will be established in the village
to keep those in line who would resist the Taliban or their
Malik. . . . The sub-commander will generally have 2-5 fighters under his control. . . . They may or may not have an IED
capability. . . . These fighters may stay in the village but
preferably are not from the village. Locals can sometimes be
pressed into service . . . , but the Taliban tend to use fighters from different villages so that when threats or physical
violence is utilized, it won't be kinsman against kinsman.
The Imam and local mosques of villages are often visited by
the Taliban [ostensibly wishing to pray] . . . . These mosque
visits afford the Taliban opportunities to gauge village sentiment and to . . . establish contacts within localities. . . .
[R]eligious leaders also . . . educate children in villages where
the Taliban have either closed or destroyed the local school.
. . . The Taliban will supplant the local Imam if needed by
supplying their own. . . . This mosque will serve as a meeting place for Taliban, storage facility, and indoctrination
center.

Sympathetic locals . . . provide food and shelter. One
way . . . is . . . to place food and blankets outside their living
quarters or in guest quarters to be used by Taliban. . . .

To control an area the Taliban will identify villages that
can be most easily subverted. They [the Taliban] will then

spread to other villages in the area one at a time, focusing their efforts on whichever node of influence seem most likely to support their effort first. Using this model the Taliban could influence and dominate or control a valley or area with a population of 1000-2500—of ten villages with 100-250 people (100-250 compounds)—with only between 20-50 active fighters and ten fighting leaders. . . .

The Taliban will have an elaborate network to support their fighters in areas they control or dominate. They will have safe houses, medical clinics, supply sites, weapons caches, transportation agents, and early warning networks to observe and report. The U.S. and Afghan forces, heavily laden with excessive body armor and equipment, are reluctant to leave their vehicles. They are blown up on the same roads and paths they entered the area on. The Taliban will use feints and lures to draw our forces away from caches and leaders in an attempt to buy them time to relocate, or into a lethal ambush. After the attack the Taliban will disperse and blend into the village. The village will usually sustain civilian casualties and the information or propaganda will be spread of U.S. and Afghan forces using excessive force. The U.S. and Afghan forces will leave or set up an outpost nearby, but the attacks will continue because the forces are not in the village, do not truly know "who's . . . [there]", and aren't able to effectively engage Taliban personnel or . . . with the village nodes of influence to their benefit.

. . . Locals are reluctant to help because to be seen talking with the Americans and Afghan security forces will result in a visit from a Taliban member. . . . The local villagers know the government has no effective plan that can counter the Taliban in their village and will typically only give information . . . to settle a blood feud. . . .

U.S. and Afghan forces . . . will need to identify individuals to [target]. . . . This requires in-depth knowledge of tribal structure, alliances, and feuds. Viable . . . choices need to be available to village leaders. . . . Just placing U.S. and Afghan soldiers at an outpost and conducting token presence patrols and occasionally bantering with locals and organizing a shura once a month are not going to work.

Afghan identity is not primarily national. . . . Afghan identity is tribal in nature. . . .

U.S. and Afghan forces must be able to infiltrate and shape the village nodes of influence and then target individuals. Right now our military embraces a centralized, top-driven approach that prevents our military and U.S.-trained Afghan counterparts from doing so. Current U.S. procedures and tactics attempt to identify the Taliban without regard to their influence or social role at a village level. Instead we attempt to link individuals to attacks and incomplete network structures through often questionable intelligence. The individuals in nodes of influence must be identified as neutral, pro, or anti-Afghan government and then dealt with. To target any other way is haphazard at best and does not gain us the initiative.

U.S. and Afghan forces must also devise and utilize tactics to fight outside and inside the village. This requires true light infantry and real counterinsurgency tactics employed by troops on the ground. . . . Being moved from place to place . . . [in] armored vehicles while hardly reengaging local leadership will not work. Targeting identified high value targets will only result in the "whack-a-mole" syndrome. . . . A light infantry force conducting specialized reconnaissance in villages, and using proven tactics like trained visual trackers to follow insurgents into and out of villages, proper ambush techniques on foot outside the village, and knowing the local village situation are the key. Infantry . . . should use also vertical envelopment of Taliban fighters by helicopter and parachute to cut off avenues of escape. Troops should foot patrol into villages at night, talk with and document compounds and inhabitants for later analysis, and have a secure patrol base locally from which to operate. . . . [U]nits and tactics should be decentralized.[19]

— Multi-tour veteran of both wars, December 2009

The Jobs/Income Variable

If Afghan men have no other way of making a living, they will turn to the Taliban for a job. If Afghan soldiers and police are earning one third of what Taliban fighters get, they will sell information or worse. So, the male citizens, soldiers, and police of each village must be given other options. And those options must be supervised.

Only by having a few NATO troops in every village and neighborhood, can this widespread a problem be solved. The easiest way is through CAP platoon participation with equal numbers of Afghan police and soldiers. Then, the most promising of the local residents must be given entrepreneurial loans or hired as sentries. If a NATO squad subsequently suspects any indigenous squad member of Taliban activity, it can send a request up its own chain of command for his "further instruction" elsewhere. At some point all three squads will click, and the local male citizenry will come to realize that the central government is now reliable and there to stay.

The Tribal Variable

Afghanistan has a tribal society, but those tribes are widely dispersed with many subsets. Just as the Yar Gul Khel subgroup of the Zali Khel clan of the Ahmed Zai Wazir tribe led the South Waziristan resistance in 2004,[20] so do the subsets of Afghan tribes frequently do what they want. (Other Wasiri clans have since cooperated with the Pakistani Army against the Mehsuds). Thus, NATO can only accomplish so much in Afghanistan by making deals with overall (and elsewhere located) tribal chieftains. More likely to succeed are local pacts and then mostly going where previously invited. The best paper on the subject is *One Tribe at a Time*, by U.S. Special Forces Major Jim Gant. He proposes victory through tiny "Tribal Engagement Teams."[21] Thus, CAP platoons more like those in Vietnam, could also work in Afghanistan. Instead of same-sized contingents of Afghan soldiers and police, American squads could work with tribal militia to monitor built-up areas astride major LoCs.

The Blood Feud Variable

Most modern Americans have no recollection of blood feuds. However, they are still an integral part of the Afghan way of life. Instead of ignoring them, CAP platoon members must make careful use of them. While some of their tips may be fabricated to get revenge, pointed questions about local-raid fatalities may help to identify neighboring-village Taliban. Then, the CAP platoons in each geographical area have only to compare notes. As for their

225

headquarters, intentionally pitting one opposition tribe or village against another will almost certainly backfire. Before the British came to India, its Muslims and Hindus generally got along.

The Hospitality Variable

By first being invited into an area by village elders, U.S. forces could automatically invoke the "hospitality to strangers" tradition that is so strong in this region. One U.S. traveler to Islamabad may have saved his own life by simply suggesting that his Taliban "assessor's" unfriendliness had violated this tradition.[22]

Pursuant to 4GW Victory

What happens in Afghanistan will ultimately depend on the Afghan government. By stressing its ceremonial heritage, NATO might indirectly discourage its corruption. (See Figure 16.1.) In a fledgling republic, that government's image must also be improved at the local level. For any low-level government employee (whether it be policeman, soldier, or tax collector), any unseemly behavior must be immediately identified as such. At first, that will take a NATO presence in every neighborhood and village along the major LoCs. Though slightly more dangerous than the current strategy, this is the cost of victory. In a 4GW environment, one must concurrently work from the bottom up.

If the Afghan situation were treated more like a law enforcement than a military problem, further prerequisites to victory might become more apparent. From a tactical standpoint, it makes more sense to let the first two responders to Columbine handle the shooters than to wait for SWAT (the special weapons assault team). Two people more easily coordinate fields of fire, etc. Of course, all Boulder police officers might first have needed additional training. Through too little appreciation for enlisted potential, most U.S. military commanders would never allow a "buddy team" of GIs enough leeway to make a strategic difference on their own. Those commanders who are senior still get nervous when anything less than a company is deployed. U.S. police chiefs do not suffer from this over-aversion to risk. They routinely cover the most volatile of neighborhoods with semi-independent two-man teams. If those police chiefs can blanket a dangerous area with buddy teams, then their military counterparts should be able to cover a slightly more dangerous area with something smaller than 220-man companies. Was it not autonomous infantry squads that "swarmed" to stop a whole German army at Stalingrad? [23] One career infantry officer (who has personally worked on squad tactics with thousands of NCOs over the last 40 years) claims that 14 U.S. Marines or soldiers can do almost anything when properly trained and led.[24]

This chapter has shown what any "soft approach" to the war in Afghanistan must eventually entail. Though full force of arms may not be required, the various "Taliban" factions cannot be beaten through political concessions, peace accords, and then lack of local supervision. That has already been attempted unsuccessfully in Pakistan. Such supervision can be most easily provided by law-enforcement-oriented CAP platoons. One can only pray that those Americans in charge will now come to realize the fantastic potential

Figure 16.1: Presidential Guard for the New Afghan Republic
(Source: DA Pam 550-21 [1985], p. 503)

of a U.S. infantry squad. There will be some opposition attempts at CAP unit annihilation of course, but only against a tiny percentage of all those deployed. To make up for the decrease in overall combat, there needs only to be commensurate successes in the other 4GW arenas. Enough economic, political, and psychological progress will not be possible without first impeding all the drug trafficking from every corner of the country.

In early February 2010, NPR's "Morning Edition" News reported that, after slightly falling over the last two years, Afghanistan's opium production was expected to stay even in the coming year.[25] In other words, despite America's fancy new strategy and military surge, 90 percent of the world's heroin would continue to come from Afghanistan. That's like admitting, "Even after all the studies by the Commander in Chief on down, the main cause of Afghanistan's destabilization would remain unaltered." Only a few conclusions are possible. Out of respect for Washington, any thought of a drug payoff at the highest levels will be eliminated. That leaves only procedural habit as the problem. After what happened in Vietnam, U.S. war planners would not again be so foolish as to try top-down strategy against a bottom-up opponent, unless they still considered organizational tradition to be more important than battlefield victory.

Epilogue

A Seemingly Impossible Mission

In December 2009, the U.S. Commander in Chief gave the Pentagon an incredibly difficult task. With 30,000 more troops, it was to stabilize Afghanistan before 2011. That task was not difficult because of any lack of desire on the part of the U.S. Armed Forces. Its members had already tremendously sacrificed over many years to achieve victory in Iraq and Afghanistan. The mission was difficult because the U.S. government, its various agencies, and military departments are not particularly good at doing anything in a hurry. The problem is in how they are structured. Washington is slow because of built-in checks and balances, and its various extensions are slow because of bureaucratic inertia. The only way for the latter to accomplish the President's directive by 2011 is to override some of their established procedures. America now has some of the best field commanders it could possibly have. Yet, those generals are still products of the establishment. They didn't acquire that much rank by regularly bucking the system. Much will depend on whether they can now put loyalty to America above that for their procedural heritage. War is no longer the wholly martial contest it once was. It now has more political, economic, and psychological overtones. As a result, one can gain considerable insight into winning modern wars by watching how natural disasters are handled.

The Haitian Earthquake

Despite Hurricane Katrina's Superdome example, the U.S. government and its military departments were painfully slow in responding to the 7.0 earthquake that struck Haiti on 12 January 2010. Not until a full week later did they finally resort to parachuting food and water to its two million victims. Only one, of what may have been several airdrops, was televised. It occurred in a huge field outside a Port-au-Prince suburb. True to the American model, Haitian troops kept all civilians away while retrieving the supplies. Some four hours later (after eating themselves), they made an orderly distribution to the local populace of whatever they hadn't deemed necessary to "confiscate."

Inside the main part of the city, the Israelis' expeditionary hospital had been up and running since two days after the quake, but U.S. equivalents didn't start to function for four more days.[1] The problem was not any lack of motivation. A smattering of U.S. advance units had been assessing the damage, running the airport, and combing the rubble for days. The problem was in the American tendency always to create order out of chaos. "Food and water could not be helicoptered in," so the reasoning went, "because without enough ground security it would only lead to violence." So, the babies, pregnant women, injured old men, and other inhabitants of Port-au-Prince went without hydration until they became desperate. Looting ensued, and the rest is just another chapter in a tragic history.

On 25 January, NPR News reported that the Haitian government had collected 150,000 corpses from the streets of Port-au-Prince but didn't know how many were still beneath the rubble. Some 132 people had been pulled out alive, but not enough heavy equipment was yet in place to begin with the recovery of the others.[2] There is no telling how many of those 150,000 might have survived if water and antibiotics had been delivered sooner. It had been far too hopeful to think that the U.S. military could do better than FEMA (the Federal Emergency Management Agency) during the initial stages of a catastrophe.

From a simplistic "non-bureaucratic" standpoint, there was another option. Helicopters can deliver supplies by extended sling without ever landing. Once the netting-covered cargo has been softly lowered, the crew chief has only to pull a lanyard or its modern equivalent to release it from the tow rope. At no time is the helicopter or any bystander in any danger.

Port-au-Prince is only 700 miles from Miami and 200 miles from the southernmost island in the Bahamas. Great Inagua Airport has a 7016 x 89 foot asphalt runway.[3] CH-53 heavy lift helicopters could have flown there from Miami, while fuel and supplies were being stockpiled by C-17. That would have meant food, water, and medical supplies for the people of Port-au-Prince within 10 hours of the quake. In a city that big, "slung" loads could have been randomly deposited so that neither gangs nor officials could get there in time to confiscate them. Only the most needy of each area's residents would have ended up with a single "arm load" of help for their respective families. After many such loads all over the city, Port-au-Prince's population would have been widely assisted in a timely manner, so as to suffer fewer casualties. However, Western military bureaucracies don't work that way. They all have massive support establishments with volume upon volume of established procedure. Everything must be carefully staffed and then deliberately done. For political reasons, safeguarding U.S. lives takes precedence over all other considerations. As a result, that which is random or quick is seldom even attempted in combat. Within this unpleasant (though thoroughly valid) comparison lies a slim hope for Afghanistan. Only required will be a leap of faith by the top brass.

Too Little Certainty Is Not the Adversary

"Uncertainty" is a fairly neutral commodity. It can be just as detrimental to the oppressor as to the liberator. Its opposite—predictability—causes more friendly casualties in battle. Thus, those who wish consistently to win at war learn to use uncertainty to their advantage. Just as randomly and softly depositing supplies in Port-au-Prince would have prevented criminal elements from hoarding them, so too can Afghan anarchy be exploited. There, random and subtle checks of roadway traffic could limit the movement of illicit cargo without causing its shippers to alter their routine.

Afghanistan's ancient smuggling conduits are now fully refined. The Soviets couldn't touch them with *Spetsnaz,* and neither will U.S. forces interdict them in the usual way. Instead of forcing their way into the natural flow of things (as is the Western custom), they need more closely to observe that flow and wait for an opening (as is the Eastern custom). Perhaps, an unforeseen traffic jam will provide the chance for a closer look. Or, another natural interruption will provide the cover for formal interdiction. If that interdiction does not appear to be happenstance, the smugglers will simply change their route or methodology, and the insurgency

231

will continue to prosper. In this way, U.S. forces could use the uncertainties of overland transportation in Afghanistan to their advantage.

Some Things Must Be Done in a Hurry

The U.S. has already been fighting in Afghanistan for almost nine years. Whether or not its new president had set a time limit on the effort, Congress would have eventually grown tired of its funding. Instead of looking for someone to blame (as was done after the Vietnam War), perhaps the U.S. military should try a more nontraditional strategy. That strategy will have to be much more bold than what eventually turned the tide in Iraq. To now win with one year to go in Afghanistan, "always protecting the troops" must give way to "fully employing the troops." As with all previous generations, young Americans are smart, brave, and for the most part well-principled. They have vastly more potential than their leaders give them credit. They know the risks of being fully committed and are ready to take them. What they are not willing to do is lose another war. With only a year in which to work, U.S. military leaders must try something totally unorthodox. If they continue down the same well-worn procedural paths, history and the American public may not be very happy with the result.

Too Much Structure Is the Problem

Most high-level American leaders (whether military or otherwise) will find such a paragraph heading totally preposterous. If it were true, they would be far less essential to progress than they prefer to believe. Therefore, the following is for the company grade officers and middle-enlisted ranks who—through their wartime sacrifices—have developed a subliminal hope for more organizational proficiency. As an infantry regimental commander confided to a retired service member in 1999, "Headquarters can be a bigger problem than the enemy."[4] Far from a disconsolate troublemaker, this particular officer went on to do great things in the Marine Corps. His honest admission had more to do with loyalty to God, America, and his subordinates. The first two, at least, should take precedence over organizational habit. Though rising quite high in the Fleet Marine Corps, Lewis B. "Chesty" Puller took issue with his parent command at almost every stage of his career.[5] That may be why he was never awarded the Congressional Medal of Honor or a fourth star. Still, to every succeeding Marine generation, he remains the preeminent example of leadership. Some of that same kind of greatness may again be in order. However, this time, several echelons with the infantry chain of command may have to defer to its lowest.

There are countless examples of less structure working in the Eastern World. Most applicable to Afghanistan is the one from Chechnya. In 1994, tiny rebel contingents simply "swarmed" (without any preconceived plan) to destroy their oppressor's first full-blown assault on Grozny. After a three-month bombardment, the Russians finally captured the city in February 1995.[6] The rebels easily took it back in August 1996. Then they tried—during the three years of Russian absence from their country—to organize themselves into a more Westernized fighting force. When the Russians finally returned to Grozny in January 2000, the rebels' new more organized "army" quickly caved in. The reason was simple. "[Their troops now] operated in a very centrally controlled fashion instead of in the 'defenseless defense' or 'let the situation do the organizing' mode of 1995."[7]

The Afghan Taliban are no longer hampered by much structure. After the U.S. invasion, they reverted to a loosely controlled conglomeration of factions. As was the mistake of the Soviet High Command, U.S. leaders still seem to think those factions are following some master plan from Kandahar or Pakistan. They aren't. To defeat them, outmoded U.S. procedures must be overridden. The best way to do that is by removing intermediate steps in the reporting chain. During the tactical successes of late 1917 and early 1918, German division commanders talked directly to company commanders.[8] So doing in Afghanistan wouldn't provide any more of a NATO presence in the far-flung tribal villages. That would take squad leaders answering directly to battalion commanders. If allowed to buy provisions and make decisions, tiny groups of enlisted Americans might just succeed where their parent commands have only scratched the surface. Instead of the localized and man-power-draining cordons that have come to symbolize U.S. counterinsurgency, hundreds of squad-sized village detachments might do more to alleviate countrywide unrest.

New Strategy Must Be More "Attack-Like" and Widely Applied

One seldom wins in war by having to react to what the enemy does. The Russians were forced by the *mujahideen* into a defensive posture. They too tried to protect every inch of the most vital cities and LoCs. U.S. leaders must not be seduced by the same vision. Wherever the countryside is abandoned, cities soon follow. Wasn't that Mao's most famous axiom? Watching smidgens of the vast rural expanse from satellites and then destroying whoever looks wrong in them by drone is not the same as controlling a countryside. Minimally, there must be a NATO presence in every sizable village. Just sweeping a region of Taliban fighters and then reinstalling its government leaders and police won't be enough. Without grassroots supervision, that region's problems will simply return. The following news piece points to the folly of "top-down" solutions wherever drug trafficking is likely (in almost every part of Afghanistan).

> International officials are keenly aware . . . [of] the possibility that old-style regional powerbrokers could interfere, using their political clout to install inept cronies in the local administration.[9]
> — Associated Press, 26 February 2010

From this and previous research, it would appear that U.S. military leaders must now do what is politically risky in their own culture, but widely accepted and proven to work in Asian cultures. They must use many of their 30,000 new troops as anchor squads for self-supporting and law-enforcement-oriented CAP platoons. So doing would better accomplish the President's new strategy. Instead of just providing perimeter security around Kabul and Kandahar, that same number of GIs could protect the residents of most inhabited areas throughout the country. Their nonviolent demeanor would differ sharply from that of the Taliban, and thus nurture the growing public ire against the Taliban. Any strategically vital location would have such a platoon, including all built-up areas along the major LoCs and at border crossings. Then, at least, there would be some way to slow the overall flow of opiates out and war supplies in. At present, there is far too little NATO supervision of such matters.

Police curb smuggling through spot checks at chokepoints, not telescopically watching whole stretches of road from barely defensible outposts. Like the Soviets, NATO seems to be more interested in keeping the thoroughfares open for its own supplies, than in limiting the flow of enemy goods along them. Insurgencies cannot be dried up that way. While most police departments don't have IEDs to worry about, they also tend to make better use of limited manpower.

Because of Afghanistan's mountains and lack of secondary road system, its highways are more strategically important than normal. That's why Taliban fighters routinely charge tolls on so many.[10] But, isolated outposts along those highways are not the answer.[11] With self-sufficient CAP platoons in all bisected villages, there would be less need for NATO transportation (or convoy security) and more of an impediment to the Taliban equivalent. Why couldn't the stretches between villages just be watched by satellite for the implantation of IEDs? Then, the advance guard for every NATO convoy could destroy them. In a system where the support establishment now so badly outnumbers the combat establishment, self-sufficiency among frontline units has become an almost alien concept. Alien or not, it is still possible. With a little Afghan currency, hundreds of CAP platoons could live and even rearm off of local economies.

Only through a closer relationship with local officials can enough public trust be generated to stop the Taliban. Each inhabited area will be different and require different solutions. If an indigenous CAP platoon member doesn't know enough English to act as interpreter, hand-and-arm signals should sufficiently augment a few Pashto words. For the right unit chemistry, there must be no overall commander of this platoon. By "working together" *(gung ho)*, all things are possible. Any suspected infiltrator can be recommended for further training elsewhere. That and any sister squad excess will be immediately reported up the NATO chain of command.

Because of the time constraints, each U.S. contingent need only be shown enough UW to work out an escape and evasion plan. Should it come under ground attack, there will be no artillery or airstrikes launched in its defense on any populated area. Initially, each contingent must count on its own civilian community for advance warning of any annihilation attempt. Then, it must have its own way to sidestep the attempt and hide until help can arrive. Its indigenous counterparts will similarly make their own contingency arrangements. This would be a totally reasonable expectation of any Eastern squad since WWI. Whatever Germans, Russians, Japanese, Chinese, North Koreans, and North Vietnamese can do, so should Americans.

Proof That This Could Work

The above plan may seem highly implausible to the current generation of U.S. military leaders, but it is not without precedent. There is evidence (albeit circumstantial) that the North Vietnamese Army left tiny contingents of soldiers behind in Cambodian villages during its sweep of the Khmer Rouge to the Thai border in late 1978. The job of each contingent would have been to reestablish a local cadre.[12] Even within recent U.S. history, there is a close facsimile. That's because one branch of the U.S. Armed Forces owes some of its tactical heritage to Mao's 8th Route Army. With very little additional training, U.S. Marine squads manned CAP platoons during the Vietnam War. With only an E-5 in charge (and no officer present), they easily cooperated with militia squads to defend Vietnamese villages. In the three years those CAP platoons were operational, there is no known case of any being overrun and only one of a Marine squad leader being assassinated.[13] Just as Carlson's Raiders had been scrapped in January 1944, so too was the entire CAP program in 1968. One can only guess at the reasons. Someone somewhere must have become convinced that rushing enemy machineguns with battalions was safer than allowing squads to operate alone. The question is—safer to whom? If today's expeditionary leaders are to win where no one has since Tamerlane, they must allow more enlisted infantrymen to reach their full potential—as warriors and as human beings. The only thing that Tamerlane's troops did differently from all the other occupiers was to more closely interact with Afghan society. Despite all impressions to the contrary from predeployment role-playing, most Asian Muslims are virtually identical in motivation to New World Christians.[14] The two can live and work in close proximity to one another, and any other belief would be self-defeating in a counterinsurgency environment.

Notes

SOURCE NOTES

Illustrations:

Maps on pages 3, 8, 10, 11, 23, 29, 134, 150, and 173
reproduced after written assurance from the GENERAL
LIBRARIES OF THE UNIVERSITY OF TEXAS AT
AUSTIN that they are in the public domain.

Map on page 5 reprinted after asking permission of
GLOBAL RESEARCH (Montreal, Canada). Though designated as
"fair usage" on their website (www.globalresearch.ca),
map designator "TAPI pipeline.jpg" may still have reprint restrictions.
Copyright © 2008 by Travis Lupick, straight.com.

Maps on pages 16, 39, 64, 65, and 66 reprinted under provisions
of GNU Free Documentation License, from *WIKIPEDIA
ENCYCLOPEDIA,* s.v. "Afghanistan," "NWFP," "Nimroz,"
"Helmand," and "Kandahar." Map designators are as follows:
"Afghanistan_pro...es_numbered.png," "NWFP_FATA.svg,"
"Nimroz_districts.png," "Helmand_districts.png," and"Kandahar_dis-
tricts.png." Copyrights © n.d.. All rights reserved.

Maps on pages 61 and 133 reproduced with permission of the United
Nations Cartographic Section and Office on Drugs and Crime. They
come from "Afghanistan," Map Number 3958, Revision 5, October 2005,
and a composite of Maps 3 through 5, *WORLD DRUG REPORT 2010,*
and China_India_Pakistan_map_tmp.pdf. The boundaries and names
shown and the designations used on the latter do not imply official
endorsement or acceptance by the United Nations. Copyrights © 2005
and 2010 by United Nations. All rights reserved.

Map on page 71 reproduced with permission of Pen &
Sword Books Ltd. (South Yorkshire, UK), from *BEAR TRAP:
AFGHANISTAN'S UNTOLD STORY* by Brigadier Mohammad
Yousaf and Major Mark Adkin. Both are Map 9 of the Pen & Sword
publication. Copyright © n.d. by Leo Cooper. All rights
reserved.

Picture insert on page 121 reproduced after written assurance from
Cassell PLC (London, UK), that the copyright holders for *WORLD
ARMY UNIFORMS SINCE 1939,* text by Andrew Mollo and
Digby Smith, color plates by Malcolm McGregor and Michael
Chappell, can no longer be contacted. The illustration is from
Part II, Plate 2, of an Orion Books reprint. Copyrights © 1975,
1980, 1981, 1983 by Blandford Books Ltd. All rights
reserved.

Picture insert on page 157 reproduced after written assurance from
Cassell PLC (London, UK), that the copyright holders for
UNIFORMS OF THE ELITE FORCES, text by Leroy
Thompson, color plates by Michael Chappell, can no
longer be contacted. The illustration is from Plate 5,
Number 15, of an Orion Books reprint. Copyright
© 1982 by Blandford Press Ltd. All rights
reserved.

Pictures on pages 178, 183, 194, and 195 reproduced with
permission of the SWEDISH ARMED FORCES and written
assurance from Sorman Information/Media (Vaxjo, Sweden)
that the illustrator can no longer be contacted, from *Soldf:
Soldaten I Falt,* by Forsvarsmakten, with illustrations
by Wolfgang Bartsch. These drawings appear on pages
436, 370, 436, and 189 of the Swedish publication.
Copyrights © 2001 by Wolfgang Bartsch. All rights
reserved.

Text:

Reprinted with the permission of the United Nations (New York,
NY), from *WORLD DRUG REPORT 2009, by* United Nations Office
on Drugs and Crime. Copyright © 2009 by United Nations. All rights
reserved.

ENDNOTES

Preface

1. John Paul II, *Crossing the Threshold of Hope* (New York: Alfred A. Knopf, 1995), pp. 205, 206.
2. "Sergeant Alvin York," by Dr. Michael Birdwell, Great War Society, as retrieved from its website, www.worldwar1.com, on 15 October 2009; "Sergeant York," 134 minutes, Warner Brothers Pictures, DVD, isbn #1-4198-3829-6.

Introduction

1. *Afghanistan Online* (www.afghan-web.com), s.v. "History Chronology"; *Wikipedia Encyclopedia,* s.v. "Afghanistan," "Ptolemaic Dynasty," "Kingdom of Seleucus," "Persian Empire," "Alexander the Great," "Mongol Empire," "Timur," and "Mughal Empire."
2. Robin Batty and David Hoffman, "Afghanistan: Crisis of Impunity," *Human Rights Watch,* vol. 13, no. 3(c), July 2001, pp. 35, 36; Amir Mir, *The True Face of Jihadis* (Lahore: Mashal Books, 2004), p. 29; Jason Burke, "Waiting for a Last Battle with the Taliban," *The Observer* (UK), 27 June 1999; Anthony H. Cordesman (Arleigh A. Burke Chair in Strategy), "Iran's Developing Military Capabilities," working draft (Washington, D.C.: Center for Strategic Internat. Studies, 14 December 2004), pp. 35-38; Barbara Slavin, "Iran Helped Overthrow Taliban, Candidate Says," *USA Today,* 10 June 2005, p. 14A; "Iran Report," *Radio Free Europe/Radio Liberty,* vol. 5, no. 3, 28 January 2002.
3. Interviews with Western observers and a Taliban official in Kabul during 1999 and 2000, in "Afghanistan: Crisis of Impunity," by Batty and Hoffman, p. 23.
4. Bill Gertz, "China-Made Artillery Seized in Afghanistan," *Washington Times,* 12 April 2002; *Dragon on Terrorism: Assessing China's Tactical Gains and Strategic Losses Post-September 11,* by Mohan Malik (Carlisle, PA: Strategic Studies Inst., U. S. Army War College, October 2002, table 1; Scott Baldauf, "How Al Qaeda Seeks to Buy Chinese Arms," *Christian Science Monitor,* 23 August 2002; Bill Gertz and Rowan Scarborough, "China-Trained Taliban," Inside the Ring, *Washington Times,* 21 June 2002.
5. Headlines Today (New Delhi News Channel), 12-15 August 2009, as viewed by author from Chennai during this period; *Wikipedia Encyclopedia,* s.v. "Coco Islands."; "Match China Pearls," *Deccan Chronicle* (Bangalore), 14 August 2009, p. 1.

6. H.E. Mu. Mohsen Amiuzadeh (Deputy Minister of External Affairs of Asia-Oceania of the Islamic Republic of Iran), "Special Address to the Federation of Indian Chambers of Commerce and Industry," New Delhi, 22 July 2003; *Wikipedia Encyclopedia,* s.v. "Hazara."

7. Akhtar Rehman (Pakistani ISI head), as quoted in *Silent Soldier,* by Brigadier Yousaf (South Yorkshire, UK: Leo Cooper, n.d.).

Chapter 1: *What Lies behind All the Afghan Turmoil?*

1. "Central Asia Pipeline Deal Signed," by Ian McWilliam, BBC News Online, 27 December 2002; "Energy Profile of Afghanistan," ed. Langdon D. Clough, *Encyclopedia of Earth,* 31 January 2007; Nojumi, *The Rise of the Taliban in Afghanistan,* pp. 176, 189, 198-201, 223.

2. "Renewed Hope for Afghan Pipeline," by Raouf Liwal, *Asia Times Online,* 23 November 2004; *Wikipedia Encyclopedia,* s.v. "Gwadar."

3. "Trio Sign Up for Turkmen Gas," *Upstream* (International Oil and Natural Gas Newspaper, Norway), 25 April 2008; "Afghan Pipeline Raises Security Questions," by Travis Lupick, *Global Research,* 21 July 2008; *Wikipedia Encyclopedia,* s.v. "Trans-Afghan Pipeline."

4. *Global Security* (globalsecurity.org), s.v. "Hamid Karzai."

5. "Analysis: Mr. Karzai Goes to Washington," by Marc Erikson, *Asia Times Online,* 29 January 2002; *Wikipedia Encyclopedia,* s.v. "Zalmay Khalilzad" and "Unocal."

6. ABC's Nightly News, 12 July 2005; "China Oil Firm in Unocal Bid War," BBC Radio News, 23 June 2005.

7. Amiuzadeh (Deputy Minister of . . . Iran), "Special Address to the Federation of Indian Chambers of Commerce and Industry," New Delhi, 22 July 2003; *Wikipedia Encyclopedia,* s.v. "Hazara."

8. "Ambassadors in Pakistan Visit Gwadar Port," Xinjua News Agency, 11 January 2002: *Wikipedia Encyclopedia,* s.v. "Karakoram Highway."

9. Carlotta Gall, "Afghan-Iranian Road Opens," *New York Times,* 28 January 2005.

10. "Caspian Oil and Gas: Production and Prospects," by Bernard A. Gelb, CRS Report for Congress, 8 September 2006.

11. "China, Turkmenistan Sign Landmark Gas Deal," *Central Asia News Online* (Turkmenistan), 18 July 2007.

12. "India, Pakistan and the 'Peace' Pipeline," *Asia Times Online,* 15 September 2004; "Trio Sign Up for Turkmen Gas"; "Peace Pipeline Progress," *Asia Monitor,* June 2007; "Iran, Pakistan Sign Peace Pipeline Deal," Press TV (Tehran), 24 May 2009.

13. "Russia's Georgia Invasion May Be About Oil," by Rachel Martin, ABC News Online, 16 August 2008.

14. "Inside Pakistan-Administered Kashmir," by Aamer Ahmed Khan, BBC News Online, 6 April 2005; *Wikipedia Encyclopedia,* s.v. "Pakistan-Administered Kashmir."

15. "Aksai Chin: China's Disputed Slice of Kashmir," CNN Online, 24 May 2002; *Wikipedia Encyclopedia,* s.v. "Aksai Chin."

16. "Ambassadors in Pakistan Visit Gwadar Port"; Niazi, Assoc. for Asian Research, "Gwadar: China's Naval Outpost on the Indian Ocean," in *Wikipedia Encyclopedia,* s.v. "Gwadar."

17. NPR's "Morning Edition" News, 22 October 2009.

18. "Beijing's Afghan Gamble," by Robert D. Kaplan, *New York Times,* 7 October 2009.

19. "Gilgit Baltistan Reforms Aimed at Providing Better Security Cover for Chinese Investments," *South East Asia News* (Bahrain), 4 September 2009.

20. "Chinese Interests Caught in Drone Threat," by Syed Fazl-e-Haider, *Asia Times Online,* 26 March 2009.

21. Ibid.

22. "Factbox: Baluchistan—Pakistan's Biggest but Poorest Province," from Reuters, 14 October 2009.

23. "Chinese Interests Caught in Drone Threat."

24. "H. E. Mr. Chen Shanmin, the Consul General Visits Quetta, Balochistan 2007-09-11," Chinese Consulate in Karachi, n.d.

25. *Wikipedia Encylopedia,* s.v. "Balochistan Liberation Army."

26. "ISI's Attempt to Discredit the Balochis," *India Defence,* 14 March 2006.

27. "Everyone Wants a Cut in Afghan Drug Trade," from McClatchy Newspapers, *Jacksonville Daily News* (NC), 10 May 2009, p. A8.

28. Al Santoli, "The Panama Canal in Transition: Threats to U.S. Security and China's Growing Role in Latin America," American Foreign Policy Council Investigative Report, 23 June 1999.

29. *CIA—The World Factbook* (www.cia.gov), s.v. "China."

30. "Do I Look Dangerous to You," Part I, Partners in Crime Series, by Frederic Dannen, *The New Republic,* 14 & 21 July 1997.

31. Santoli, "The Panama Canal in Transition." Bill Gertz, *The China Threat: How the People's Republic Targets America* (Washington, D.C.: Regnery Publishing, 2000), p. 94.

32. "Do I Look Dangerous to You," by Dannen.

33. Gretchen Peters, *Seeds of Terror: How Heroin Is Bankrolling the Taliban and al-Qaeda* (New York: Thomas Dunne Books, 2009), pp. 136, 155; James Risen, "Reports Link Karzai's Brother to Afghan Heroin Trade," *New York Times,* 4 October 2008; "Afghan Leader Accused of Hurting Drug Fight," from AP, *Jacksonville Daily News* (NC), 25 July 2008, p. 5A.

34. NPR's Morning News, 2 September 2009.

Chapter 2: *The Afghan Taliban's Karachi Home*

1. Amir Mir, *The True Face of Jihadis* (Lahore: Mashal Books, 2004), p. 282.

2. Ibid., pp. 195-198.

3. Amir Mir, *Talibanisation of Pakistan* (New Delhi: Pentagon Press, 2010), p. 196; Robert T. McLean, "Can Pakistan Reform," *FrontPage Magazine,* 5 January 2006, in *Wikipedia Encyclopedia,* s.v. "madrassah"; South Asia Intelligence Review database, s.v. "Pakistan Backgrounder"; Wilson John, Observer Research Foundation, *Coming Blowback: How Pakistan Is Endangering the World* (New Delhi: Rupa & Co., 2009), p. 24.

4. Ali Jalali and Lester W. Grau, *Afghan Guerrilla Warfare: In the Words of the Mujahideen Fighters* (St. Paul, MN: MBI Publishing, 2001), first published as *The Other Side of the Mountain* (Quantico, VA: Marine Corps Combat Development Cmd., 1995), p. 410; Rohan Gunaratna, *Inside al-Qaeda: Global Network of Terror* (Lahore: Vanguard, 2002), p. 40.

5. Neamatollah Nojumi, *The Rise of the Taliban in Afghanistan: Mass Mobilization, Civil War, and the Future of the Region* (New York: Palgrave, 2002), p. 120; "Jaish-e-Mohammed (JEM) Backgrounder," South Asia Analysis Group (India), paper no. 3320, 10 March 2001; Zia Sarhadi, "Turning Pakistan into a Sectarian Battleground," *Muslimedia* (London), 1 February 1998.

6. Nojumi, *The Rise of the Taliban in Afghanistan*, p. 122.

7. Ibid.

8. "Pakistani Madrassahs: A Balanced View," Report for U.S. Inst. of Peace, August 2005.

9. John L. Esposito, *Unholy War: Terror in the Name of Islam* (London: Oxford Univ. Press, 2002), pp. 15-17.

10. Khaled Ahmed, *Pakistan: Behind the Ideological Mask* (Lahore: Vanguard, 2004), pp. 223, 226.

11. *Patterns of Global Terrorism, 2003 Report* (Washington, D.C.: U.S. Dept. of State, April 2004). (This work will henceforth be cited as *Patterns of Global Terrorism, 2003.)*

12. Mir, *The True Face of Jihadis,* pp. 123-135; Nojumi, *The Rise of the Taliban in Afghanistan,* p. 128.

13. H. John Poole, *Militant Tricks: Battlefield Ruses of the Islamic Insurgent* (Emerald Isle, NC: 2005), Figure 6.1; South Asia Intelligence Review database, s.v. "Lashkar i-Jhangvi."

14. Aaron Mannes, *Profiles in Terror: Guide to Middle East Terror Organizations* (Lanham, MD: Rowman & Littlefield, 2004), p. 67; Wilson John, Observer Research Foundation, *Coming Blowback: How Pakistan Is Endangering the World* (New Delhi: Rupa & Co., 2009), p. 99.

15. *Patterns of Global Terrorism, 2003.*
16. John K. Cooley, *Unholy Wars: Afghanistan, America, and International Terrorism* (n.p., n.d.), in *Pakistan: Behind the Ideological Mask,* by Khaled Ahmed (Lahore: Vanguard, 2004), p. 225; Mir, *The True Face of Jihadis,* pp. 105, 183, 184; South Asia Intelligence Review database, s.v. "Lashkar-e-Toiba."
17. Interviews with senior Pakistani military officer at Lahore and Pakistani religious party recruits and Taliban prisoners in 1999, in "Afghanistan: Crisis of Impunity," by Batty and Hoffman, p. 28.
18. Nojumi, *The Rise of the Taliban in Afghanistan,* p. 119.
19. Ibid., p. 120.
20. Jalali and Grau, *Afghan Guerrilla Warfare,* p. 409.
21. Nojumi, *The Rise of the Taliban in Afghanistan,* p. 122.
22. Ahmed, *Pakistan: Behind the Ideological Mask,* p. 223; Mir, *The True Face of Jihadis,* p. 21.
23. Jalali and Grau, *Afghan Guerrilla Warfare,* p. 410.
24. K.J.M. Varma, "PoK Also Banns Jihadi Outfits," from *PTI* (Pakistan), 5 December 2003; Mannes, *Profiles in Terror,* p. 67; Mir, *The True Face of Jihadis,* pp. 103, 104.
25. South Asia Intelligence Review database, s.v. "Lashkar i-Jhangvi."
26. Mir, *The True Face of Jihadis,* pp. 31, 328.
27. South Asia Intelligence Review database, s.v. "Harkat-ul-Jihad-al-Islami."
28. "Islam's Medieval Outposts," by Husain Haqqani, *Foreign Policy* (Washington, D.C.), November/December 2002.
29. "Talibanism: Pakistani-Style," *The Friday Times,* vol. XI, no. 52, 25 February-2 March 2000; Owais Tohid, "In Death, As in Life," *Newsline,* October 2003.
30. Memorandum for the record by H.J. Poole.
31. Pranab Dhal Samanta, "India Wants Him, Pak Uses Jaish Chief to Defuse Mosque Tension," *India Express* (New Delhi), 7 July 2009; "Talibanism: Pakistani-Style."
32. Wilson John, "The Karachi Connection," *The Pioneer* (New Delhi), 23 January 2002.
33. South Asia Intelligence Review database, s.v. "Sipah-e-Sahaba Pakistan."
34. Cooley, *Unholy Wars,* as quoted in "The Great Banuri Town Seminary," by Shaykh, *Sunni Forum,* 12 August 2005.
35. "The Great Banuri Town Seminary," by Shaykh, *Sunni Forum,* 12 August 2005.

36. Federation of American Scientists database, s.v. "Harakat ul-Jihad-I-Islami (HUJI)."

37. "Talibanism: Pakistani-Style."

38. Tim McGirk, Phil Zabriskie, Helen Gibson, Ghulam Hasnain, and Zamira Loebis, "Islam's Other Hot Spots," *Time,* 15 September 2003.

39. "The Binori Town Madrassah," by Yahya Durrani, www.paklinks.com, 16 January 2000.

40. "Talibanism: Pakistani-Style."

41. Pepe Escobar, review of *Who Killed Daniel Pearl,* by Bernard-Henri Levy, *Asia Times Online,* 28 June 2003.

42. "Pakistani Madrassahs: A Balanced View."

43. Samanta, "India Wants Him, Pak Uses Jaish Chief to Defuse Mosque Tension."

44. NPR's "Morning Edition" News, 27 June 2009.

45. McGirk et al, "Islam's Other Hot Spots."

46. "Pakistani Madrassahs: A Balanced View"; "Pakistan under Siege," PBS's *Frontline World,* NC Public TV, 14 April and 26 May 2009.

47. Huma Yusuf, "Taliban Rising? Ask the Women," *Christian Science Monitor,* 24 May 2009, p. 8.

48. Wilson John, Observer Research Foundation, *Coming Blowback: How Pakistan Is Endangering the World* (New Delhi: Rupa & Co., 2009), p. 167; Mir, *The True Face of Jihadis,* p. 21; Nojumi, *The Rise of the Taliban in Afghanistan,* p. 124; Mark Rice-Oxley and Owais Tohid, "British Keep a Wary Eye on Pakistan," *Christian Science Monitor,* 27 July 2005, pp. 1, 4; Ahmed Rashid, *Taliban: Militant Islam, Oil and Fundamentalism in Central Asia* (New Haven, Ct.: Yale Univ. Press, March 2001), in *Wikipedia Encyclopedia,* s.v. "al-Qaeda"; "Islam's Medieval Outposts"; "The 'University of Holy War'," by Haroon Rashid, BBC News Online, 2 October 2003.

49. "Jaish-e-Mohammed (JEM) Backgrounder," South Asia Analysis Group (India), paper no. 332, 3 October 2001; *Wikipedia Encyclopedia,* s.v. "Jamia Ashrafia."

50. Issam Ahmed, "Pakistan's Old Jihadis Pose New Threat," *Christian Science Monitor,* 6 December 2009, pp. 8, 9; Mir, *Talibanisation of Pakistan,* p. 57.

51. Ibid.; Robert D. Kaplan, *Soldiers of God: With Islamic Warriors in Afghanistan and Pakistan* (New York: Vintage Books, 1990), pp. 234, 235.

52. Mir, *The True Face of Jihadis,* p. 20.

53. Ben Arnoldy, "The Taliban: A Threat Overrated," *Christian Science Monitor,* 7 June 2009, pp. 13-16.

54. *Global Security* (globalsecurity.org) and *Wikipedia Encyclopedia,* s.v. "Muttahida-e-Majlis-e-Amal."

55. "Pak Raids Unravel Taliban-Drugs Link," *The Times of India,* 25 August 2009; Chanakya Sen, review of *Karachi: A Terror Capital in the Making,* by Wilson John, *Asia Times Online,* 17 January 2004; Nojumi, *The Rise of the Taliban in Afghanistan,* p. 120; South Asia Intelligence Review database, s.v. "Lashkar-e-Toiba" and "Harkat-ul-Mujahideen Al-alami"; Mir, *The True Face of Jahadis,* pp. 183, 184; "Lashkar-e-Jhangvi: Sectarian Violence in Pakistan and Ties to International Terrorism," by Animesh Roul, in Unmasking Terror, vol. I, ed. Christopher Heffelfinger (Washington, D.C: Jamestown Foundation, 2005), pp. 97, 325-329.

56. Mir, *The True Face of Jihadis,* p. 237.

57. Robert D. Kaplan, *Soldiers of God: With Islamic Warriors in Afghanistan and Pakistan,* revised ed. (New York: Vintage Books, 2001), pp. 234, 235; Nojumi, *The Rise of the Taliban in Afghanistan,* p. 122.

58. South Asia Intelligence Review database, s.v. "Lashkar-e-Toiba"; Gretchen Peters and Aleem Agha, "Weary Taliban Coming In from the Cold," *Christian Science Monitor,* 14 December 2004, pp. 1, 7.

59. South Asia Intelligence Review database, s.v. "Lashkar i-Jhangvi" and "Harkat-ul-Jihad-al-Islami."

60. Mir, *The True Face of Jihadis,* p. 33.

61. South Asia Intelligence Review database, s.v. "Lashkar-e-Toiba"; "Jaish-e-Mohammed (JEM) Backgrounder."

62. A.G. Noorani, "Pakistan's Burden," *Frontline* (India), 3-16 January 2009; *Wikipedia Encyclopedia,* s.v. "Lashkar e-Taiba."

63. "Pakistani Madrassahs: A Balanced View."

64. South Asia Intelligence Review database, s.v. "Sipah-e-Sahaba Pakistan."

65. Amir Mir, *Talibanisation of Pakistan,* pp. 118-120; Samanta, "India Wants Him, Pak Uses Jaish Chief to Defuse Mosque Tension."

66. South Asia Intelligence Review database, s.v. "Lashkar-e-Toiba."

67. Ibid., s.v. "Lashkar i-Jhangvi."

68. Ibid., s.v. "Sipah-e-Sahaba Pakistan" and "Lashkar i-Jhangvi."

69. Nishit Dholabhai, "Lid off Lashkar's Manipur Mission," *The Telegraph* (Calcutta), 28 December 2006, in *Wikipedia Encyclopedia,* s.v. "Lashkar e-Taiba"; Mir, *The True Face of Jihadis,* p. 96; South Asia Intelligence Review database, s.v. "Lashkar-e-Toiba."

70. Mir, *The True Face of Jihadis,* p. 97; Mir, *Talibanisation of Pakistan,* pp. 78, 79.

71. Mir, *Talibanisation of Pakistan,* pp. 65, 66; Mir, *The True Face of Jihadis,* p. 97; South Asia Intelligence Review database, s.v. "Lashkar-e-Toiba."

72. Nojumi, *The Rise of the Taliban in Afghanistan,* p. 120; South Asia Intelligence Review database, s.v. "Lashkar i-Jhangvi."

73. South Asia Intelligence Review database, s.v. "Lashkar i-Jhangvi" and "Sipah-e-Sahaba Pakistan."

74. John, *Coming Blowback*, p. 167.

75. Ibid., pp. 5-17.

76. "Markets Closed, Traffic Thin: 135 Arrested in Lahore," by Intikhab Hanif and Ahmad Fraz Khan, *Dawn Newspaper Group Online* (Karachi), 10 November 2001; John, *Coming Blow-Back*, p. 20.

77. South Asia Intelligence Review database, s.v. "Lashkar e-Toiba"; Mir, *The True Face of Jahadis,*pp. 183, 184; John, *Coming Blow-Back,* p. 42.

78. John, *Coming Blow-Back,* pp. 39, 58.

79. "Jaish-e-Mohammed (JEM) Backgrounder," South Asia Analysis Group (India), paper no. 332, 3 October 2001; *Wikipedia Encyclopedia,* s.v. "Jamia Ashrafia."

80. Ahmed, "Pakistan's Old Jihadis Pose New Threat," pp. 8, 9; Mir, *Talibanisation of Pakistan,* p. 57.

81. South Asia Intelligence Review database, s.v. "Lashkar i-Jhangv"; John, *Coming Blow-Back,* pp. 31, 32.

82. Ibid., s.v. "Lashkar e-Toiba."

83. Ibid., s.v. "Lashkar i-Jhangvi."

84. Ibid., s.v. "Lashkar e-Toiba."

85. "Harakat ul-Mujahidin," *Patterns of Global Terrorism, 2002 Report* (Washington, D.C.: U.S. Dept. of State, April 2003).

86. "The Marriott Blast: Was Denmark the Target," by B. Rahman of the South Asia Analysis Group, *International Terrorism Monitor,"* Paper No. 449, 22 September 2008, in *Wikipedia Encyclopedia,* s.v. "Islamabad Marriott Hotel Bombing."

87. South Asia Intelligence Review database, s.v. "Harkat-ul-Ansar."

88. Ibid, s.v. "Lashkar i-Jhangvi"; Australian Govt. National Security Website (www.ag.gov.au), s.v. "Lashkar e-Jhangvi."

89. Ibid., s.v. "Lashkar e-Toiba."

90. Ibid., s.v. "Harkat-ul-Ansar"; "Jaish-e-Mohammed (JEM) Backgrounder"; "Harakat ul-Mujahidin," *Patterns of Global Terrorism, 2002 Report.*

91. Mir, *The True Face of Jihadis,* pp. 24, 96, 105; Noorani, "Pakistan's Burden"; *Wikipedia Encyclopedia,* s.v. "Lashkar e-Taiba."

92. Tariq Naqash and Syed Irfan Raza, "Operation against LeT-Dawa Launched in AJK," *Dawn Newspaper Group Online* (Karachi), 9 December 2008; Nirupama Subramanian, "Shut Down LeT Operations, India Tells Pakistan," *The Hindu* (India) 8 December 2008; both from *Wikipedia Encyclopedia,* s.v. "Lashkar e-Taiba."

93. South Asia Intelligence Review database, s.v. "Hizb-ul-Mujahideen."

94. Mir, *The True Face of Jihadis,* pp. 129 and 123-135; Nojumi, *The Rise of the Taliban in Afghanistan,* p. 128.

95. Nojumi, *The Rise of the Taliban in Afghanistan,* pp. 101, 189.

96. "Clash of Canons," by Riyaz Wani, *Indian Express,* 9 December 2006; Nojumi, *The Rise of the Taliban in Afghanistan,* pp. 101, 189.

97. South Asia Intelligence Review database, s.v. "Lashkar-e-Toiba" and "Hizb-ul-Mujahideen."

98. "Jaish-e-Mohammed (JEM) Backgrounder."

99. Rohan Gunaratna, *Inside al-Qaeda: Global Network of Terror* (Lahore: Vanguard, 2002), pp. 40, 206; Ahmed Rashid, "Taliban Ready for 'Decisive' Push, *Daily Telegraph* (London), 22 July 1999, in "Afghanistan: Crisis of Impunity," by Batty and Hoffman, p. 32; South Asia Intelligence Review database and *Wikipedia Encyclopedia,* s.v. "Tehreek-e-Nafaz-e-Shariat-e-Mohammadi"; Mir, *The True Face of Jihadis,* pp. 123-135; Nojumi, *The Rise of the Taliban in Afghanistan,* p. 128.

100. "Pakistan Bans LET, JuD, and 23 Outfits," *Deccan Herald* (India), 6 August 2009; South Asia Intelligence Review database, s.v. "Lashkar-e-Toiba."

101. South Asia Intelligence Review database, s.v. "Sipah-e-Sahaba Pakistan"; *Wikipedia Encyclopedia,* s.v. "Sipah-e-Sahaba Pakistan."

102. South Asia Intelligence Review database, s.v. "Harkat-ul-Jihad-al-Islami."

103. *CIA—The World Factbook* (www.cia.gov), s.v. "Pakistan"; South Asia Intelligence Review database, s.v. "Jaish-e-Mohammed."

104. Ibid., s.v. "Lashkar i-Jhangvi"; "Lashkar-e-Jhangvi & Al Qaeda," by B. Raman, South Asia Analysis Group, Paper No. 2526, 31 December 2007, and *International Terrorism Monitor,* Paper No. 337, n.d.; Mir, *The True Face of Jihadis,* p. 218; "Jaish-e-Mohammed (JEM) Backgrounder."

105. "Mehsud's Pals in High Places," *Newsweek,*13 April 2009.

106. "Pakistan under Siege."

107. Ibid.

108. Halima Kazem, "U.S. Thins Taliban's Ranks, But their Ideological Grip Remains Strong," *Christian Science Monitor,* 18 September 2003, p. 7.

109. Nic Robertson, "Pakistan: Taliban Buying Children for Suicide Attacks," CNN Online, 7 July 2009; "Mehsud Buying Children to Make Suicide Bombers," *News Outlook* (India), 3 July 2009.

110. Fergus M. Bordewich, "Fading Glory," *Smithsonian,* December 2008, pp. 60, 61.

111. Ibid.

112. "Pakistan Project," International Center for Religion and Diplomacy (Washington, D.C.), n.d.

113. South Asia Intelligence Review database, s.v. "Sipah-e-Sahaba Pakistan."

Chapter 3: *The Pakistani Taliban's Islamabad Offensive*

1. "Pakistan Conflict Map," from BBC News Online, South Asia section, 22 June 2009.

2. Ben Arnoldy, "Pakistan Accepts Islamic Law in Swat Valley," *Christian Science Monitor,* 17 February 2009; Decian Walsh, "Pakistan Bows to Demand for Sharia Law in Taliban-Controlled Swat Valley," *Guardian* (UK), 14 April 2009.

3. "Constitution of Pakistan," as retrieved from pakistani.org on 20 July 2009; CIA—*The World Factbook* (www.cia.gov), s.v. "Pakistan."

4. *Pakistan: A Country Study,* Federal Research Div. (Washington, D.C.: Library of Congress, 1995), chapt. 1, "Historical Setting (Zia ul-Haq and Military Domination, 1977-88), and chapt. 4, "The Government and Politics (Zia ul-Haq, 1977-88); *Wikipedia Encyclopedia,* s.v. "Pakistan."

5. *Pakistan: A Country Study,* chapt. 4, "The Government and Politics (Judiciary)."

6. Ibid., chapt. 5, "Internal Security (Islamic Provisions)."

7. Pakistani Government (pak.gov.pk), s.v. "Constitution of Pakistan"; *Wikipedia Encyclopedia,* s.v. "Constitution of Pakistan."

8. *Pakistan: A Country Study.*

9. H. John Poole, *Dragon Days: Time for "Unconventional" Tactics* (Emerald Isle, NC: Posterity Press, 2007), p. 133; *Wikipedia Encyclopedia,* s.v. "Bajaur."

10. "Pakistan Conflict Map."

11. Ibid.

12. Ibid.

13. Ibid.; "Pakistan Captures Mehsud's Hometown," UPI.com, 24 October 2009.

14. "Pakistan Conflict Map."

15. Ibid.

16. Ibid.

17. Ibid.

18. Ibid.

19. Ibid.

20. Arnoldy, "Pakistan Accepts Islamic Law in Swat Valley."

21. Decian Walsh, "Pakistan Bows to Demand for Sharia Law in Taliban-Controlled Swat Valley," *Guardian* (UK), 14 April 2009.

22. Arnoldy, "Pakistan Accepts Islamic Law in Swat Valley."

23. "Pakistan Conflict Map."

24. Ibid.

25. Ibid.

26. Esposito, *Unholy War,* pp. 15-17; Ahmed, *Pakistan: Behind the Ideological Mask,* pp. 223, 226.

27. *Pakistan Country Study,* Areas Handbook Series (Washington, D.C.: Library of Congress, 2003); Tini Tran, AP, "Tape Targets Clerics," *Jacksonville Daily News* (NC), 25 November 2004, pp. 1A, 4A.

28. Nojumi, *The Rise of the Taliban in Afghanistan,* pp. 101, 189.

29. South Asia Intelligence Review database and *Wikipedia Encyclopedia,* s.v. "Tehreek-e-Nafaz-e-Shariat-e-Mohammadi."

30. Ibid.

31. Ibid.; *Wikipedia Encyclopedia,* s.v. "Bajaur."

32. South Asia Intelligence Review database and *Wikipedia Encyclopedia,* s.v. "Tehreek-e-Nafaz-e-Shariat-e-Mohammadi."

33. Hassan Abbas, "The Black-Turbaned Brigade: The Rise of TNSM in Pakistan," Jamestown Foundation, 12 April 2006, in *Wikipedia Encyclopedia,* s.v. "Tehreek-e-Nafaz-e-Shariat-e-Mohammadi."

34. Nahal Toosi, "Taliban to Cease Fire in Pakistan's Swat Valley," Yahoo News, 15 February 2009, in *Wikipedia Encyclopedia,* s.v. "Tehreek-e-Nafaz-e-Shariat-e-Mohammadi"; "Pakistan Conflict Map."

35. Kamran Rehmat, "Swat: Pakistan's Lost Paradise," Al Jazeera, 27 January 2009, in *Wikipedia Encyclopedia,* s.v. "Tehreek-e-Nafaz-e-Shariat-e-Mohammadi."

36. "Pakistan Troops Seize Radical Cleric's Base", Agence France Presse, 28 November 2007, in *Wikipedia Encyclopedia,* s.v. "Tehreek-e-Nafaz-e-Shariat-e-Mohammadi."

37. Hassan Abbas, "A Profile of Tehrik-I-Taliban Pakistan," Combating Terrorism Center (West Point), *CTC Sentinel,* January 2008, in *Wikipedia Encyclopedia,* s.v. "Tehrik-i-Taliban Pakistan."

38. Carlotta Gall et al, "Pakistani and Afghan Taliban Unify in Face of U.S. Influx," *New York Times,* 26 March 2009; Haji Mujtaba Khan, "Taliban Rename Their Group," *The Nation* (Pakistan), 23 February 2009; "Three Taliban Factions Form Shura Ittehad-ul-Mujahiden," *The News* (Pakistan), 23 February 2009; all in *Wikipedia Encyclopedia,* s.v. "Tehrik-i-Taliban Pakistan."

39. B. Raman, "The New Trojan Horse of Al Qaeda," South Asia Analysis, *International Terrorism Monitor,* Paper No. 301, 10 November 2007.

40. South Asia Intelligence Review database, s.v. "Tehreek-e-Nafaz-e-Shariat-e-Mohammadi"; "Pakistan Conflict Map"; *Wikipedia Encyclopedia,* s.v. "Bajaur."

41. "Pakistan Conflict Map."

42. Delawar Jan, "100 Militants Killed in Maidan," *The News* (Pakistan), 22 July 2009.

43. South Asia Intelligence Review database, s.v. "Tehreek-e-Nafaz-e-Shariat-e-Mohammadi"; "Pakistan Conflict Map."

44. Pepe Escobar, "The Roving Eye," *Asia Times Online,* 15 November 2001.

45. Sami Yousafzai and Ron Moreau, "Rumors of bin Laden's Lair," *Newsweek*, 8 September 2003, pp. 24-27; Nojumi, *The Rise of the Taliban in Afghanistan*, p. 226.

46. Gunaratna, *Inside al-Qaeda*, p. 206.

47. "Pakistan Conflict Map"; Issam Ahmed, "Stakes High for Pakistan's Push," *Christian Science Monitor*, 1 November 2009, p. 8.

48. Raman, "The New Trojan Horse of Al Qaeda."

49. "Iran Report," *Radio Free Europe/Radio Liberty*, vol. 5, no. 3, 28 January 2002.

50. Raman, "The New Trojan Horse of Al Qaeda."

51. "Pakistan: Timeline on Swat Valley Turbulence," IRIN (irinnews.org), 31 July 2009; "Desperate Moves On to Secure Swat— the Lost Valley," by Ismail Khan, *Dawn Newspaper Group Online* (Karachi), 15 January 2009; "Militants Gain Despite Decree by Musharraf," by Jane Perlez and Ismail Khan, *New York Times*, 15 November 2007; "Pakistan Hunting Swat Militants," BBC News Online, 8 December 2007; all in *Wikipedia Encyclopedia*, s.v. "Swat."

52. "Pakistan Troops Seize Radical Cleric's Base: Officials," from AFP, 28 November 2007.

53. Ben Arnoldy, "Pakistan's Not-So-Epic Offensive," *Christian Science Monitor*, 18 October 2009, p. 8; Owais Tohid and Faye Bowers, "U.S. Pakistan Tighten Net on Al Qaeda," *Christian Science Monitor*, 22 March 2004, pp. 1, 10; Kim Barker *(Chicago Tribune)*, "Pakistani Tribes Fight Alleged al-Qaida Allies," *Seattle Times*, 24 April 2007.

54. Peters, *Seeds of Terror*, p. 144.

55. James Risen, "U.S. Inaction Seen After Taliban P.O.W.'s Died," *New York Times*, Asia Pacific ed., 10 July 2009.

56. Memorandum for the record by H.J. Poole.

57. "19-Hour Siege of GHQ Block Ends," by Shakeel Anjum, *The International News Online* (Pakistan), 12 October 2009; "Militants Take Hostages at Pakistan Army HQ," News Briefs Wire Reports (AP), *Jacksonville Daily News* (NC), 11 October 2009.

58. "Suicide Attack Kills 30 in Pakistan," World News in Brief, *Christian Science Monitor*, 28 May 2009.

59. NPR's "Morning Edition" News, 12 October 2009.

60. *Global Security* (globalsecurity.org), s.v. "Baittulah Mehsud."

61. Anonymous U.S. Special Forces member (after multiple tours to Iraq and Afghanistan), in telephone conversation with author on 30 July 2009.

62. "Pakistani Islamists Sign Deal With China," by Farhan Bokhari, CBS News World Watch, 18 February 2009; "Markets Closed, Traffic Thin: 135 Arrested in Lahore," by Hanif and Khan.

63. Matthew Pennington, AP, "Pakistan Unsure If Target Is al-Zawahri," *Jacksonville Daily News* (NC), 21 March 2004, p. 5A.

64. Geo Pakistan News Online (www.geo.tv), 19 June 2009.

65. "Munawar sworn in as JI Ameer," The International News Online (Pakistan), 6 April 2009.

66. "Pakistan's 'New Zone of Militancy'," BBC News Online, 12 October 2009.

67. South Asia Intelligence Review database, s.v. "Sipah-e-Sahaba Pakistan" and "Lashkar i-Jhangvi."

68. Mir, *The True Face of Jihadis,* p. 282.

69. "Jaish-e-Mohammed (JEM) Backgrounder."

70. "Lashkar-e-Jhangvi & Al Qaeda," by B. Raman, South Asia Analysis Group, Paper No. 2526, 31 December 2007, and *International Terrorism Monitor,* Paper No. 337, n.d.; South Asia Intelligence Review database, s.v. "Lashkar i-Jhangvi."

71. "Taliban Claim Pakistan Army Raid," BBC News Online, 12 October 2009; *Wikipedia Encyclopedia,* s.v. "Azam Tariq."

72. Ahmed, "Pakistan's Old Jihadis Pose New Threat," p. 9; "19-Hour Siege of GHQ Block Ends," by Anjum.

73. "Pakistani Commandos Break Siege on Army Headquarters," by Bill Roggio, *Long War Journal,* 10 October 2009.

74. "Waziristan-Based Terror Group Takes Credit for Lahore Assault," by Bill Roggio, *Long War Journal,* 30 March 2009.

75. Arnoldy, "Pakistan's Not-So-Epic Offensive," p. 8.

76. "Pakistan Cuts Deal with Anti-American Taliban," News Briefs Wire Reports (AP), *Jacksonville Daily News* (NC), 20 October 2009, p. 11.

77. "Pakistan Conflict Map"; Peters, *Seeds of Terror,* p. 110.

78. "Pakistan Conflict Map."

79. Gall et al, "Pakistani and Afghan Taliban Unify in Face of U.S. Influx"; Khan, "Taliban Rename Their Group," *The Nation* (Pakistan), 23 February 2009; "Three Taliban Factions Form Shura Ittehad-ul-Mujahiden," *The News* (Pakistan), 23 February 2009; all in *Wikipedia Encyclopedia,* s.v. "Tehrik-i-Taliban Pakistan."

80. NPR's "Morning Edition" News, 22 October 2009.

81. Ibid., 2 November 2009.

82. "Attack Aimed at Pakistan Military Mosque," UPI, 4 December 2009.

83. NPR's "Morning Edition" News, 12 March 2010.

84. Noorani, "Pakistan's Burden"; *Wikipedia Encyclopedia,* s.v. "Lashkar e-Taiba."

85. Nishit Dholabhai, "Lid off Lashkar's Manipur Mission," *The Telegraph* (Calcutta), 28 December 2006, in *Wikipedia Encyclopedia*, s.v. "Lashkar e-Taiba"; Mir, *The True Face of Jihadis,* pp. 96, 97; South Asia Intelligence Review database, s.v. "Lashkar-e-Toiba."
86. South Asia Intelligence Review database, s.v. "Lashkar i-Jhangvi."
87. "Taliban Leader's Death Confirmed," News Briefs/Wire Reports (AP), *Jacksonville Daily News* (NC), 11 February 2010, p. 13.
88. "Pakistan Conflict Map."

Chapter 4: *Al-Qaeda's Hidden Presence*

1. "Al Qaeda Message Urges Pakistanis to Back Militants," CNN Online, 15 July 2009.
2. Al-Zawahiri, as quoted in "Al Qaeda Message Urges Pakistanis to Back Militants."
3. "Al Qaeda: Profile and Threat Assessment," by Kenneth Katzman, CRS Report for Congress, Order Code RL33038, 17 August 2005.
4. Federation of American Scientists database, s.v. "al-Qaeda"; Mir, *The True Face of Jihadis,* p. 282.
5. Raman, "The New Trojan Horse of Al Qaeda."
6. "Documents Show American Trained at Al Qaeda Camps in Pakistan," from AP, 23 July 2009.
7. Pennington, "Pakistan Unsure If Target Is al-Zawahri," p. 5A.
8. Owais Tohid and Faye Bowers, "U.S. Pakistan Tighten Net on Al Qaeda," *Christian Science Monitor,* 22 March 2004, pp. 1, 10.
9. Arnoldy, "Pakistan's Not-So-Epic Offensive."
10. "Pakistan Blames IMU Militants for Afghan Border Unrest," by Alisher Sidikov, Radio Free Europe/Radio Liberty, 2 July 2008; Peters, *Seeds of Terror,* pp. 130, 131.
11. "International Relations and Security Network [of] al-Qaeda," by Jayshree Bajoria, Council on Foreign Relations (New York, NY), 18 April 2008.
12. Mir, *The True Face of Jihadis,* p. 23.
13. Ibid., p. 33.
14. *Patterns of Global Terrorism, 2003.*
15. Cooley, *Unholy Wars, in Pakistan: Behind the Ideological Mask,* by Ahmed, p. 225; Gunaratna, *Inside al-Qaeda,* p. 207.
16. "Documents Show American Trained at Al Qaeda Camps in Pakistan."
17. "Suicide Bomber Kills Peacekeeper, Civilian in Afghan Capital," World Brief Wire Reports (AP), *Jacksonville Daily News* (NC), 28 January 2004.

18. Yoni Fighel and Yael Shahar, "The Al-Qaida-Hizballah Connection," as posted on 26 February 2002 at the ICT website; Howard LaFranchi, "Anti-Iran Sentiment Hardening Fast," *Christian Science Monitor,* 22 July 2004, pp. 1, 10; "Who Did It? Foreign Report Presents an Alternative View," *Jane's Foreign Report 19, 2001,* in *Seeds of Hate,* by Pintak, p. 307; Nicholas Blanford, "Hizbullah Reelects Its Leader," *Christian Science Monitor,* 19 August 2004, p. 6.

19. "Pakistan Bans LET, JuD, and 23 Outfits"; South Asia Intelligence Review database, s.v. "Lashkar-e-Toiba."

20. Ibid.

21. South Asia Intelligence Review database, s.v. "Sipah-e-Sahaba Pakistan"; *Wikipedia Encyclopedia,* s.v. "Sipah-e-Sahaba Pakistan."

22. South Asia Intelligence Review database, s.v. "Sipah-e-Sahaba Pakistan" and "Lashkar i-Jhangvi"; "Lashkar-e-Jhangvi & Al Qaeda," by B. Raman.

23. "Al Qaeda Deploys Paramilitary 'Shadow Army'," by Bill Roggio, *Long War Journal,* 10 February 2009.

24. Gunaratna, *Inside al-Qaeda,* pp. 40, 206; Ahmed Rashid, "Taliban Ready for 'Decisive' Push," *Daily Telegraph* (London), 22 July 1999, in "Afghanistan: Crisis of Impunity," by Batty and Hoffman, p. 32.

25. South Asia Intelligence Review database and *Wikipedia Encyclopedia,* s.v. "Tehreek-e-Nafaz-e-Shariat-e-Mohammadi"; Mir, *The True Face of Jihadis,* pp. 123-135; Nojumi, *The Rise of the Taliban in Afghanistan,* p. 128.

26. "Chinese-Made Ammo in al Qaeda Caves Confirms," *DEBKAfile* (Israel), 17 December 2001.

27. Gertz, "China-Made Artillery Seized in Afghanistan.

28. "India Wants Him, Pak Uses Jaish Chief to Defuse Mosque Tension," by Pranab Dhal Samanta, *India Express* (Delhi), 7 July 2009.

29. Mir, *The True Face of Jihadis,* p. 218.

Chapter 5: *Afghanistan's Drug Barons*

1. Peters, *Seeds of Terror,* pp. 29-31; "GOP Begins Cleanup of Smugglers Den at Sohrab Goth," U.S. State Dept cable, in *Seeds of Terror,* by Peters, p. 31.

2. DEA Chief Jack Dawn in testimony before the Senate Intelligence Committee, and CIA assessment in September 1988, as quoted in *Seeds of Terror,* by Peters, pp. 28, 51.

3. Lt.Col. Patrick Myers and Patrick Poole, "Hezbollah, Illegal Immigration, and the Next 9/11," *Front Page Magazine,* 28 April 2006; Cilluffo, "Threat Posed by the Convergence of Organized Crime, Drug Trafficking, and Terrorism," in *Seeds of Terror,* by Peters, pp. 10, 11.

4. Peters, *Seeds of Terror,* pp. 74, 86, 95; Ron Moreau, "America's New Nightmare," *Newsweek,* 3 August 2009, pp. 38-41; NPR's "Morning Edition" News, 15 February 2010.

5. NPR's "Morning Edition" News, 8 December 2009; "Afghanistan: U.S. Escalates the Illegal Drug Industry," by John W. Warnock, *Global Research* (www.globalresearch.ca), 25 February 2009; *Global Security* (globalsecurity.org), s.v. "Abdul Rashid Dostum"; "Former Warlord in Standoff With Police at Kabul Home," by Ahmad Masood (Reuters), *New York Times,* Asia Pacific ed., n.d.

6. Peters, *Seeds of Terror,* p. 177.

7. Ibid., pp. 130, 131; "Pakistan Blames IMU Militants for Afghan Border Unrest," by Sidikov; Arnoldy, "Pakistan's Not-So-Epic Offensive," p. 8.

8. "Here Comes Trouble," *The Economist,* 11 June 2009.

9. Peters, *Seeds of Terror,* pp. 132, 133.

10. Ibid., pp. 53, 111, 155, 160; an Afghan confederate of Noorzai, in *Seeds of Terror,* by Peters, p. 74.

11. Peters, *Seeds of Terror,* p. 37.

12. Ibid., pp. 38, 39.

13. Ibid., p. 129.

14. Batty and Hoffman, "Afghanistan: Crisis of Impunity," pp. 35, 36; Bonner, "Afghan Rebels Victory Garden: Opium," in *Seeds of Terror,* by Peters, p. 32.

15. Rupert and Coll, "U.S. Declines to Probe Afghan Drug Trade; Rebels, Pakistani Officers Implicated," in *Seeds of Terror,* by Peters, p. 34.

16. Rubin, "The Fragmentation of Afghanistan," in *Seeds of Terror,* by Peters, p. 35.

17. Gunaratna, *Inside al-Qaeda,* p. 40; Nojumi, *The Rise of the Taliban in Afghanistan,* pp. 23, 95; *Country Profiles,* BBC News Online, s.v. "Afghanistan: Timeline."

18. Edgar O'Ballance, *Afghan Wars: Battles in the Hostile Land, 1839 to Present* (Karachi: Oxford Univ. Press, 2002), p. 242.

19. Mir, *The True Face of Jihadis,* p. 282.

20. Peters, *Seeds of Terror,* p. 93.

21. Ibid.

22. History Commons (www.historycommons.org), s.v. "Profile: Haji Bashir Noorzai"; *Wikipedia Encyclopedia,* s.v. "Haji Bashir Noorzai."

23. Peters, *Seeds of Terror,* pp. 94, 109; *Country Profiles,* BBC News Online, s.v. "Afghanistan: Timeline."

24. Marc W. Herold, "The Failing Campaign," *Frontline* (India), vol. 19, issue 3, 2-15 February 2002.

25. Peters, *Seeds of Terror,* p. 110.

26. Unnamed senior Western counternarcotics official, in *Seeds of Terror,* by Peters, p. 128.

27. Mir, *The True Face of Jihadis,* p. 138; "Iran Report"; Herold, "The Failing Campaign."

28. Peters, *Seeds of Terror,* p. 129.

29. Ibid., pp. 35, 36; "Afghanistan," by Warnock; Macdonald, *Drugs in Afghanistan,* p. 88, in *Seeds of Terror,* by Peters, p. 36; O'Ballance, *Afghan Wars,* p. 116; *The Rise of the Taliban in Afghanistan,* p. 222; Gunaratna, *Inside al-Qaeda,* p. 17; Mir, *The True Face of Jihadis,* p. 130.

30. Brigadier Mohammad Yousaf and Mark Adkin, *Bear Trap: Afghanistan's Untold Story* (South Yorkshire, UK: Leo Cooper, n.d.); O'Ballance, *Afghan Wars,* p. 164.

31. Batty and Hoffman, "Afghanistan: Crisis of Impunity," pp. 35, 36; O'Ballance, *Afghan Wars,* pp. 242, 243.

32. "Haqqani Network," Inst. for the Study of War (Washington, D.C.), n.d.

33. "Opium Trade Is Halal in Islam: Bara Scholar," *Pakistan Daily News,* 21 January 2005, in *Seeds of Terror,* by Peters, p. 143.

34. Ibid; *Global Security* (globalsecurity.org), s.v. "Mawlawi Jalaluddin Haqqani."

35. "Afghan Linked to Taliban Sentenced to Life in Drug Trafficking Case," by Benjamin Weiser, *New York Times,* 1 May 2009; "Afghan Arrested in New York Said to Be a Heroin Kingpin," by Julia Peterson, *New York Times,* 26 April 2005; "In Drug Trial, Sharply Differing Portraits of Afghan With Ties to the Taliban," by Benjamin Weiser, *New York Times,* 11 September 2008; Peters, *Seeds of Terror,* p. 196; H. John Poole, *Homeland Siege: Tactics for Police and Military* (Emerald Isle, NC: Posterity Press, 2009), chapt. 3.

36. Peters, *Seeds of Terror,* pp. 43, 74, 193, and chapt. 3, endnote 13.

37. Ibid.

38. Bob Clarke, former DEA agent in Islamabad, 2 February 2008, as quoted in *Seeds of Terror,* by Peters, p. 86.

39. Unnamed U.S. official, as quoted in *Seeds of Terror,* by Peters, p. 150.

40. Peters, *Seeds of Terror,* p. 145.

41. General Ali Shah Paktiawal, as quoted in *Seeds of Terror,* by Peters, p. 145.

42. Peters, *Seeds of Terror,* p. 148.

43. Ibid., pp. 149, 152.

44. Ibid., p. 151.

45. Ibid.

46. Ibid., pp. 153, 154.

47. Former SAS commander, as quoted in *Seeds of Terror,* by Peters, p. 115.

48. Peters, *Seeds of Terror,* pp. 154, 155.

49. Ibid., p. 159.

50. Ibid., pp. 106, 107.

51. *Global Security* (globalsecurity.org), s.v. "Mohammad Qasim Fahim."

52. "Games in Afghan Poppy Land," *Calcutta Telegraph* (India), 6 September 2005; Afghanistan's Presidential Election: A Mockery of Democracy, *Tribune* (Pakistan), 4 October 2004, in *Wikipedia Encyclopedia,* s.v. "Hazrat Ali."

53. David Kaplan and Aamir Latif, "A Stash to Beat All," *U.S News and World Report,* 10 August 2005, in *Seeds of Terror,* by Peters, p. 187.

54. Dean Nelson, "Hamid Karzai Blames Britain for Taliban Resurgence," *The Times Online* (UK), 7 September 2008, in *Seeds of Terror,* by Peters, chapt, 7, endnote 10.

55. "Afghan Leader Accused of Hurting Drug Fight," from AP, *Jacksonville Daily News* (NC), 25 July 2008, p. 5A.

56. Declan Walsh, "How Anti-Corruption Chief Once Sold Heroin in Las Vegas," *Guardian* (UK), 28 August 2007, in *Seeds of Terror,* by Peters, p. 186.

57. Peters, *Seeds of Terror,* p. 209; Gall and Cloud, "U.S. Memo Faults Afghan Leader on Heroin Fight," in *Seeds of Terror,* by Peters, p. 209.

58. Peters, *Seeds of Terror,* p. 137.

59. Ibid., p. 155.

60. Sifton and Coursen-Neff, "Killing You Is a Very Easy Thing for Us," Human Rights Watch report, n.d, in *Seeds of Terror,* by Peters, p. 198.

61. Brian Ross and Gretchen Peters, "U.S. Military Link's Karzai's Brother to Drugs," ABC News Online, 22 June 2006, in *Seeds of Terror,* by Peters, chapt. 7, endnote 38.

62. Peters, *Seeds of Terror,* p. 208.

63. Ibid., p. 30.

64. "Pakistan: Countering an Expanding Drug Industry," CIA intelligence assessment, in *Seeds of Terror,* by Peters, pp. 42, 43.

65. Peters, *Seeds of Terror,* pp. 26, 56; "Afghanistan," by Warnock.

66. Ahmed Rashid, *The Taliban* (New Haven, CT: Yale Univ. Press, March 2001), p. 122, in *Seeds of Terror,* by Peters, p. 95.

67. Peters, *Seeds of Terror,* p. 116.

68. "Dawood's ISI Links Could Trouble Musharraf," by Wilson John, Observer Research Foundation (New Delhi), *Strategic Trends,* vol. I, issue 5, 4 November 2003; Peters, *Seeds of Terror,* p. 157.

69. Ibid., p. 159.

70. Ibid., p. 51; Mannes, *Profiles in Terror*, p. 66; *Patterns of Global Terrorism, 2003.*

71. "Dawood's ISI Links Could Trouble Musharraf," by John; Peters, *Seeds of Terror*, p. 129.

72. Peters, *Seeds of Terror*, pp. 65, 96, 173.

73. Ibid., pp. 12, 82, 110; Rashid, *The Taliban* (New Haven, CT: Yale Univ. Press, March 2001) in *Seeds of Terror*, by Peters, p. 118.

74. Peters, *Seeds of Terror*, p. 84.

75. Ibid., pp. 12, 122, 123.

76. Ibid., pp. 116, 117.

77. Ibid., pp. 5, 12.

78. Ahmadullah Alizai interview of July 2004, in *Seeds of Terror*, by Peters, p. 3.

79. "Opium Trade Is Halal in Islam: Bara Scholar," *Pakistan Daily News*, 21 January 2005, in *Seeds of Terror*, by Peters, p. 143.

80. Chanakya Sen, review of *Karachi: A Terror Capital in the Making*, by Wilson John, *Asia Times Online*, 17 January 2004; Peters, *Seeds of Terror*, p. 31; Lawrence Lifschultz, "Pakistan, the Empire of Heroin," in McCoy and Block, *War on Drugs*, p. 320, and Lifschultz, *Heroin Empire*, pp. 71-72, and *The Herald* (Pakistan) during 1985, all in *Seeds of Terror*, by Peters, p. 37.

81. *Patterns of Global Terrorism, 2003;* "Jaish e-Mohammed Profile," Overseas Security Advisor Council, *Global Security News & Reports*, n.d.; Mariane Pearl, *A Mighty Heart: The Inside Story of the Al Qaeda Kidnapping of Danny Pearl* (New York: Scribner, 2003), p. 74; Danny Pearl, as quoted in *A Mighty Heart*, by Mariane Pearl, p. 75; Mir, *The True Face of Jihadis*, p. 218.

82. Mir, *The True Face of Jihadis*, pp. 123-135; Nojumi, *The Rise of the Taliban in Afghanistan*, p. 128; "Heroin in Pakistan: Sowing the Wild Wind," CIA report, in *Seeds of Terror*, by Peters, p. 64.

83. Mir, *The True Face of Jihadis*, p. 33.

84. Mannes, *Profiles in Terror*, p. 66; South Asia Intelligence Review database, s.v. "Lashkar-e-Toiba" and "Hizb-ul-Mujahideen"; Gunaratna, *Inside al-Qaeda*, pp. 40, 206; Ahmed Rashid, "Taliban Ready for 'Decisive' Push," *Daily Telegraph* (London), 22 July 1999, in "Afghanistan: Crisis of Impunity," by Batty and Hoffman, p. 32; South Asia Intelligence Review database and *Wikipedia Encyclopedia*, s.v. "Tehreek-e-Nafaz-e-Shariat-e-Mohammadi"; Mir, *The True Face of Jihadis*, pp. 123-135; Nojumi, *The Rise of the Taliban in Afghanistan*, p. 128; "Al Qaeda Deploys Paramilitary 'Shadow Army'," by Roggio.

85. Peters, *Seeds of Terror,* p. 160.

86. The Memorial Institute for the Prevention of Terrorism (MIPT) Knowledge Base, s.v. "FARC." [This source will henceforth be cited as MIPT Knowledge Base.]

87. Ibid.

88. "Colombia's Most Powerful Rebels," BBC News Online, 19 September 2003.

89. "Nicaragua Corredor de Armas"; "Colombia Says FARC Rebels Operating in Bolivia, Paraguay," Xinhua, *People's Daily on Line* (Beijing), 23 June 2006; Davidson, "Terrorism and Human Smuggling Rings . . . ," in *Unmasking Terror,* vol. III, ed. Jonathan Hutzley (Washington, D.C.: Jamestown Foundation, 2007), p. 500; "Terrorist and Organized Crime Groups in the Tri-Border Area"; Fed. of American Scientists (www.fas.org), s.v. "FARC"; *Wikipedia Encyclopedia,* s.v. "Revolutionary Armed Forces of Colombia."

90. H. John Poole, *Tequila Junction: 4th-Generation Counterinsurgency* (Emerald Isle, NC: Posterity Press, 2008), pp. 72-75; *Wikipedia Encyclopedia,* s.v. "Jacobo Arenas."

91. "Do I Look Dangerous to You," by Dannen.

92. Peters, *Seeds of Terror,* pp. 5, 12.

93. Poole, *Dragon Days,* pp. 112-126.

94. "Smoking Al Qaeda Out of Karachi," by B. Raman, South Asia Analysis Group, Paper No. 519, 14 September 2002; "Dawood Gang Provided Logistics to Lashkar Militants," Press Trust of India, NDTV website (Mumbai), 29 November 2008; *Wikipedia Encyclopedia,* s.v. "Dawood Ibrahim"; "Dawood's Drug Net Financed 26/11: Russian Intelligence," NDTV website (Mumbai), 18 December 2008; Craig Whitlock and Karen DeYoung, "Attributes Suggest Outside Help," *Washington Post,* 28 November 2008, p. 1.

95. Sudip Mazumdar, "Captors of the Liberated Zone," *Newsweek,* 18 May 2009, Maoist activity map on p. 43.

96. Perl, "The Taliban and the Drug Trade," in *Seeds of Terror,* by Peters, pp. 86, 87.

97. Sen, review of *Karachi,* by John; Peters, *Seeds of Terror,* p. 31; Lawrence Lifschultz, "Pakistan, the Empire of Heroin," in McCoy and Block, "War on Drugs," p. 320, and Lifschultz, *Heroin Empire,* pp. 71-72, and *The Herald* (Pakistan) during 1985, all in *Seeds of Terror,* by Peters, p. 37.

98. "Dawood Ibrahim: The Global Terrorist," by B. Raman, South Asia Analysis Group, Paper No. 818, 19 October 2003; "Dawood Ibrahim," Interpol Special Notice, 2 October 2009.

99. Sen, review of *Karachi,* by John.

100. "Dawood's ISI Links Could Trouble Musharraf," by John.

101. Sen, review of *Karachi,* by John.

102. "Pak Raids Unravel Taliban-Drugs Link."

103. "Dawood Ibrahim," Interpol Special Notice, 2 October 2009.

104. Peters, *Seeds of Terror*, p. 161.

105. Quetta interview with Pakistani intelligence official of December 2008, in *Seeds of Terror*, by Peters, p. 161.

106. Sen, review of *Karachi*, by John; Ron Moreau, "Sheltered in Karachi," *Newsweek*, 7 December 2009, p. 16.

107. Gilbert King, *The Most Dangerous Man in the World* (New York: Chamberlain Bros., a Penguin imprint, 2004), pp. 11, 12; Sen, review of *Karachi*, by John.

108. "U.S. Puts Afghan Drug Lords on Hitlist to Disrupt Taliban Finances," by Richard Norton-Taylor and Jon Boone, *The Guardian Online* (UK), 10 August 2009.

109. Sly, "Opium Cash Fuels Terror, Experts Say," and Dept. of Homeland Security report cited in Rabasa et al, "Ungoverned Territories," p. 66, both from *Seeds of Terror*, by Peters, p. 110, 111.

110. "Heroin in Pakistan: Sowing the Wind," a CIA report leaked to and printed by Pakistan's *Friday Times*, 3 September 1995, in *Seeds of Terror*, by Peters, p. 60.

111. Peters, *Seeds of Terror*, p. 126.

112. "Pakistan and the Taliban," by Ahmed Rashid, *The Nation* (Lahore), 11 April 1998.

113. Peters, *Seeds of Terror*, p. 214.

114. Kabul interview with Western official in 2004, from *Seeds of Terror*, by Peters, pp. 3, 4.

115. McGirk, "Terrorism's Harvests," and multiple interviews in *Seeds of Terror*, by Peters, pp. 152, 153.

116. Sen, review of *Karachi*, by John.

117. "Organized Crime, Intelligence and Terror: The D-Company's Role in the Mumbai Attacks," by Tom Burghardt, *Global Research*, 13 December 2008; "A Godfather's Lethal Mix of Business and Politics," *U.S. News & World Report Online*, 5 December 2005; "Dawood Ibrahim Has Agents in Bangladesh," from Indo-Asian News Service, 1 June 2009; King, *The Most Dangerous Man in the World*, p. 20.

118. Mir, *Talibanisation of Pakistan*, p. 174.

119. "Organized Crime, Intelligence and Terror: The D-Company's Role in the Mumbai Attacks," by Tom Burghardt; King, *The Most Dangerous Man in the World*, p. 119.

120. "Africa Drug Trade Fuelling Terrorism and Crime, Says UN," BBC News Online, 9 December 2009; "Mystery Surrounds Alleged Hezbollah Links to Drug Arrests in Curacao," by Chris Zambelis, Jamestown Foundation, *Terrorism Monitor*, vol. 7, issue 18, 25 June 2009; "Why West Africa Cannot Break Its Drug Habit," by Rose Skelton, BBC News Online, 21 June 2010.

121. "Africa Drug Trade Fuelling Terrorism and Crime, Says UN."

122. Memorandum for the record by H.J. Poole.

123. "U.S. Designates Dawood Ibrahim As Terrorist Supporter," U.S. Treasury Dept. Press Release, 16 October 2003.

124. "Dawood Ibrahim," U.S. Treasury Dept. Fact Sheet, n.d.

125. Peters, *Seeds of Terror*, p. 189; Matt Pennington, "Afghanistan Stops Paying Farmers to Give Up Growing Opium," from AP, 25 August 2003.

126. "U.S. Puts Afghan Drug Lords on Hitlist . . . ," by Norton-Taylor and Boone; Barbara Slavin, "Iran Helped Overthrow Taliban, Candidate Says," *USA Today*, 10 June 2005, p. 14A.

127. Peters, *Seeds of Terror*, p. 12.

128. Ibid., p. 183.

129. "Obama's War," PBS's *Frontline*, NC Public TV, October 2009.

130. Peters, *Seeds of Terror*, p. 216; *CIA—The World Factbook* (www.cia.gov), s.v. "Afghanistan."

131. *Country Profiles*, BBC News Online, s.v. "Afghanistan."

132. Peters, *Seeds of Terror*, p. 216.

133. Ibid.; Peters, *Seeds of Terror*, p. 216.

134. Peters, *Seeds of Terror*, p. 4.

135. Marvin Weinbaum, former U.S. State Dept. intelligence analyst, as quoted in *Seeds of Terror*, by Peters, p. 9.

136. Peters, *Seeds of Terror*, p. 12.

Chapter 6: *Foreign Destabilization of Afghanistan*

1. *Country Profiles*, BBC News Online, s.v. "Afghanistan: Timeline."

2. "Clash of Canons," by Wani; "Reluctance to Slate Suicide Bombing," by Kunwar Idris, *Dawn Newspaper Group Online* (Karachi), 21 June 2009.

3. *Pakistan Country Study;* Tini Tran, AP, "Tape Targets Clerics," *Jacksonville Daily News* (NC), 25 November 2004, pp. 1A, 4A; Nojumi, *The Rise of the Taliban in Afghanistan*, pp. 101, 189.

4. South Asia Intelligence Review database, s.v. "Tehreek-e-Nafaz-e-Shariat-e-Mohammadi"; "Pakistan Conflict Map"; *Wikipedia Encyclopedia*, s.v. "Bajaur."

5. "Al Qaeda: Profile and Threat Assessment," by Katzman.

6. Peters, *Seeds of Terror*, p. 34.

7. Herold, "The Failing Campaign"; Peters, *Seeds of Terror*, p. 110.

8. Gall et al, "Pakistani and Afghan Taliban Unify in Face of U.S. Influx"; Khan, "Taliban Rename Their Group"; "Three Taliban Factions Form Shura Ittehad-ul-Mujahiden"; all in *Wikipedia Encyclopedia*, s.v. "Tehrik-i-Taliban Pakistan."

9. Anonymous U.S. Special Forces member (after multiple tours to Afghanistan), in telephone conversation with author on 11 December 2009.

10. Louis Meixler, AP, "Extremists Send Recruits into Iraq via Iranian Border," *Jacksonville Daily News* (NC), 8 November 2004, p. 4A.

11. "Afghanistan's President: Partner Or Obstacle," by Soraya Sarhaddi Nelson, NPR's "Morning Edition" News, 24 March 2010; Rahimullah Samander and Rahim Gul Sarwan, "Concern That Jihad Chieftains Will Set Political Agenda," Inst. for War and Peace Reporting, ARR No. 88, 18 December 2003; Nojumi, *The Rise of the Taliban in Afghanistan*, p. 132; "Karzai's Cabinet Rejected," from AP, *Jacksonville Daily News* (NC), 3 January 2010, p. 12; Edgar O'Ballance, *Afghan Wars: Battles in a Hostile Land, 1839 to Present* (Karachi: Oxford Univ. Press, 2002), pp. 234, 235; "Iran Report."

12. Peters, *Seeds of Terror*, p. 138.

13. "The Presence of U.S. Troops and Alleged Support for the Insurgency," Afghanistan Project Themes: Iran and Afghanistan, Inst. for the Study of War (Washington, D.C.), n.d.

14. Rubin, "The Fragmentation of Afghanistan," p. 263, in *Seeds of Terror*, by Peters, p. 34.

15. "Afghanistan: Opium Winter Assessment" and "Responding to drug use and HIV in Iran," United Nations Office on Drugs and Crime, January 2009 and 19 November 2008, respectively, in "The Presence of U.S. Troops and Alleged Support for the Insurgency."

16. Richard Clarke (former U.S. antiterrorism czar), on ABC's Morning News, 7 June 2007.

17. Jason Straziuso, AP, "Afghan Bomber Deadlier," *Jacksonville Daily News* (NC), 3 June 2007, pp. 1A, 8A.

18. Richard Clarke, on ABC's Morning News, 7 June 2007.

19. ABC's Nightly News, 6 June 2007.

20. "Military: Iran Teaching Iraqi Militia to Build Bombs," from AP, *Jacksonville Daily News* (NC), 12 April 2007, p. 5A; Scott Peterson, "Shiites Rising—Part One," *Christian Science Monitor*, 6 June 2007, pp. 1, 13-16.

21. Poole, *Militant Tricks*, pp. 139-141; "Afghanistan: Crisis of Impunity," by Batty and Hoffman, pp. 35-39.

22. ABC's Morning News, 14 December 2005.

23. Jason Burke, "Waiting for a Last Battle with the Taliban," *The Observer* (UK), 27 June 1999; Mir, *The True Face of Jihadis*, p. 29.

24. Anthony H. Cordesman, "Iran's Developing Military Capabilities," working draft (Washington, D.C.: Center for Strategic Internat. Studies, 14 December 2004), pp. 35-38.

25. Barbara Slavin, "Iran Helped Overthrow Taliban, Candidate Says," *USA Today*, 10 June 2005, p. 14A.

26. "Iran Report."

27. Ahmad Qurishi, "Landmine Depot Smuggled from Iran Discovered," *Pajhwok News Agency*, 26 January 2008, and "Iran 'Iranian Weapons Cache Found in Afghanistan: U.S.'," *AFP*, 10 September 2009, both in "The Presence of U.S. Troops and Alleged Support for the Insurgency."

28. Stephen Graham, AP, "Latest Assault Leaves 2 Brits, Afghan Interpreter Dead," *Jacksonville Daily News* (NC), 6 May 2004, p. 8A.

29. Kochay and Rahim, as quoted in *Afghan Guerrilla Warfare*, by Jalali and Grau, pp. 59-61 and p. 21, respectively; H. John Poole, *Phantom Soldier: The Enemy's Answer to U.S. Firepower* (Emerald Isle, NC: Posterity Press, 2001), p. 138.

30. Greg Miller, "U.S. Says Pakistan, Iran Helping Taliban," *Los Angeles Times Online,* 22 September 2009.

31. Heidi Vogt and Rahim Faiez, AP, "NATO General in Afghanistan: Taliban Train, Get Weapons in Iran," *Jacksonville Daily News* (NC), 31 May 2010, p. 11.

31. Muhammad Tahir, "Iranian Involvement in Afghanistan," Jamestown Foundation, *Terrorism Monitor,* vol. 5, Issue 1, 21 February 2007.

32. Amin Tarzi, "Afghanistan: Kabuls Mulls Relations with Iran," *Radio Free Europe/Radio Liberty,* 17 March 2007, in "The Presence of U.S. Troops and Alleged Support for the Insurgency."

33. "Inside America's Empire," PBS's *America at a Crossroads,* NC Public TV, 11 September 2007.

34. "Pakistani Islamists Sign Deal With China," by Farhan Bokhari, CBS News World Watch, 18 February 2009.

35. Ibid.

36. *Dragon on Terrorism: Assessing China's Tactical Gains and Strategic Losses Post-September 11,* by Mohan Malik (Carlisle, PA: Strategic Studies Inst., U.S. Army War College, October 2002).

37. H. John Poole, *Homeland Siege: Tactics for Police and Military* (Emerald Isle, NC: Posterity Press, 2009), introduction; "Guinea Confirms Huge China Deal," BBC News Online, 13 October 2009; BBC News, 8 November 2009; ABC's Nightly News, 7 January 2007.

38. NPR's "Morning Edition" News, 22 October 2009.

39. "Ecuador Offers Concession of Manta Air Base to China, Declines to Renew Contract with U.S.," by Vittorio Hernandez, AHN News (Ecuador), 26 November 2007.

40. *China's Rising Power in Africa,* Part 3, "China, Congo Trade for What the Other Wants," by Gwen Thompkins, NPR, 30 July 2008.

41. Escobar, "The Roving Eye"; "Osama's Secret Citadel," *DEBKA-Net-Weekly,* 28 September 2001.

42. "Beijing's Afghan Gamble," by Kaplan.

43. Amiuzadeh (Deputy Minister of . . . Iran), Special Address to the Federation of Indian Chambers of Commerce and Industry (New Delhi, 22 July 2003); *Wikipedia Encyclopedia*, s.v. "Hazara."

Chapter 7: *Unresolved Issues within Pakistan*

1. *Global Security* (globalsecurity.org) and *Wikipedia Encyclopedia*, s.v. "Muttahida-e-Majlis-e-Amal."
2. Sreeram Chaulia, review of *Pakistan: In the Shadow of Jihad and Afghanistan*, by Mary Anne Weaver, *Asia Times Online*, 1 March 2003.
3. "Terrorists Hit Pak N-Sites Thrice in 2 Yrs.," *Times Global* (Chennai), 12 August 2009, p. 1.
4. South Asia Intelligence Review database, s.v. "Lashkar i-Jhangvi."
5. "Obama's War."
6. "Pakistan Bans LET, JuD, and 23 Outfits"; Varma, "PoK Also Banns Jihadi Outfits."
7. "Pakistan Trims Top ISI Chairs," from PTI Islamabad, *The Economic Times* (Chennai), 13 August 2009, p. 3.
8. *Global Security* (globalsecurity.org), s.v. "Mawlawi Jalaluddin Haqqani."
9. Peters, *Seeds of Terror*, p. 110.
10. *Global Security* (globalsecurity.org), s.v. "Baittulah Mehsud."
11. Ibid.
12. Peters, *Seeds of Terror*, p. 129.
13. "Pakistan Conflict Map."
14. Imtiaz Gul, *The Al-Qaeda Connection: The Taliban and Terror in Pakistan's Tribal Areas* (New Delhi: Viking, an imprint of Penguin, 2009)p. 276; "Pakistan Conflict Map"; Peters, *Seeds of Terror*, p. 110.
15. "Pakistan Conflict Map."
16. Tohid, Owais and Faye Bowers, "U.S. Pakistan Tighten Net on Al Qaeda," *Christian Science Monitor*, 22 March 2004, pp. 1, 10.
17. Ibid.; Gul, *The Al-Qaeda Connection*, p. 275.
18. Patrick McDowell, AP, "Pakistan Goes After Terrorists on Border," *Jacksonville Daily News* (NC), 9 January 2004, p. 6A.
19. "Maulvi Nazir Group Decides to Stay Neutral," by Iqbal Khattak, *Daily Times* (Pakistan), 19 October 2009.
20. Gall et al, "Pakistani and Afghan Taliban Unify in Face of U.S. Influx"; Khan, "Taliban Rename Their Group," *The Nation* (Pakistan), 23 February 2009; "Three Taliban Factions Form Shura Ittehad-ul-Mujahiden," *The News* (Pakistan), 23 February 2009; all in *Wikipedia Encyclopedia*, s.v. "Tehrik-i-Taliban Pakistan."

21. "Pakistan Cuts Deal with Anti-American Taliban," p. 11.

22. Raman, "The New Trojan Horse of Al Qaeda"; "Here Comes Trouble."

23. Raman, "The New Trojan Horse of Al Qaeda."

24. Peters, *Seeds of Terror,* pp. 130, 131; "Pakistan Blames IMU Militants for Afghan Border Unrest," by Sidikov; Arnoldy, "Pakistan's Not-So-Epic Offensive," p. 8.

25. Australian Govt. National Security Website (www.ag.gov.au), s.v. "Lashkar e-Jhangvi."

26. Raman, "The New Trojan Horse of Al Qaeda"; Mir, *The True Face of Jihadis,* pp. 183, 184.

27. South Asia Intelligence Review database and *Wikipedia Encyclopedia,* s.v. "Tehreek-e-Nafaz-e-Shariat-e-Mohammadi" and "Bajaur"; Ahmed, "Stakes High for Pakistan's Push," p. 8.

28. "Pakistan Conflict Map"; Peters, *Seeds of Terror,* p. 110.

29. Ibid.

30. "Opium Trade Is Halal in Islam: Bara Scholar," *Pakistan Daily News,* 21 January 2005, in *Seeds of Terror,* by Peters, p. 143.

31. Ibid; *Global Security* (globalsecurity.org), s.v. "Mawlawi Jalaluddin Haqqani."

32. *CIA—The World Factbook* (www.cia.gov), s.v. "Afghanistan."

33. South Asia Intelligence Review database, s.v. "Hizb-ul-Mujahideen."

34. Ibid., s.v. "Lashkar-e-Toiba."

35. "Jaish e-Mohammed profile," Overseas Security Advisory Council, *Global Security News & Reports,* n.d.; Raman, "The New Trojan Horse of Al Qaeda"; Mannes, *Profiles in Terror,* p. 66.

36. Mariane Pearl, *A Mighty Heart: The Inside Story of the Al Qaeda Kidnapping of Danny Pearl* (New York: Scribner, 2003), p. 74; "*Jaish e-Mohammed* profile"; *Patterns of Global Terrorism, 2003;* Danny Pearl, as quoted in *A Mighty Heart,* by Mariane Pearl, p. 75; Mir, *The True Face of Jihadis,* p. 218.

37. Mir, *The True Face of Jihadis,* pp. 123-135; Nojumi, *The Rise of the Taliban in Afghanistan,* p. 128; "Heroin in Pakistan: Sowing the Wild Wind," CIA report, in *Seeds of Terror,* by Peters, p. 64.

38. Mir, *The True Face of Jihadis,* p. 282; "Jaish-e-Mohammed (JEM) Backgrounder."

39. Gunaratna, *Inside al-Qaeda,* pp. 40, 206; Ahmed Rashid, "Taliban Ready for 'Decisive' Push, *Daily Telegraph* (London), 22 July 1999, in "Afghanistan: Crisis of Impunity," by Batty and Hoffman, p. 32; South Asia Intelligence Review database and *Wikipedia Encyclopedia,* s.v. "Tehreek-e-Nafaz-e-Shariat-e-Mohammadi"; Mir, *The True Face of Jihadis,* pp. 123-135; Nojumi, *The Rise of the Taliban in Afghanistan,* p. 128.

40. South Asia Intelligence Review database, s.v. "Lashkar i-Jhangvi."

41. Ibid.

42. Mir, *The True Face of Jihadis,* pp. 31, 328; Raman, "The New Trojan Horse of Al Qaeda."

43. Kaplan, *Soldiers of God,* p. 217; Gunaratna, *Inside al-Qaeda,* p. 40; Brigadier Mohammad Yousaf, *The Silent Soldier: The Man behind the Afghan Jehad* (South Yorkshire, UK: Leo Cooper, n.d.); Mannes, *Profiles in Terror,* p. 18.

44. Ibid.; Yousaf and Adkin, *Bear Trap.*

45. Owais Tohid, "Al Qaeda Supporters Strike Back in Pakistan," *Christian Science Monitor,* 25 March 2004.

46. Tohid and Bowers, "U.S. Pakistan Tighten Net on Al Qaeda," pp. 1, 10.

47. Ibid.

48. Ibid.

49. Owais Tohid, "Pakistan Marks Pro-Al Qaeda Clan," *Christian Science Monitor,* 23 March 2004; Tohid, "Al Qaeda Supporters Strike Back in Pakistan."

50. Tohid, "Pakistan Marks Pro-Al Qaeda Clan."

51. Owais Tohid, "Pakistan Gains in Al Qaeda Hunt," *Christian Science Monitor,* 16 March 2004.

52. David Montero, "In Border Zone, Pakistan Backs Off from Taliban," *Christian Science Monitor,* 26 September 2006, p. 5.

53. Tohid, "Pakistan Gains in Al Qaeda Hunt."

54. "South Waziristan's Maulvi Nazir: The New Face of the Taliban," by Hassan Abbas, The Jamestown Foundation, *Terrorism Monitor,* vol. 5, issue 9, 14 May 2007.

55. Arnoldy, "Pakistan's Not-So-Epic Offensive," p. 8; Tohid and Bowers, "U.S. Pakistan Tighten Net on Al Qaeda," *Christian Science Monitor,* pp. 1, 10; Kim Barker *(Chicago Tribune),* "Pakistani Tribes Fight Alleged al-Qaida Allies," *Seattle Times,* 24 April 2007.

56. Howard LaFranchi, "Pakistan: U.S. Ally, U.S. Dilemma," *Christian Science Monitor,* 29 March 2007, pp. 1, 10.

57. Kim Barker *(Chicago Tribune),* "Pakistani Tribes Fight Alleged al-Qaida Allies," *Seattle Times,* 24 April 2007.

58. *The Guardian* (UK), 5 April 2007, in "South Waziristan's Maulvi Nazir," by Abbas.

59. Arnoldy, "Pakistan's Not-So-Epic Offensive," p. 8; Tohid and Bowers, "U.S. Pakistan Tighten Net on Al Qaeda," pp. 1, 10; Barker, "Pakistani Tribes Fight Alleged al-Qaida Allies."

60. Barker, "Pakistani Tribes Fight Alleged al-Qaida Allies."

61. Tohid, "Pakistan Marks Pro-Al Qaeda Clan."

62. "Pakistan Conflict Map"; "Pakistan Captures Mehsud's Hometown," UPI.com, 24 October 2009.

63. "Maulvi Nazir Group Decides to Stay Neutral," by Khattak.

64. "Pakistan Conflict Map"; "Pakistan Captures Mehsud's Hometown," UPI.com, 24 October 2009.

65. Ibid.

66. NPR's "Morning Edition" News, 18 November 2009.

67. "Militants Overrun Pakistan Fort," BBC News Online, 17 January 2008.

68. Arnoldy, "Pakistan's Not-So-Epic Offensive," p. 8.

69. "Pakistan Cuts Deal with Anti-American Taliban," p. 11.

70. Gall et al, "Pakistani and Afghan Taliban Unify in Face of U.S. Influx"; Khan, "Taliban Rename Their Group," *The Nation* (Pakistan), 23 February 2009; "Three Taliban Factions Form Shura Ittehad-ul-Mujahiden," *The News* (Pakistan), 23 February 2009; all in *Wikipedia Encyclopedia,* s.v. "Tehrik-i-Taliban Pakistan."

71. *Boston Globe,* 21 April 2007, in "South Waziristan's Maulvi Nazir," by Abbas.

72. Peters, *Seeds of Terror,* p. 129.

73. *Friday Times* (Pakistan), 30 March 2007, *Daily Times* (Pakistan), 9 January 2009, in "South Waziristan's Maulvi Nazir," by Abbas.

74. "South Waziristan's Maulvi Nazir," by Abbas.

75. *Global Security* (globalsecurity.org), s.v. "Mawlawi Jalaluddin Haqqani."

76. "Pakistani Military Hits Taliban in Orakzai," by Bill Roggio, *Long War Journal,* 17 November 2009.

77. "Heroin in Pakistan: Sowing the Wind," a CIA report leaked to and printed by Pakistan's *Friday Times,* 3 September 1995, in *Seeds of Terror,* by Peters, p. 60.

78. "Pakistani Military Hits Taliban in Orakzai," by Roggio.

79. Gordon Lubold, "Mullen's Charm Offensive," *Christian Science Monitor,* 17 January 2010., p. 19.

80. Samina Ahmed, International Crisis Group, as quoted in "Crackdown On Taliban Shifts U.S.-Pakistan Ties," by Julie McCarthy, NPR's "Morning Edition" News, 10 March 2010; South Asia Intelligence Review database, s.v. "Harkat-ul-Ansar"; "Jaish-e-Mohammed (JEM) Backgrounder"; "Harakat ul-Mujahidin," *Patterns of Global Terrorism, 2002 Report.*

81. Mir, *The True Face of Jihadis,* p. 282; "Jaish-e-Mohammed (JEM) Backgrounder"; "Secrets of Brigade 055," by Daniel Eisenberg, *Time,* 28 October 2001.

82. Gunaratna, *Inside al-Qaeda,* pp. 40, 206; Ahmed Rashid, "Taliban Ready for 'Decisive' Push," *Daily Telegraph* (London), 22 July 1999, in "Afghanistan: Crisis of Impunity," by Batty and Hoffman, p. 32.

83. "Al Qaeda Deploys Paramilitary 'Shadow Army'," by Roggio.

84. Ibid.

85. Ben Arnoldy, "One Path to Taliban Talks," *Christian Science Monitor,* 13 December 2009, p. 11.

86. South Asia Intelligence Review database, s.v. "Hizb-ul-Mujahideen"; "Pakistan's Old Jihadis Pose New Threat," by Ahmed.

87. Anonymous U.S. Special Forces member (after multiple tours to Iraq and Afghanistan), in telephone conversations with author on 11 December 2009 and 31 May 2010; "Iran Role in the Recent Uprising in Iraq," Special Dispatch No. 692, 9 April 2004, from Middle East Media Research Inst.

88. "Pakistan's Old Jihadis Pose New Threat," by Ahmed.

89. "South Waziristan's Maulvi Nazir," by Abbas.

90. Mannes, *Profiles in Terror,* p. 66; South Asia Intelligence Review database, s.v. "Lashkar-e-Toiba" and "Hizb-ul-Mujahideen"; Gunaratna, *Inside al-Qaeda,* pp. 40, 206; Ahmed Rashid, "Taliban Ready for 'Decisive' Push," *Daily Telegraph* (London), 22 July 1999, in "Afghanistan: Crisis of Impunity," by Batty and Hoffman, p. 32; South Asia Intelligence Review database and *Wikipedia Encyclopedia,* s.v. "Tehreek-e-Nafaz-e-Shariat-e-Mohammadi"; Mir, *The True Face of Jihadis,* pp. 123-135; Nojumi, *The Rise of the Taliban in Afghanistan,* p. 128; "Al Qaeda Deploys Paramilitary 'Shadow Army'," by Roggio.

91. "Al Qaeda Deploys Paramilitary 'Shadow Army'," by Roggio.

92. "Pakistani Commandos Break Siege on Army Headquarters," by Roggio.

93. "Pakistani Military Hits Taliban in Orakzai," by Roggio.

94. NPR's "Morning Edition" News, 8 December 2009.

95. South Asia Intelligence Review database, s.v. "Lashkar-e-Toiba."

96. Peters, *Seeds of Terror,* pp. 74, 86, 95; Ron Moreau, "America's New Nightmare," *Newsweek,* 3 August 2009, pp. 38-41; NPR's "Morning Edition" News, 15 February 2010.

97. ABC's Nightly News, 15 February 2010; NPR's "Morning Edition" News, 16 February 2010.

98. *CIA—The World Factbook* (www.cia.gov), s.v. "Pakistan."

99. Afghan Interior Minister Younis Qanooni, as quoted in "Pakistan Spy Service 'Aiding Bin Laden'," BBC News Online, 30 September 2001.

100. "Who Really Killed Daniel Pearl," *Guardian Online* (UK), 5 April 2002.

101. "A Godfather's Lethal Mix of Business and Politics," *U.S. News & World Report Online,* 5 December 2005; "Dawood's ISI Links Could Trouble Musharraf," by John; John, *Coming Blowback,* p. 187.

102. "Dawood Ibrahim: The Global Terrorist," by Raman.

103. "A Godfather's Lethal Mix of Business and Politics."

104. "How Pakistan's ISI Funds Its Proxy War," by Syed Nooruzzaman, *The Tribune* (India), 28 November 1999.

105. "A Godfather's Lethal Mix of Business and Politics."

106. Escobar, review of *Who Killed Daniel Pearl,* by Levy; "Who Really Killed Daniel Pearl," *Guardian Online.*

107. "Hunting for Dawood Ibrahim," by B. Raman, South Asia Analysis Group, Paper No 1952, 16 September 2006, and *International Terrorism Monitor,* Paper No. 122, n.d.; King, *The Most Dangerous Man in the World,* p. 15.

108. "Organized Crime, Intelligence and Terror: The D-Company's Role in the Mumbai Attacks," Tom Burghardt; King, *The Most Dangerous Man in the World,* chapt. 7; "Dawood Ibrahim Had Played an Important Role in the Smuggling of Nuclear Weapons," by S. Balakrishnan, *Times of India,* 4 August 2004.

109. King, *The Most Dangerous Man in the World,* p. 21; Mariane Pearl, *A Mighty Heart,* p. 16; *Wikipedia Encyclopedia,* s.v. "Daniel Pearl."

110. Mariane Pearl, *A Mighty Heart,* p. 198.

111. Ibid., p. 233; *Wikipedia Encyclopedia,* s.v. "Saud Memon."

112. Mir, *Talibanisation of Pakistan,* p. 173.

113. Ibid., pp. 173, 174.

114. "Mumbai Bombing Sentencing Delay," BBC News Online, 13 September 2006; *Wikipedia Encyclopedia,* s.v. "Yakub Memon," "Tiger Memon," and "1993 Mumbai Bombings."

115. John, *Coming Blowback,* p. 222.

116. King, *The Most Dangerous Man in the World,* as quoted in *Talibanisation of Pakistan,* by Mir, p. 174.

117. Wajid Shamsul Hasan (former Pakistani High Commissioner to Britain), as quoted in "Profile: Pakistan's Military Intelligence Agency," by David Chazan, BBC News Online, 9 January 2002.

118. Memorandum for the record by H.J. Poole.

119. "Profile: Pakistan's Military Intelligence Agency," by David Chazan, BBC News Online, 9 January 2002.

120. Ibid.

121. Sen, review of *Karachi,* by John; Peters, *Seeds of Terror,* p. 31; Lawrence Lifschultz, "Pakistan, the Empire of Heroin," in McCoy and Block, "War on Drugs," p. 320, and Lifschultz, *Heroin Empire,* pp. 71-72, and *The Herald* (Pakistan) during 1985, all in *Seeds of Terror,* by Peters, p. 37.

122. *World Drug Report 2009,* U.N. Office on Drugs and Crime.

123. "Pakistan Reels Under A Jihadi Guerilla War," by B. Raman, South Asia Analysis Group, Paper No. 3462, 15 October 2009, and *International Terrorism Monitor,* Paper No. 568, n.d.

124. Vali Nasr, *The Vanguard of the Islamic Revolution: The Jama'at-i-Islami of Pakistan* (Berkeley: Univ. of California Press, 1994), in *Coming-Blowback,* by John, p. 38.

125. John, *Coming Blowback,* p. 39.

126. Ibid., p. 184.

127. "Pakistani Islamists Sign Deal With China," by Bokhari; South Asia Intelligence Review database and *Wikipedia Encyclopedia,* s.v. "Tehreek-e-Nafaz-e-Shariat-e-Mohammadi."

128. Poole, *Homeland Siege,* pp. xxi, xxii, and appendix.

129. NPR's "Morning Edition" News, 18 February 2010; Anuj Chopra, "Maoist Rebels Spread across Rural India," *Christian Science Monitor,* 22 August 2006, p. 6.

130. "Maoists Attack," The World, *Time,* 19 April 2010, p. 19.

131. "Are India's Maoist Rebels Winning the War," BBC News Online, 28 May 2010.

Chapter 8: *Reasons behind the Soviet Failure*

1. *The Soviet-Afghan War: How a Superpower Fought and Lost,* by the Russian General Staff, ed. Lester Grau and Michael A. Gress (Lawrence, KS: Univ. of Kansas Press, 2002), p. 106.

2. Ibid., editor's comments, pp. 30, 310, 311.

3. Jalali and Grau, *Afghan Guerrilla,* editor's commentary, p. 256.

4. Yousaf and Adkin, *Bear Trap.*

5. *The Soviet-Afghan War,* by the Russian General Staff, editor's comments, pp. 313, 314.

6. Ibid., editor's comments, pp. 232, 233.

7. Ibid., editor's comments, pp. 310, 311.

8. Ibid., editor's comments, pp. 232, 233.

9. Yousaf and Adkin, *Bear Trap.*

10. Memorandum for the record, by H.J. Poole.

11. *The Soviet-Afghan War,* by the Russian General Staff, editor's comments, pp. 232, 233.

12. Anonymous U.S. Special Forces member (multiple-tour veteran of both Iraq and Afghanistan), in telephone conversation with author in 2005.

13. H. John Poole, *Phantom Soldier: The Enemy's Answer to U.S. Firepower* (Emerald Isle, NC: Posterity Press, 2001), chapt. 6.

14. C.J. Dick, "Mujahideen Tactics in the Soviet-Afghan War" (Sandhurst, UK: Conflict Studies Research Centre, Royal Mil. Acad., n.d.), p. 7; *The Soviet-Afghan War,* by the Russian General Staff, editor's comments, p. 312.

15. Akbar and Hemat, as quoted in *Afghan Guerrilla Warfare,* by Jalali and Grau, pp. 6, 9.

16. Kaplan, *Soldiers of God,* p. 159.

17. Jalali and Grau, *Afghan Guerrilla Warfare,* editor's commentary, p. 41.

18. *The Soviet-Afghan War,* by the Russian General Staff, editor's comments, p. 233.

19. Dick, "Mujahideen Tactics," p. 6.

20. Akhtarjhan, as quoted in "Night Stalkers and Mean Streets," by Ali A. Jalali and Lester W. Grau (Ft. Leavenworth, KS: Foreign Mil. Studies Office, 1998), *Infantry Magazine,* January-April 1999.

21. Kaplan, *Soldiers of God,* p. 18.

22. Shabuddin, as quoted in *Afghan Guerrilla,* by Jalali and Grau, p. 385.

23. Yakub, as quoted in *Afghan Guerrilla,* by Jalali and Grau, p. 368.

24. Kaplan, *Soldiers of God,* p. 162.

25. Rod Nordland, "Al-Sadr Strikes," *Newsweek,* 10 April 2006, pp. 45-47; ABC's Nightly News, 26 March 2006.

26. Max Boot, Frederick Kagan, and Kimberly Kagan, "How to Surge the Taliban," Op-Ed piece, *New York Times,* 13 March 2009.

27. Peters, *Seeds of Terror,* pp. 29-31.

28. Batty and Hoffman, "Afghanistan: Crisis of Impunity," pp. 35, 36; Bonner, "Afghan Rebels Victory Garden: Opium," in *Seeds of Terror,* by Peters, p. 32.

29. Rupert and Coll, "U.S. Declines to Probe Afghan Drug Trade; Rebels, Pakistani Officers Implicated," in *Seeds of Terror,* by Peters, p. 34.

30. Rubin, "The Fragmentation of Afghanistan," in *Seeds of Terror,* by Peters, p. 35.

31. Peters, *Seeds of Terror,* pp. 53, 111, 155, 160; an Afghan confederate of Noorzai, in *Seeds of Terror,* by Peters, p. 74.

32. Peters, *Seeds of Terror,* pp. 25, 36, 129; "Afghanistan," by Warnock; Macdonald, *Drugs in Afghanistan,* p. 88, in *Seeds of Terror,* by Peters, p. 36; O'Ballance, *Afghan Wars,* p. 116; *The Rise of the Taliban in Afghanistan,* p. 222; Gunaratna, *Inside al-Qaeda,* p. 17; Mir, *The True Face of Jihadis,* p. 130.

33. Yousaf and Adkin, *Bear Trap;* O'Ballance, *Afghan Wars,* p. 164.

34. "Return of the Taliban"; Gunaratna, *Inside Al Qaeda,* p. 42.

35. Omar and Haqani, as quoted in *Afghan Guerrilla,* by Jalali and Grau, pp. 317-321; Peters, *Seeds of Terror,* p. 129.

36. Sen, review of *Karachi,* by John; Peters, *Seeds of Terror,* p. 31; Lawrence Lifschultz, "Pakistan, the Empire of Heroin," in McCoy and Block, "War on Drugs," p. 320, and Lifschultz, *Heroin Empire,* pp. 71-72, and *The Herald* (Pakistan) during 1985, all in *Seeds of Terror,* by Peters, p. 37.

37. "Heroin in Pakistan: Sowing the Wind," a CIA report leaked to and printed by Pakistan's *Friday Times,* 3 September 1995, in *Seeds of Terror,* by Peters, p. 60.

38. "Mexico's Drug Cartels," by Colleen W. Cook, CRS Report for Congress, Order Code RL34215 (Washington, D.C: Library of Congress, 25 February 2008, pp. CRS-8, CRS-9, CRS-13; "Mexico's Internal Drug War," *Power and Interest News Report (PINR),* 14 August 2006; *Wikipedia Encyclopedia,* s.v. "Guzman-Loera" and "Los Negros."

39. Anonymous U.S. Special Forces member (multiple-tour veteran of both Iraq and Afghanistan), in telephone conversation with author in November 2009.

40. "Suicide Bomber Kills Peacekeeper, Civilian in Afghan Capital."

41. Return of the Taliban," PBS's *Frontline,* NC Public TV, 8 January 2007.

42. Shahin, as quoted in *Afghan Guerrilla,* by Jalali and Grau, pp. 379, 380.

43. Dick, "Mujahideen Tactics," p. 4.

Chapter 9: *Traditional Afghan Conduits and Lairs*

1. Poole, *Phantom Soldier,* chapts. 11-13.

2. *The Soviet-Afghan War: How a Superpower Fought and Lost,* by the Russian General Staff, ed. Lester Grau and Michael A. Gress (Lawrence, KS: Univ. of Kansas Press, 2002), p. 71.

3. Jalali and Grau, *Afghan Guerrilla,* p. 267.

4. Yousaf and Adkin, *Bear Trap.*

5. Omar and Haqani, as quoted in *Afghan Guerrilla,* by Jalali and Grau, pp. 317-321.

6. Ibid., p. 317.

7. Qader, as quoted in *Afghan Guerrilla,* by Jalali and Grau, p. 261.

8. Jalali and Grau, *Afghan Guerrilla,* p. 267.

9. Ibid., p. 402.

10. Dick, "Mujahideen Tactics in the Soviet-Afghan War," pp. 9, 10; Gunaratna, *Inside al-Qaeda,* pp. 23, 42.

11. Mannes, *Profiles in Terror,* p. 19; Gunaratna, *Inside al-Qaeda,* pp. 19, 23.

12. Gunaratna, *Inside al-Qaeda,* pp. 23, 42.

13. O'Ballance, *Afghan Wars,* p. 158.

14. "DoD News Briefing—ASD PA Clarke and Rear Adm. Stufflebeem," 14 January 2002.

15. Bruce B. Auster, "The Recruiter for Hate," *U.S. News & World Report,* 31 August 1998, p. 49, from *Inside al-Qaeda,* by Gunaratna, p. 20.

16. Gunaratna, *Inside al-Qaeda,* p. 58; O'Ballance, *Afghan Wars,* p. 253.

17. Gunaratna, *Inside al-Qaeda,* p. 60.

18. Ibid., p. 42; "Return of the Taliban," PBS's *Frontline,* NC Public TV, 8 January 2007.

19. Peters, *Seeds of Terror,* p. 129.
20. Ibid., p. 34.
21. Ibid., p. 129.
22. Ibid.
23. Ibid., p. 110.
24. "Return of the Taliban."
25. *World Drug Report 2010,* U.N. Office on Drugs and Crime, Map 5; "Al Qaeda Deploys Paramilitary 'Shadow Army'," by Roggio.
26. Yousaf and Adkin, *Bear Trap.*
27. "Militants Free 40 Kidnapped Passengers," by Hussain Afzai, *Dawn* (Karachi), 17 May 2010, p. 1.
28. Peters, *Seeds of Terror,* p. 151.
29. *The Soviet-Afghan War,* by the Russian General Staff, editors' comments, pp. 232, 233.
30. Ibid., p. 60.

Chapter 10: *Changes in How the Taliban Fights*

1. "Govt Blames LeT for Parliament Attack, Asks Pak to Restrain Terrorist Outfits," *Rediff News* (India), 14 December 2001.
2. ABC's Noon News, 18 January 2010.
3. "Suicide Attack on Afghan Ministry Kills Five," from IANS, *Thaindian News,* 30 October 2008.
4. "Taliban Attacks Afghan Ministry," videocast from Al Jazeera, Youtube, 11 February 2009.
5. "Taliban Launches Brazen Attack on Kabul," from AP, MSNBC Online News, 18 January 2010.
6. "Taliban Attack Afghan Presidential Palace, Ministries," from IANS, Kerala News (India), 18 January 2010.
7. Poole, *Homeland Siege,* chapt. 9.
8. "Taliban Launches Brazen Attack on Kabul," from AP.
9. "Taliban Attack Afghan Presidential Palace, Ministries," from IANS.
10. "Taliban Launches Brazen Attack on Kabul," from AP.
11. Ibid.; "Taliban Attack Afghan Presidential Palace, Ministries," from IANS.
12. "Taliban Launches Brazen Attack on Kabul," from AP.
13. Ibid.; "Taliban Attack Afghan Presidential Palace, Ministries," from IANS.
14. Ibid.; "Taliban Attack Afghan Presidential Palace, Ministries," from IANS.
15. "Suicide Attack on Afghan Ministry Kills Five," from IANS.
16. "Taliban Attack Afghan Presidential Palace, Ministries," from IANS.

17. "Govt Blames LeT for Parliament Attack, Asks Pak to Restrain Terrorist Outfits."

18. Poole, *Homeland Siege,* chapt. 9.

19. "Taliban Attack Afghan Presidential Palace, Ministries," from IANS.

20. Mir, *The True Face of Jihadis,* pp. 183, 184.

21. Cooley, *Unholy Wars,* in *Pakistan,* by Ahmed, p. 225; Mir, *The True Face of Jihadis,* pp. 105, 183, 184; South Asia Intelligence Review database, s.v. "Lashkar-e-Toiba."

22. *Patterns of Global Terrorism, 2003.*

23. Poole, *Homeland Siege,* chapt. 9.

24. Anonymous U.S. Special Forces member (after multiple tours to Iraq and Afghanistan), in telephone conversation with author on 30 July 2009.

25. Ibid.

26. Ibid.

27. "Suicide Bomber Kills Peacekeeper, Civilian in Afghan Capital."

28. Pauline Jelinek, AP, "U.S. Plans Spring Offensive in Afghanistan," AOL News, 30 January 2004.

29. "NATO Force Could Patrol Afghanistan," from AP, *Jacksonville Daily News* (NC), 5 August 2005, p. 4A; ABC's Morning News, 18 August 2009; ABC's Nightly News, 21 August 2005.

30. Straziuso, "Afghan Bomber Deadlier," pp. 1A, 8A; Richard Clarke, on ABC's Morning News, 7 June 2007; ABC's Nightly News, 6 June 2007; "Military: Iran Teaching Iraqi Militia to Build Bombs," from AP, p. 5A; Scott Peterson, "Shiites Rising—Part One," *Christian Science Monitor,* 6 June 2007, pp. 1, 13-16.

31. *Global Security* (globalsecurity.org), s.v. "Salafi Islam."

32. NPR's "Morning Edition" News, 1 March 2010.

33. H. John Poole, *The Tiger's Way: A Private's Best Chance for Survival* (Emerald Isle, NC: Posterity Press, 2003), pp. 122, 123.

34. Jalali and Grau, *Afghan Guerrilla,* editor's commentary, p. 72.

35. Tom A. Peter, "U.S. Soldiers: Iraq, This Isn't," *Christian Science Monitor,* 29 November 2009, p. 10.

36. Yousaf and Adkin, *Bear Trap.*

37. Ibid.

38. Gunaratna, *Inside al-Qaeda,* pp. 40, 206; Ahmed Rashid, "Taliban Ready for 'Decisive' Push, *Daily Telegraph* (London), 22 July 1999, in "Afghanistan: Crisis of Impunity," by Batty and Hoffman, p. 32.

39. "Al Qaeda Deploys Paramilitary 'Shadow Army'," by Roggio.

40. "South Waziristan's Maulvi Nazir," by Abbas.

41. "Here Comes Trouble," *The Economist,* 11 June 2009.

42. Mir, *The True Face of Jihadis,* p. 23.

43. "Region under Taliban Control," PBS's *Frontline World,* NC Public TV, 24 February 2010.

Chapter 11: *The Drug Runners' Modus Operandi*

1. DEA Chief Jack Dawn in testimony before the Senate Intelligence Committee, and CIA assessment in September 1988, as quoted in *Seeds of Terror,* by Peters, pp. 28, 51.

2. Sen, review of *Karachi,* by John; Peters, *Seeds of Terror,* p. 31; Lawrence Lifschultz, "Pakistan, the Empire of Heroin," in McCoy and Block, *War on Drugs,* p. 320, and Lifschultz, *Heroin Empire,* pp. 71-72, and *The Herald* (Pakistan) during 1985, all in *Seeds of Terror,* by Peters, p. 37.

3. Ahmed Rashid, *The Taliban* (New Haven, CT: Yale Univ. Press, March 2001), p. 122, in *Seeds of Terror,* by Peters, p. 95.

4. Peters, *Seeds of Terror,* p. 51; Mannes, *Profiles in Terror,* p. 66; *Patterns of Global Terrorism, 2003.*

5. "Opium Trade Is Halal in Islam: Bara Scholar," *Pakistan Daily News,* 21 January 2005, in *Seeds of Terror,* by Peters, p. 143.

6. South Asia Intelligence Review database, s.v. "Hizb-ul-Mujahideen"; "Jaish e-Mohammed profile"; Raman, "The New Trojan Horse of Al Qaeda"; Mannes, *Profiles in Terror,* p. 66.

7. Kabul interview with Western official in 2004, from *Seeds of Terror,* by Peters, pp. 3, 4.

8. "Return of the Taliban," PBS's *Frontline;* Gunaratna, *Inside Al Qaeda,* p. 42.

9. "Return of the Taliban."

10. "Al Qaeda Deploys Paramilitary 'Shadow Army'," by Roggio.

11. Gertz, "China-Made Artillery Seized in Afghanistan"; Scott Baldauf, "How Al Qaeda Seeks to Buy Chinese Arms," *Christian Science Monitor,* 23 August 2002; *Dragon on Terrorism: Assessing China's Tactical Gains and Strategic Losses Post-September 11,* by Mohan Malik (Carlisle, PA: Strategic Studies Inst., U. S. Army War College, October 2002), table 1.

12. Peters, *Seeds of Terror,* p. 129.

13. "Dawood's ISI Links Could Trouble Musharraf," by John.

14. Peters, *Seeds of Terror,* p. 129.

15. "Heroin in Pakistan: Sowing the Wind," a CIA report leaked to and printed by Pakistan's *Friday Times,* 3 September 1995, in *Seeds of Terror,* by Peters, p. 60.

16. "U.S. Turns to Drug Baron to Rally Support," by Syed Saleem Shahzad, *Asia Times Online,* 4 December 2001; "Drug Baron Ayub Afridi Appears in SC [Supreme Court] Today," *Daily Times* (Pakistan), 17 November 2005.

17. "Afghanistan/Pakistan: U.S. Indicts 11 in Connection with Drug Ring," by Ron Synovitz, *Radio Free Europe/Radio Liberty,* 17 September 2003.

18. *World Drug Report 2009,* U.N. Office on Drugs and Crime.

19. "Transnational Activities of Chinese Crime Organizations," by Glenn E. Curtis, Seth L. Elan, Rexford A. Hudson, and Nina A. Koll, Fed. Research Div., Library of Congress, April 2003, pp. 23, 24.

20. "Operation Hardtac," FBI case study, 1998, as retrieved from its website in October 2008.

21. "Transnational Activities of Chinese Crime Organizations," by Glenn E. Curtiset al, pp. 23, 24.

22. *National Drug Threat Assessment (for) 2008,* "Drug Transportation," NDIC, October 2007.

23. "Terrorism's Pacific Gateway," by Patrick Lloyd Hatcher, Univ. of San Francisco Center for the Pacific Rim, Report No. 38, June 2005.

24. "Pakistan Closes Torkham Border Crossing, Shuts Down NATO's Supply Line," by Bill Rogio, *Long War Journal,* 6 September 2008.

25. "Suicide Bomber Kills 22 Border Guards at Torkham Crossing in Pakistan," by Bill Roggio, *Long War Journal,* 27 August 2009.

26. Peters, *Seeds of Terror,* pp. 65, 96, 173.

27. "Suicide Bomber Kills 22 Border Guards at Torkham Crossing in Pakistan," by Roggio.

28. Gul, *The Al-Qaeda Connection,* p. 72; "Taliban Group Chooses New Name," *Daily Times* (Pakistan), 27 April 2008.

28. "Opium Trade Is Halal in Islam: Bara Scholar," *Pakistan Daily News,* 21 January 2005, in *Seeds of Terror,* by Peters, p. 143.

Chapter 12: *Present U.S. Strategy*

1. NPR's "Morning Edition" News, 31 March 2009.

2. Robert Morton, "Who Needs the Panama Canal," *Washington Times,* Nat. Weekly Ed., 1-8 March 1999.

3. Barbara Slavin, "Iran Helped to Overthrow Taliban," *USA Today,* 10 June 2005. p. 14A.

4. Mir, *The True Face of Jihadis,* p. 29; Jason Burke, "Waiting for the Last Battle with the Taliban," *The Observer* (UK); 27 June 1999; Kaplan, *Soldiers of God,* pp. 234, 235.

5. "New Afghan Strategy Puts Troops Out Front," from AP, *Jacksonville Daily News* (NC), 21 March 2009, p. A1.

6. Ibid.

7. Ibid.

8. Gen. David Petraeus, on NPR's "Morning Edition" News, 29 May 2009.

9. Jason Straziuso, AP, "General Says Troops Need New View of Afghan War," *Boston Globe,* 25 June 2009.

10. Ibid.

11. Gen. David Petraeus, on NPR's "Morning Edition" News, 29 May 2009.

12. ABC's Nightly News, 31 August 2009.

13. "General Seeks New Afghan Approach," *Philadelphia Inquirer,* 1 August 2009.

14. NPR's "Morning Edition" News, 25 September 2009.

15. "McCrystal's War," by Evan Thomas, *Newsweek,* 5 October 2009, pp. 28-33.

16. Ibid.

17. Ibid.

18. Ibid.

19. "General Petraeus Gives a War Briefing," by Col. Jack Jacobs, *Parade Magazine,* 29 November 2009, pp. 8-11.

20. Ibid.

21. Ibid.

22. ABC's Nightly News, 28 October 2009.

23. President Barack Obama, in his address to the nation, on ABC TV, 1 December 2009.

24. "Karzai Upset by Taliban Capture," from AP, *Jacksonville Daily News* (NC), 16 March 2010, p. 10; "Karzai Considers Proposals from Militant Group," from AP, *Jacksonville Daily News* (NC), 23 March 2010, p. 24.

25. Gen. McCrystal, during an interview on NPR's "Morning Edition" News, 3 December 2009.

26. ABC's Nightly News, 11 January 2010.

27. Ibid.

28. ABC's Nightly News, 12 January 2010.

29. Peters, *Seeds of Terror,* p. 183.

30. "Harvesting Change," Christina Wood, *Military Officer,* May 2009, pp. 50, 51.

31. "DEA Agents among U.S. Troop Casualties," Nation/World Newswatch, from AP, *Jacksonville Daily News* (NC), 27 October 2009.

32. DEA Chief Jack Dawn in testimony before the Senate Intelligence Committee, and CIA assessment in September 1988, as quoted in *Seeds of Terror,* by Peters, pp. 28, 51.

33. *National Drug Threat Assessment (for) 2009,* Nat. Drug Intell. Center, December 2008; *National Drug Threat Assessment (for) 2008,* Nat. Drug Intell. Center, October 2007; "Asian Criminal Enterprises," FBI's Organized Crime Section, retrieved in September 2008; "Asian Transnational Organized Crime and Its Impact on the United States," by James O. Finckenauer and Ko-lin Chin, U.S. Dept. of Justice Special Report, January 2007.

34. "U.S. Puts Afghan Drug Lords on Hitlist to Disrupt Taliban Finances," by Norton-Taylor and Boone.

35. NPR's "Morning Edition" News, 24 February 2010.

36. "Afghan and U.S. Forces Battle Taliban in Northern Helmand Stronghold," by Bill Roggio, *Long War Journal,* 22 May 2009.

37. ABC's Nightly News, 29 March 2010.

Chapter 13: *Drug Interdiction Tactics*

1. Samander and Sarwan, "Concern That Jihad Chieftains Will Set Political Agenda"; Nojumi, *The Rise of the Taliban in Afghanistan,* p. 132; "Karzai's Cabinet Rejected," from AP, *Jacksonville Daily News* (NC), 3 January 2010, p. 12; O'Ballance, *Afghan Wars,* pp. 234, 235; "Iran Report."

2. Peters, *Seeds of Terror,* pp. 154, 155.

3. Ibid., pp. 53, 74, 111, 155, 160.

4. Peters, *Seeds of Terror,* pp. 149, 151, 152, 154, 155, 159; Quetta interview with Pakistani intelligence official of December 2008, in *Seeds of Terror,* by Peters, p. 161.

5. Ibid., pp. 53, 111, 155, 160; an Afghan confederate of Noorzai, in *Seeds of Terror,* by Peters, p. 74.

6. Ibid., pp. 132, 133, 177.

7. Rupert and Coll, "U.S. Declines to Probe Afghan Drug Trade; Rebels, Pakistani Officers Implicated," in *Seeds of Terror,* by Peters, p. 34.

8. Peters, *Seeds of Terror,* pp. 94, 109; *Country Profiles,* BBC News Online, s.v. "Afghanistan: Timeline."

9. "Afghan Linked to Taliban Sentenced to Life in Drug Trafficking Case," by Weiser; "Afghan Arrested in New York Said to Be a Heroin Kingpin," by Julia Peterson, *New York Times,* 26 April 2005; "In Drug Trial, Sharply Differing Portraits of Afghan With Ties to the Taliban," by Benjamin Weiser, *New York Times,* 11 September 2008; Peters, *Seeds of Terror,* p. 196.

10. Peters, *Seeds of Terror,* p. 151; former SAS commander, as quoted in *Seeds of Terror,* by Peters, p. 115.

11. Peters, *Seeds of Terror,* p. 151.

12. Ibid., p. 129.

13. Rubin, "The Fragmentation of Afghanistan," in *Seeds of Terror,* by Peters, p. 35.

14. Peters, *Seeds of Terror,* pp. 35, 36; "Afghanistan," by Warnock; Macdonald, *Drugs in Afghanistan,* p. 88, in *Seeds of Terror,* by Peters, p. 36; O'Ballance, *Afghan Wars,* p. 116; *The Rise of the Taliban in Afghanistan,* p. 222; Gunaratna, *Inside al-Qaeda,* p. 17; Mir, *The True Face of Jihadis,* p. 130.

15. "Pakistan: Countering an Expanding Drug Industry," CIA intelligence assessment, in *Seeds of Terror,* by Peters, pp. 42, 43.

16. Peters, *Seeds of Terror,* pp. 26, 56; "Afghanistan," by Warnock.

17. DEA Chief Jack Dawn in testimony before the Senate Intelligence Committee, and CIA assessment in September 1988, as quoted in *Seeds of Terror,* by Peters, pp. 28, 51.

18. Jalali and Grau, *Afghan Guerrilla,* p. 402.

19. Peters, *Seeds of Terror,* p. 84.

20. NPR's "Morning Edition" News, 8 December 2009; "Afghanistan: U.S. Escalates the Illegal Drug Industry," by John W. Warnock, *Global Research* (www.globalresearch.ca), 25 February 2009; *Global Security* (globalsecurity.org), s.v. "Abdul Rashid Dostum."

21. "Dawood's ISI Links Could Trouble Musharraf," by John.

Chapter 14: *New Techniques on Offense*

1. Poole, *Phantom Solider,* chapt. 6.

2. Attributed to Rodney Walker.

3. *100 Strategies of War: Brilliant Tactics in Action,* trans. Yeo Ai Hoon (Singapore: Asiapac Books, 1993), p. 31.

4. Poole, *The Tiger's Way,* pp. 280-283.

5. H.J. Poole, *The Last Hundred Yards: The NCO's Contribution to Warfare* (Emerald Isle, NC: Posterity Press, 1997), chapt. 9.

Chapter 15: *New Techniques on Defense*

1. "Across the Reef: The Marine Assault on Tarawa," by Col. Joseph H. Alexander, *Marines in WWII Commemorative Series* (Washington, D.C.: History and Museums Div., HQMC, 1993.)

2. Jalali and Grau, *Afghan Guerrilla Warfare,* editors' commentaries.

3. Poole, *Phantom Soldier,* chapt. 6.

4. Poole, *The Tiger's Way,* chapts. 12 and 19.

5. Ibid., chapts. 23, 24, and appendix B.

6. Poole, *Phantom Soldier,* chapt. 9.

7. Ibid.

8. Gul, as quoted in *Afghan Guerrilla Warfare,* by Jalali and Grau, p. 97.

Chapter 16: *The Village Contingent Option*

1. NPR's "Morning Edition" News, 14 December 2009.
2. "The Gang That Couldn't Shoot Straight," by T. Christian Miller, Mark Hosenball, and Ron Moreau, *Newsweek,* 29 March 2010, pp. 25-31.
3. Ibid.
4. "Mission Impossible," by John Barry and Michael Hirsh, *Newsweek,* 14 December 2009, pp. 12.
5. "The Khost Attack and the Intelligence War Challenge," *Stratfor Weekly,* 11 January 2010.
6. Peters, *Seeds of Terror,* p. 238.
7. "Doing It the Dutch Way in Afghanistan," Graeme Smith and Tirin Kot, *Globe and Mail* (Toronto), 3 December 2006.
8. Ibid., in *Seeds of Terror,* by Peters, p. 222.
9. Moore, "NATO Confronts Surprisingly Fierce Taliban," in *Seeds of Terror,* by Peters, p. 222.
10. Bill Lind (father of 4GW theory), as quoted in "Homeland Siege," by H. John Poole (Emerald Isle, NC: Posterity Press, 2009), pp. 97, 98.
11. "Doing It the Dutch Way in Afghanistan," Smith and Kot.
12. Anonymous multi-tour U.S. Special Forces veteran of Afghanistan, in telephone conversation with the author of 11 December 2009.
13. "Doing It the Dutch Way in Afghanistan," Smith and Kot.
14. Peters, *Seeds of Terror,* p. 222.
15. Memorandum for the record by H.J. Poole.
16. Seth Jones. "America Is Making a Difference in Eastern Afghanistan," *Globe and Mail* (Toronto), 1 April 2008, in *Seeds of Terror,* by Peters, p. 222.
17. "Obama's War."
18. Peter Stiff, *The Silent War: South African Recce Operations, 1969-1994* (Alberton, South Africa: Galago Publishing, 1999), pp. 289, 290.
19. "How the Taliban Take a Village," by Mark Sexton, ed. William S. Lind, *On War #325,* 7 December 2009.
20. Tohid and Bowers, "U.S. Pakistan Tighten Net on Al Qaeda," pp. 1, 10.
21. Maj. Jim Gant, *One Tribe at a Time: A Strategy of Success in Afghanistan* (N.p.: Steven Pressfield Online, n.d.).
22. Memorandum for the record by H.J. Poole.
23. Poole, *The Tiger's Way,* pp. 280-283
24. Memorandum for the record by H.J. Poole.

25. NPR's "Morning Edition" News, 10 February 2010.

Epilogue

1. ABC's Nightly News, 18 January 2010.
2. NPR's "Morning Edition" News, 25 January 2010.
3. *World Aero Data* (worldaerodata.com), s.v. "Great Inagua Airport (MYIG)."
4. Marine Regimental Commander, during hushed verbal exchange with author in late summer of 1999.
5. Burke Davis, *Marine* (New York: Bantam, 1964).
6. Maj. Norman L. Cooling, "Russia's 1994-96 Campaign for Chechnya: A Failure in Shaping the Battlespace," *Marine Corps Gazette,* October 2001, pp. 62-66.
7. Lt.Col. Timothy L. Thomas and Lester W. Grau, "Russian Lessons Learned from the Battles for Grozny," *Marine Corps Gazette,* April 2000, p. 48.
8. Bruce I. Gudmundsson, *Stormtroop Tactics — Innovation in the German Army 1914-1918* (New York: Praeger, 1989.
9. "Afghans Raise Flag in Former Taliban Stronghold," from AP, *Jacksonville Daily News* (NC), 26 February 2010, p. 16.
10. NPR's "Morning Edition" News, 23 December 2009.
11. "Marine Engineers Fortify Observation Posts in Afghanistan," by L.Cpl. Walter Marino, *Camp Lejeune Globe* (NC), 7 January 2010, p. 1.
12. Poole, *Tequila Junction,* pp. 218, 219.
13. Memorandum for the record from H.J. Poole.
14. Ibid.

Glossary

AAF	Anti-Afghan Forces	Term applied to all government foes in Afghanistan
ABC	American Broadcasting Company	U.S. TV network
AP	Associated Press	U.S. news service
BBC	British Broadcasting Corporation	British electronic media network
BGB	Bureau of Geophysical Prospecting	Chinese company operating in Baluchistan
BLA	Baloch Liberation Army	Resistance army in Baluchistan
C-17	U.S. military designator	Most modern U.S. Air Force heavy lift airplane
CAP	Combined Action Platoon	Unit consisting of squad of GIs with two squads of indigenous troops & police, or tribal militia
CBS	Columbia Broadcasting System	U.S. TV network
CENTCOM	U.S. Central Command	Protects U.S. interests in 20 nations from the Middle East to Central Asia
CH-53	U.S. military designator	Marine heavy lift helicopter
CIA	Central Intelligence Agency	U.S. spy agency
CNN	Cable News Network	U.S. TV network

COSCO	China Ocean Shipping Company	Civilian cargo vessels that work as an extension of the PLA
D.C.	District of Columbia	Federal enclave containing the U.S. capitol complex
DEA	Drug Enforcement Administration	U.S. counter-narcotics bureau
DRA	Democratic Republic of Afghanistan	Soviets' Afghan puppet regime
DRC	Democratic Republic of the Congo	Sovereign country in Central Africa
E-5	U.S. enlisted pay grade designator	Pay grade for the lowest ranking sergeant
E&E	Escape and Evasion	Ability to elude a pursuer
EFP	Explosively Formed Projectile	Sophisticated IED for penetrating armor
FARC	*Fuerzas Armadas Revolutionarias de Colombia*	Maoist rebels in Colombia
FATA	Federally Administered Tribal Areas	Series of Pakistani tribal agencies along Afghan border
FBI	Federal Bureau of Investigation	U.S. law enforcement agency
FEMA	Federal Emergency Management Agency	U.S. bureau that coordinates natural disaster relief
4GW	Fourth-Generation Warfare	War conducted within martial and nonmartial arenas simultaneously
GDP	Gross Domestic Product	Market value of all final goods and services produced by a nation's citizens in a year
GI	Government Issue	Slang name for junior U.S. enlisted man

GPS	Global Positioning System	Device that determines one's location on the ground from satellite signals
Hezb	*Hezb-ul-Mujahideen*	*JI's* military wing, founded by Hekmatyar in Azad Kashmir
HI	*Hizb i-Islami*	Hekmatyar's Islamic party begun in Pakistan in 1975
HIG	*Hizb i-Islami Gulbuddin*	Hekmatyar's *JI*-supported Afghan militia
HIK	*Hizb i-Islami-Khalis*	Khalis' Afghan offshoot of *HI*
HMA	*Harakat ul Mujahideen al-Alami*	Militant faction, an offshoot of the merger between *HUM* and *HUJI*
HUJI	*Harakat ul-Jehad i-Islami*	Deobandi affiliate of *JUI/F*
HUM	*Harakat ul-Mujahideen*	*JUI/F's* military wing
IED	Improvised Explosive Device	Remotely detonated mine
IIF	International Islamic Front	Osama bin Laden's alliance of Pakistani religious party militias
IJT	*Islami Jamiat Talaba*	Student wing of *JI*
IRGC	Islamic Revolution Guards Corps	Overseers of the Iranian revolution
ISI	Inter-Service Intelligence	Pakistan's spy agency
JEM	*Jaish-e-Mohammed*	Militant faction, an offshoot of the merger between *HUM* and *HUJI*
JI	*Jamaat-i-Islami*	Legal Pakistani religious political party, primary supporter of *Hezb* and *HIG*

287

JuD	*Jamaat-ul-Dawa*	Pakistani militant faction, previously called *MDI*
JUI	*Jamiat Ulema-i-Islam*	Pakistani religious political party, forerunner of *JUI/F*
JUI/F	*Jamiat Ulema-i-Islam* Fazlur Rehman faction	Legal Pakistani religious political party, primary supporter of Afghan Taliban
LeJ	*Lashkar i-Jhangvi*	*SSP's* military wing
LET	*Lashkar-e-Toiba*	*JuD's* military wing
LI	*Lashkar-e-Islam*	Khyber Agency faction, offshoot or affiliate of the *TTP*
LoC	Line of Communication	Term applied to the major roads in Afghanistan
M-16	U.S. military designator	Main service rifle
M-4	U.S. military designator	M-16 configuration with shorter muzzle and lower velocity, can host a "silencer"
MCC	Metallurgical Construction Corporation	Chinese company operating in Baluchistan
MDI	*Markaz-ud-Dawa-wal-Irshad*	Pakistani militant faction, forerunner of *JuD*
MI6	U.K agency designator	British intelligence bureau
MMA	*Muttahida Majlis Amal*	Pakistani religious party alliance with *JI* and *JUI/F*
MRDL	Chinese business acronym	MCC subsidiary operating in Baluchistan
NAFTA	North American Free Trade Agreement	Economic pact between Western Hemisphere nations
NATO	North Atlantic Treaty Organization	European military alliance

NCO	Noncommissioned Officer	Junior enlisted leader
NLC	National Logistics Cell	Pakistani-Army-run trucking firm during Soviet-Afghan War
9/11	11 September 2001	Date of attack on World Trade Center and Pentagon
NPR	National Public Radio	U.S. educational network
NWFP	Northwest Frontier Province	Pakistani province
PBS	Public Broadcasting System	U.S. educational TV network
PLA	People's Liberation Army	Armed forces of the PRC
PRC	People's Republic of China	Communist China
RL	Rocket Launcher	Pakistani term for RPG tube
RPG	Rocket-Propelled Grenade	Eastern-bloc bazooka round
SA-7	Chinese military designator	Anti-aircraft missile
SAS	British Special Air Service	British special operations organization
SAW	Squad Automatic Weapon	U.S. light machinegun
SIM	*Shura Ittehad-ul-Mujahideen*	Alliance between Baitullah Mehsud, Maulavi Nazir, and Hafiz Gul Bahadur to aid Mullah Omar & bin Laden
SSP	*Sipah-e Sahaba*	Pakistani militant faction
SWAT	Special Weapons Assault Team	Police paramilitary squad
TJD	*Tubala Jamat-ud Dawa*	Student wing of the *JuD*
TNSM	*Tehreek-e-Nafaz-e-Shariat-e-Mohammadi*	Radical offshoot of *JI*
TRADOC	Training and Doctrine Command	U.S. Army's headquarters section that writes manuals

TTP	*Tehrik-i-Taliban*	Baitullah Mehsud's "Pakistani Taliban"
TV	Television	Video medium
U.K.	United Kingdom	Great Britain
U.N.	United Nations	World peace organization
UNOCAL	Union Oil Company of California	Company trying to build the trans-Afghan gas pipeline
UNODC	United Nations Office on Drugs and Crime	U.N. section in charge of tracking narcotics and crime
U.S.	United States	America
U.S.F.	University of San Francisco	Institution of higher learning in the Bay Area
U.S.S.R.	Union of Soviet Socialist Republics	Soviet Union prior to its break-up in 1990
UW	Unconventional Warfare	For infantrymen, it consists mostly of E&E in enemy territory and fighting like a guerrilla
WWI	World War One	First global conflagration
WWII	World War Two	Second global conflagration

Bibliography

U.S. Government Publications, Databases, and News Releases

"Across the Reef: The Marine Assault on Tarawa." By Col. Joseph H. Alexander. *Marines in WWII Commemorative Series.* Washington, D.C.: History and Museums Division, Headquarters Marine Corps, 1993.

"Afghanistan/Pakistan: U.S. Indicts 11 in Connection with Drug Ring." By Ron Synovitz. *Radio Free Europe / Radio Liberty,* 17 September 2003. As retrieved from www.globalstrategy.org on 20 November 2009.

"Al-Qaeda: Profile and Threat Assessment." By Kenneth Katzman. Congressional Research Service (CRS) Report for Congress. Order Code RL33038, 17 August 2005.

"Asian Criminal Enterprises." FBI's Organized Crime Section. As retrieved from its website, www.fbi.gov, in September 2008.

"Asian Transnational Organized Crime and Its Impact on the United States." By James O. Finckenauer and Ko-lin Chin. U.S. Dept. of Justice Special Report, January 2007. As retrieved from the National Institute of Justice website, www.ojp.usdoj.gov/nij, in September 2008.

"Caspian Oil and Gas: Production and Prospects." By Bernard A. Gelb. Congressional Research Service (CRS) Report for Congress. Order Code RS21190, 8 September 2006.

CIA – The World Factbook. As updated every three months. As retrieved from its website, www.cia.gov, during the period July 2009-June 2010.

"Dawood Ibrahim." U.S. Treasury Dept. Fact Sheet, n.d. As retrieved from its website, www.ustreas.gov, on 1 October 2009.

"DoD News Briefing—ASD PA Clarke and Rear Adm. Stufflebeem," 14 January 2002. As retrieved from the DoD website, www.defenselink.mil, in early 2005.

Dragon on Terrorism: Assessing China's Tactical Gains and Strategic Losses Post-September 11. By Mohan Malik. Carlisle, PA. Strategic Studies Institute. U. S. Army War College, October 2002.

"Iran Report." *Radio Free Europe/Radio Liberty.* Volume 5, number 3, 28 January 2002. As retrieved from www.globalstrategy.org in 2005.

"Marine Engineers Fortify Observation Posts in Afghanistan." By L.Cpl. Walter Marino. *Camp Lejeune Globe* (NC), 7 January 2010.

"Mexico's Drug Cartels." By Colleen W. Cook. CRS Report for Congress. Order Code RL34215. Washington, D.C: Library of Congress, 25 February 2008.

National Drug Threat Assessment (for) 2008. National Drug Intelligence Center, October 2007. As retrieved from its website, www.usdoj.gov/dea, in October 2008.

National Drug Threat Assessment (for) 2009. National Drug Intelligence Center, December 2008. As retrieved from the NDIC website, www.usdoj.gov/ndic, in March 2009.

"Operation Hardtac." FBI case study, 1998. As retrieved from its website, www.fbi.gov, in October 2008.

Pakistan: A Country Study. By Mohan Malik. Federal Research Division. Washington, D.C.: Library of Congress, 1995. Call number DS376.9.P376 1995.

"Pakistan Blames IMU Militants for Afghan Border Unrest." By Alisher Sidikov. *Radio Free Europe/Radio Liberty,* 2 July 2008. As retrieved from its website, www.rferl.org, on 8 September 2009.

Pakistan Country Study. Areas Handbook Series. Washington, D.C.: Library of Congress, 2003.

Patterns of Global Terrorism, 2002 Report. Washington, D.C.: U.S. Dept. of State, April 2003.

Patterns of Global Terrorism, 2003 Report. Washington, D.C.: U.S. Dept. of State, April 2004.

"Transnational Activities of Chinese Crime Organizations." By Glenn E. Curtis, Seth L. Elan, Rexford A. Hudson, and Nina A. Kol. Federal Research Division, Library of Congress, April 2003.

"U.S. Designates Dawood Ibrahim As Terrorist Supporter." U.S. Treasury Dept. Press Release, 16 October 2003.

Civilian Publications

Analytical Studies and Databases

Afghanistan Online. From its website www.afghan-web.com.

Ahmed, Khaled. *Pakistan: Behind the Ideological Mask.* Lahore: Vanguard, 2004.

Australian Government National Security Website (www.ag.gov.au). Listing of Terrorism Organizations.

Country Profiles. BBC News Online. From its website, bbc.co.uk.

Davis, Burke. *Marine.* New York: Bantam, 1964.

Dick, C.J. "Mujahideen Tactics in the Soviet-Afghan War." Sandhurst, UK: Conflict Studies Research Centre, Royal Military Academy, n.d.

Encyclopedia of Earth. From its website, www.eoearth.org.

Esposito, John L. *Unholy War: Terror in the Name of Islam*. London: Oxford University Press, 2002.

Federation of American Scientists database. From its website, www.fas.org.

Gant, Maj. Jim. *One Tribe at a Time: A Strategy of Success in Afghanistan*. N.p.: Steven Pressfield Online, n.d.

Geo Pakistan News Online. From its website, www.geo.tv.

Gertz, Bill. *The China Threat: How the People's Republic Targets America*. Washington, D.C.: Regnery Publishing, 2000.

Global Security. From its website, globalsecurity.org.

Gudmundsson, Bruce I. *Stormtroop Tactics — Innovation in the German Army 1914-1918*. New York: Praeger, 1989.

Gul, Imtiaz. *The Al-Qaeda Connection: The Taliban and Terror in Pakistan's Tribal Areas*. New Delhi: Penguin, 2009.

Gunaratna, Rohan. *Inside al-Qaeda: Global Network of Terror*. Lahore: Vanguard, 2002.

Jalali, Ali and Lester W. Grau. *Afghan Guerrilla Warfare: In the Words of the Mujahideen Fighters*. St. Paul, MN: MBI Publishing, 2001. First published as *The Other Side of the Mountain*. Quantico, VA: Marine Corps Combat Development Command, 1995.

John, Wilson. Observer Research Foundation. *Coming Blowback: How Pakistan Is Endangering the World*. New Delhi: Rupa & Co., 2009.

John Paul II. *Crossing the Threshold of Hope*. New York: Alfred A. Knopf, 1995.

Kaplan, Robert D. *Soldiers of God: With Islamic Warriors in Afghanistan and Pakistan*. New York: Vintage Books, 2001.

King, Gibert. *The Most Dangerous Man in the World*. New York: Chamberlain Brothers, a Penguin imprint, 2004.

Mannes, Aaron. *Profiles in Terror: Guide to Middle East Terror Organizations*. Lanham, MD: Rowman & Littlefield, 2004.

The Memorial Institute for the Prevention of Terrorism (MIPT) Knowledge Base. From its website, www.tkb.org.

Mir, Amir. *Talibanisation of Pakistan*. New Delhi: Pentagon Press, 2010.

Mir, Amir. *The True Face of Jihadis*. Lahore: Mashal Books, 2004.

Nojumi, Neamatollah. *The Rise of the Taliban in Afghanistan: Mass Mobilization, Civil War, and the Future of the Region*. New York: Palgrave, 2002.

O'Ballance, Edgar. *Afghan Wars: Battles in the Hostile Land, 1839 to Present*. Karachi: Oxford University Press, 2002.

100 Strategies of War: Brilliant Tactics in Action. Translated by Yeo Ai Hoon. Singapore: Asiapac Books, 1993.

Pearl, Marianne. *A Mighty Heart: The Inside Story of the Al Qaeda Kidnapping of Danny Pearl.* New York: Scribner, 2003.

Peters, Gretchen. *Seeds of Terror: How Heroin Is Bankrolling the Taliban and al-Qaeda.* New York: Thomas Dunne Books, 2009.

Pintak, Lawrence. *Seeds of Hate: How America's Flawed Middle East Policy Ignited the Jihad.* London: Pluto Press, 2003.

Poole, H. John. *Dragon Days: Time for "Unconventional" Tactics.* Emerald Isle, NC: Posterity Press, 2007.

Poole, H. John. *Homeland Siege: Tactics for Police and Military.* Emerald Isle, NC: Posterity Press, 2009.

Poole, H. John. *The Last Hundred Yards: The NCO's Contribution to Warfare.* Emerald Isle, NC: Posterity Press, 1997.

Poole, H. John. *Militant Tricks: Battlefield Ruses of the Islamic Insurgent.* Emerald Isle, NC: Posterity Press, 2005.

Poole, H. John. *One More Bridge to Cross: Lowering the Cost of War.* Emerald Isle, NC: Posterity Press, 1999.

Poole, H. John. *Phantom Soldier: The Enemy's Answer to U.S. Firepower.* Emerald Isle, NC: Posterity Press, 2001.

Poole, H. John. *Tactics of the Crescent Moon: Militant Muslim Combat Methods.* Emerald Isle, NC: Posterity Press, 2004.

Poole, H. John. *Terrorist Trail: Backtracking the Foreign Fighter.* Emerald Isle, NC: Posterity Press, 2006.

Poole, H. John. Tequila Junction: 4th-Generation Counterinsurgency. Emerald Isle, NC: Posterity Press, 2008.

Poole, H. John. *The Tiger's Way: A U.S. Private's Best Chance of Survival.* Emerald Isle, NC: Posterity Press, 2003.

South Asia Intelligence Review. South Asia Terrorist Portal database. Institute for Conflict Management (New Delhi). From its website, www.satp.org.

The Soviet-Afghan War: How a Superpower Fought and Lost. By the Russian General Staff. Edited by Lester Grau and Michael A. Gress. Lawrence, KS: University of Kansas Press, 2002.

Stiff, Peter. *The Silent War: South African Recce Operations, 1969-1994.* Alberton, South Africa: Galago Publishing, 1999.

Unmasking Terror: A Global Review of Terrorist Activities. Volumes I, II, and III. The first two edited by Christopher Heffelfinger, and the third by Jonathan Hutzley. Washington, D.C: Jamestown Foundation, 2005 through 2007.

Wikipedia Encyclopedia. From its website, www.wikipedia.org.

World Aero Data. From its website, worldaerodata.com.

World Drug Report 2009. U.N. Office on Drugs and Crime. As retreived from its website, www.unodc.org, in November 2009.

World Drug Report 2010. U.N. Office on Drugs and Crime. As retreived from its website, www.unodc.org, on 25 June 2010.

Yousaf, Brigadier Mohammed. *The Silent Soldier: The Man behind the Afghan Jehad.* South Yorkshire, UK: Leo Cooper, n.d.

Yousaf, Brigadier Mohammad and Mark Adkin. *Bear Trap: Afghanistan's Untold Story.* South Yorkshire, UK: Leo Cooper, n.d.

Videotapes, Movies, DVDs, TV Programs, Slide Shows, and Illustrations

China's Rising Power in Africa. Five-part series. NPR, 28 July - 1 August 2008.

"Inside America's Empire." PBS's *America at a Crossroads.* NC Public Television, 11 September 2007.

"Obama's War." PBS's *Frontline.* NC Public Television, October 2009.

"Pakistan under Siege." PBS's *Frontline World.* NC Public Television, 14 April and 26 May 2009.

"Region under Taliban Control. " PBS's *Frontline World.* NC Public Television, 24 February 2010.

"Return of the Taliban." PBS's *Frontline.* NC Public Television, 8 January 2007.

"Sergeant York." 134 minutes. Warner Brothers Pictures. DVD, isbn #1-4198-3829-6.

"Taliban Attacks Afghan Ministry." Videocast from Al Jazeera. Youtube, 11 February 2009. As retrieved on 19 January 2010 from following url: www.youtube.com/watch?v=v8F2MfXvI2k.

Letters, E-Mail, and Verbal Conversations

Anonymous U.S. Special Forces member (multiple-tour veteran of both Iraq and Afghanistan). In telephone conversations with author between March 2005 and May 2010.

Marine Regimental Commander. During hushed verbal exchange with author in late summer of 1999.

Newspaper, Magazine, Radio, and Website Articles

"Afghan and U.S. forces Battle Taliban in Northern Helmand Stronghold." By Bill Roggio. *Long War Journal,* 22 May 2009.

"Afghan Arrested in New York Said to Be a Heroin Kingpin." By Julia Peterson. *New York Times,* 26 April 2005.

"Afghan Leader Accused of Hurting Drug Fight." From Associated Press. *Jacksonville Daily News* (NC), 25 July 2008.

"Afghan Linked to Taliban Sentenced to Life in Drug Trafficking Case." By Benjamin Weiser. *New York Times,* 1 May 2009.

"Afghan Pipeline Raises Security Questions." By Travis Lupick. *Global Research* (Canada), 21 July 2008. As retrieved from its website, www.globalresearch.ca, on 31 August 2009.

"Afghanistan's President: Partner Or Obstacle." By Soraya Sarhaddi Nelson. NPR's "Morning Edition" News, 24 March 2010.

"Afghanistan: U.S. Escalates the Illegal Drug Industry." By John W. Warnock. *Global Research*, 25 February 2009. As retrieved from its website, www.globalresearch.ca, in February 2010.

"Afghans Raise Flag in Former Taliban Stronghold." From Associated Press. *Jacksonville Daily News* (NC), 26 February 2010.

"Africa Drug Trade Fuelling Terrorism and Crime, Says UN." BBC News Online, 9 December 2009.

Ahmed, Issam. "Pakistan's Old Jihadis Pose New Threat." *Christian Science Monitor,* 6 December 2009.

Ahmed, Issam. "Stakes High for Pakistan's Push" *Christian Science Monitor,* 1 November 2009.

Ahmed, Samina. International Crisis Group. As quoted in "Crackdown On Taliban Shifts U.S.-Pakistan Ties." By Julie McCarthy, NPR's "Morning Edition" News, 10 March 2010.

"Aksai Chin: China's Disputed Slice of Kashmir." CNN Online, 24 May 2002.

"Al Qaeda Message Urges Pakistanis to Back Militants." CNN Online, 15 July 2009.

"Ambassadors in Pakistan Visit Gwadar Port." Xinjua News Agency, 11 January 2002. As retrieved from its website, news.xinhuanet.com, on 15 September 2009.

Amiuzadeh, H.E. Mu. Mohsen (Deputy Minister of External Affairs of Asia-Oceania of the Islamic Republic of Iran). "Special Address to the Federation of Indian Chambers of Commerce and Industry." New Delhi, 22 July 2003.

"Analysis: Mr. Karzai Goes to Washington." By Marc Erikson. *Asia Times Online,* 29 January 2002.

"Are India's Maoist Rebels Winning the War." BBC News Online, 28 May 2010.

Arnoldy, Ben "One Path to Taliban Talks." *Christian Science Monitor,* 13 December 2009.

Arnoldy, Ben. "Pakistan Accepts Islamic Law in Swat Valley." *Christian Science Monitor,* 17 February 2009.

Arnoldy, Ben. "Pakistan's Not-So-Epic Offensive." *Christian Science Monitor,* 18 October 2009.

Arnoldy, Ben. "The Taliban: A Threat Overrated." *Christian Science Monitor,* 7 June 2009.

"Attack Aimed at Pakistan Military Mosque." United Press International, 4 December 2009.

Baldauf, Scott. "How Al Qaeda Seeks to Buy Chinese Arms." *Christian Science Monitor,* 23 August 2002.

Barker, Kim *(Chicago Tribune).* "Pakistani Tribes Fight Alleged al-Qaida Allies." *Seattle Times,* 24 April 2007.

Batty, Robbin and David Hoffman. "Afghanistan: Crisis of Impunity." *Human Rights Watch.* Volume 13, number 3(c), July 2001.

"Beijing's Afghan Gamble." By Robert D. Kaplan. *New York Times,* 7 October 2009.

"The Binori Town Madrassah." By Yahya Durrani. Posted at www.paklinks.com on 16 January 2000 and retrieved in June 2009.

Blanford, Nicholas. "Hizbullah Reelects Its Leader." *Christian Science Monitor,* 19 August 2004.

Boot, Max and Frederick Kagan, and Kimberly Kagan. "How to Surge the Taliban." Opinion-Editorial piece. *New York Times,* 13 March 2009.

Bordewich, Fergus M. "Fading Glory." *Smithsonian,* December 2008.

Burke, Jason. "Waiting for a Last Battle with the Taliban." *The Observer* (UK), 27 June 1999.

"Central Asia Pipeline Deal Signed." By Ian McWilliam. BBC News Online, 27 December 2002.

Chaulia, Sreeram. Review of *Pakistan: In the Shadow of Jihad and Afghanistan,* by Mary Anne Weaver. *Asia Times Online,* 1 March 2003.

"China Oil Firm in Unocal Bid War." BBC Radio News, 23 June 2005.

"China, Turkmenistan Sign Landmark Gas Deal." *Central Asia News Online* (Turkmenistan), 18 July 2007. As retrieved from its website, www.newscentralasia.net, on 3 September 2009.

"Chinese Interests Caught in Drone Threat." By Syed Fazl-e-Haider. *Asia Times Online,* 26 March 2009.

"Chinese-Made Ammo in al Qaeda Caves Confirms." *DEBKAfile* (Israel), 17 December 2001.

Chopra, Anuj. "Maoist Rebels Spread across Rural India." *Christian Science Monitor,* 22 August 2006.

"Clash of Canons." By Riyaz Wani. *Indian Express* (India), 9 December 2006. As retrieved in November 2009 from the following url: www.indianexpress.com/story_print.php?storyId=18227.

"Colombia Says FARC Rebels Operating in Bolivia, Paraguay." Xinhua. *People's Daily on Line* (Beijing), 23 June 2006.

"Colombia's Most Powerful Rebels." BBC News Online, 19 September 2003.

Constable, Pamela. "Islamic Law Instituted In Pakistan's Swat Valley." *Washington Post,* 17 February 2009.

"Constitution of Pakistan." As retrieved from pakistani.org on 20 July 2009.

Cooling, Maj. Normal L. "Russia's 1994-96 Campaign for Chechnya: A Failure in Shaping the Battlespace." *Marine Corps Gazette,* October 2001.

Cordesman, Anthony H. (Arleigh A. Burke Chair in Strategy). "Iran's Developing Military Capabilities." Working draft. Washington, D.C.: Center for Strategic International Studies, 14 December 2004.

"Dawood Gang Provided Logistics to Lashkar Militants." Press Trust of India. NDTV website (Mumbai), 29 November 2008.

"Dawood Ibrahim." Interpol Special Notice, 2 October 2009. As retrieved from its website, www.interpol.int, on 1 October 2009.

"Dawood Ibrahim: The Global Terrorist." By B. Raman. South Asia Analysis Group. Paper No. 818, 19 October 2003.

"Dawood Ibrahim Had Played an Important Role in the Smuggling of Nuclear Weapons." By S. Balakrishnan. *Times of India,* 4 August 2004.

"Dawood Ibrahim Has Agents in Bangladesh." From Indo-Asian News Service, 1 June 2009. As retrieved from the Thaindia News website, www.thaindian.com, on 2 October 2009.

"Dawood's Drug Net Financed 26/11: Russian Intelligence." NDTV website (Mumbai), 18 December 2008.

"Dawood's ISI Links Could Trouble Musharraf." By Wilson John. Observer Research Foundation (New Delhi). *Strategic Trends.* Volume I, issue 5, 4 November 2003. As retrieved from its website, www.observerindia.com, on 1 October 2009.

"DEA Agents among U.S. Troop Casualties." Nation/World Newswatch. From Associated Press. *Jacksonville Daily News* (NC), 27 October 2009.

"Do I Look Dangerous to You." Part I. Partners in Crime Series, by Frederic Dannen. *The New Republic,* 14 & 21 July 1997.

"Documents Show American Trained at Al Qaeda Camps in Pakistan." From Associated Press, 23 July 2009. As retrieved from foxnews.com on 27 July 2009.

"Drug Baron Ayub Afridi Appears in SC [Supreme Court] Today." *Daily Times* (Pakistan), 17 November 2005.

"Ecuador Offers Concession of Manta Air Base to China, Declines to Renew Contract with U.S." By Vittorio Hernandez. AHN News Online (Ecuador), 26 November 2007.

Escobar, Pepe. Review of *Who Killed Daniel Pearl,* by
  Bernard-Henri Levy. *Asia Times Online,* 28 June 2003.
Escobar, Pepe. "The Roving Eye." *Asia Times Online,* 15 November
  2001.
"Everyone Wants a Cut in Afghan Drug Trade." From McClatchy
  Newspapers. *Jacksonville Daily News* (NC), 10 May
  2009.
"Factbox: Baluchistan—Pakistan's Biggest but Poorest Province." From
  Reuters, 14 October 2009. As retrieved from its website,
  www.reuters.com, on 30 October 2009.
Fighel, Yoni and Yael Shahar. "The Al-Qaida-Hizballah Connection."
  As posted 26 February 2002 at the International Policy Institute for
  Counter-Terrorism (ICT) website.
"Former Warlord in Standoff With Police at Kabul Home." By Ahmad
  Masood (Reuters). *New York Times.* Asia Pacific edition, n.d.
  As retrieved from their website, nytimes.com, on 1 October 2009.
Gall, Carlotta. "Afghan-Iranian Road Opens." *New York Times,*
  28 January 2005.
"Games in Afghan Poppy Land." *Calcutta Telegraph*
  (India), 6 September 2005.
"The Gang That Couldn't Shoot Straight." By T. Christian Miller,
  Mark Hosenball, and Ron Moreau. *Newsweek,* 29 March 2010.
"General Seeks New Afghan Approach." *Philadelphia Inquirer,*
  1 August 2009.
Gertz, Bill. "China-Made Artillery Seized in Afghanistan."
  Washington Times, 12 April 2002.
Gertz, Bill and Rowan Scarborough. "China-Trained Taliban." Inside
  the Ring. *Washington Times,* 21 June 2002. Unedited version
  from www.gertzfile.com.
"Gilgit Baltistan Reforms Aimed at Providing Better Security Cover for
  Chinese Investments." *South East Asia News* (Bahrain),
  4 September 2009. As retrieved from its website,
  www.southeastasianews.net, in November 2009.
"A Godfather's Lethal Mix of Business and Politics." *U.S. News &
  World Report Online,* 5 December 2005.
"Govt Blames LeT for Parliament Attack, Asks Pak to
  Restrain Terrorist Outfits." *Rediff News* (India),
  14 December 2001. As retrieved from its website,
  rediff.com, on 18 January 2010.
Graham, Stephen. Associated Press. "Latest Assault Leaves
  2 Brits, Afghan Interpreter Dead." *Jacksonville Daily News*
  (NC), 6 May 2004.
"The Great Banuri Town Seminary." By Shaykh. *Sunni Forum,*
  12 August 2005. As retrieved from its website,
  www.sunniforum.com, on 12 in June 2009.

"Haqqani Network." Institute for the Study of War (Washington, D.C.), n.d. As retrieved from their website, www.understandingwar.org, on 26 September 2009.

"Harvesting Change." Christina Wood. *Military Officer,* May 2009.

"H. E. Mr. Chen Shanmin, the Consul General Visits Quetta, Balochistan 2007-09-11." Chinese Consulate in Karachi. As retrieved in October 2009 from the following url: http://karachi.china-consulate.org/eng/zlghd/t361142.htm.

"Here Comes Trouble." *The Economist,* 11 June 2009.

Herold, Marc W. "The Failing Campaign." *Frontline* (India). Volume 19, issue 3, 2-15 February 2002.

"How Pakistan's ISI Funds Its Proxy War." By Syed Nooruzzaman. *The Tribune* (India), 28 November 1999. From the following url: http://www.tribuneindia.com/1999/99nov28/head6.htm#1

"How the Taliban Take a Village." By Mark Sexton. Edited by William S. Lind. *On War #325,* 7 December 2009. From the following url: http://globalguerrillas.typepad.com/lind/2009/12/on-war-325.

"Hunting for Dawood Ibrahim" By B. Raman. South Asia Analysis Group. Paper No 1952, 16 September 2006. And *International Terrorism Monitor,* Paper No. 122, n.d.

"In Drug Trial, Sharply Differing Portraits of Afghan With Ties to the Taliban." By Benjamin Weiser. *New York Times,* 11 September 2008.

"India, Pakistan and the 'Peace' Pipeline." *Asia Times Online,* 15 September 2004

"India Wants Him, Pak Uses Jaish Chief to Defuse Mosque Tension." By Pranab Dhal Samanta. *India Express* (Delhi), 7 July 2009. As retrieved from indiaexpress.com on 25 July 2009.

"Inside Pakistan-Administered Kashmir." By Aamer Ahmed Khan. BBC News Online, 6 April 2005.

"International Relations and Security Network [of] al-Qaeda." By Jayshree Bajoria. Council on Foreign Relations (New York, NY), 18 April 2008. As retrieved from www.cfr.org on 27 July 2009.

"Iran, Pakistan Sign Peace Pipeline Deal," Press TV (Tehran), 24 May 2009. As retrieved from its website, www.presstv.com, on 2 September 2009.

"Iran Role in the Recent Uprising in Iraq." Special Dispatch No. 692, 9 April 2004. From Middle East Media Research Institute. As retrieved from the following url in March 2005: http://www.memri.org/bin/opener_latest.cgi?ID=SD69204.

"ISI's Attempt to Discredit the Balochis." *India Defence,* 14 March 2006. As retrieved from their website, www.india-defence.com, in November 2009.

"Islam's Medieval Outposts." By Husain Haqqani. *Foreign Policy* (Washington, D.C.), November/December 2002.

"Jaish-e-Mohammed (JEM) Backgrounder." South Asia Analysis Group (India), paper no. 3320, 10 March 2001. As retrieved from its website, southasiaanalysis.org/default.asp, on 7 July 2009.

"Jaish e-Mohammed Profile." Overseas Security Advisor Council. *Global Security News & Reports,* n.d. From its website, www.ds-osac.org.

Jan, Delawar. "100 Militants Killed in Maidan." *The News* (Pakistan), 22 July 2009.

Jelinek, Pauline. Associated Press. "U.S. Plans Spring Offensive in Afghanistan." AOL News, 30 January 2004.

John, Wilson. "The Karachi Connection." *The Pioneer* (New Delhi), 23 January 2002.

"Karzai Considers Proposals from Militant Group." From Associated Press. *Jacksonville Daily News* (NC), 23 March 2010.

"Karzai Upset by Taliban Capture." From Associated Press. *Jacksonville Daily News* (NC), 16 March 2010.

"Karzai's Cabinet Rejected." From Associated Press. *Jacksonville Daily News* (NC), 3 January 2010.

Kazem, Halema. "U.S. Thins Taliban's Ranks, But their Ideological Grip Remains Strong." *Christian Science Monitor,* 18 September 2003.

"The Khost Attack and the Intelligence War Challenge." *Stratfor Weekly,* 11 January 2010. As retrieved from its website, www.stratfor.com, on 11 January 2010.

LaFranchi, Howard. "Anti-Iran Sentiment Hardening Fast." *Christian Science Monitor,* 22 July 2004.

LaFranchi, Howard. "Pakistan: U.S. Ally, U.S. Dilemma." *Christian Science Monitor,* 29 March 2007.

"Lashkar-e-Jhangvi & Al Qaeda." By B. Raman. South Asia Analysis Group. Paper No. 2526, 31 December 2007. And *International Terrorism Monitor,* Paper No. 337, n.d.

Lubold, Gordon. "Mullen's Charm Offensive." *Christian Science Monitor,* 17 January 2010.

"Markets Closed, Traffic Thin: 135 Arrested in Lahore." By Intikhab Hanif and Ahmad Fraz Khan. *Dawn Newspaper Group Online* (Karachi), 10 November 2001.

"Match China Pearls." *Deccan Chronicle* (Bangalore), 14 August 2009.

"Maulvi Nazir Group Decides to Stay Neutral." By Iqbal Khattak, *Daily Times* (Pakistan), 19 October 2009. As retrieved from its website, www.dailytimes.com.pk, in November 2009.

Mazumdar, Sudip. "Captors of the Liberated Zone."
Newsweek, 18 May 2009.

"McCrystal's War." By Evan Thomas. *Newsweek*, 5 October 2009.

McDowell, Patrick. Associated Press. "Pakistan Goes After Terrorists on Border." *Jacksonville Daily News* (NC), 9 January 2004.

McGirk, Tim and Phil Zabriskie, Helen Gibson, Ghulam Hasnain, and Zamira Loebis. "Islam's Other Hot Spots." *Time*, 15 September 2003.

"Mehsud Buying Children to Make Suicide Bombers." *News Outlook* (India), 3 July 2009. As retrieved from itw website, news.outlookindia.com, in August 2009.

"Mehsud's Pals in High Places." *Newsweek*, 13 April 2009.

Meixler, Louis. Associated Press. "Extremists Send Recruits into Iraq via Iranian Border." *Jacksonville Daily News* (NC), 8 November 2004.

"Mexico's Internal Drug War." *Power and Interest News Report (PINR)*, 14 August 2006. As retrieved from its website, www.pinr.com, in July 2007.

"Militants Free 40 Kidnapped Passengers." By Hussain Afzai. *Dawn* (Karachi), 17 May 2010.

"Militants Overrun Pakistan Fort." BBC News Online, 17 January 2008.

"Militants Take Hostages at Parkistan Army HQ." News Briefs Wire Reports (AP). *Jacksonville Daily News* (NC), 11 October 2009.

"Military: Iran Teaching Iraqi Militia to Build Bombs." From Associated Press. *Jacksonville Daily News* (NC), 12 April 2007.

Miller, Greg. "U.S. Says Pakistan, Iran Helping Taliban." *Los Angeles Times Online,* 22 September 2009.

"Mission Impossible." By John Barry and Michael Hirsh. *Newsweek,* 14 December 2009.

"Maoists Attack." The World. *Time,* 19 April 2010.

Montero, David. "In Border Zone, Pakistan Backs Off from Taliban." *Christian Science Monitor,* 26 September 2006.

Moreau, Ron. "America's New Nightmare." *Newsweek,* 3 August 2009.

Moreau, Ron. "Sheltered in Karachi." *Newsweek,* 7 December 2009.

Morton, Robert. "Who Needs the Panama Canal." *Washington Times.* National weekly edition, 1-8 March 1999.

"Mumbai Bombing Sentencing Delay." BBC News Online, 13 September 2006.

"Munawar Sworn in As JI Ameer." *The International News Online* (Pakistan), 6 April 2009.

Myers, Lt.Col. Patrick and Patrick Poole. "Hezbollah, Illegal
    Immigration, and the Next 9/11." *Front Page Magazine,* 28 April
    2006.
"NATO Force Could Patrol Afghanistan." From Associated Press.
    Jacksonville Daily News (NC), 5 August 2005.
"New Afghan Strategy Puts Troops Out Front." From Associated Press.
    Jacksonville Daily News (NC), 21 March 2009.
"Nicaragua Corredor de Armas." By Elizabeth Romero. *La Prensa,*
    17 April 2005.
"Night Stalkers and Mean Streets." By Ali A. Jalali and Lester W. Grau.
    Ft. Leavenworth, KS: Foreign Military Studies Office, 1998).
    Infantry Magazine, January-April 1999.
"19-Hour Siege of GHQ Block Ends." By Shakeel Anjum. *The
    International News Online* (Pakistan), 12 October 2009.
Noorani, A.G. "Pakistan's Burden." *Frontline* (India), 3-16 January
    2009. As retrieved on 3 July 2009 from the following url:
    http://www.frontlineonnet.com/stories/20090116260108400.htm.
Nordland, Rod. "Al-Sadr Strikes." *Newsweek,* 10 April 2006.
Obama, President Barack. In his address to the nation. ABC Television,
    1 December 2009.
"Organized Crime, Intelligence and Terror: The D-Company's Role in
    the Mumbai Attacks." By Tom Burghardt. *Global Research,*
    13 December 2008. As retrieved from its website,
    www.globalresearch.ca, on 26 May 2010.
"Osama's Secret Citadel." *DEBKA-Net-Weekly,* 28 September
    2001.
"Pak Raids Unravel Taliban-Drugs Link." *The Times of India,*
    25 August 2009. As retrieved from its website,
    www.timesofindia.indiatimes.com, on 2 October 2009.
"Pakistan and the Taliban." By Ahmed Rashid. *The Nation*
    (Lahore), 11 April 1998.
"Pakistan Bans LET, JuD, and 23 Outfits." *Deccan Herald* (India),
    6 August 2009.
"Pakistan Captures Mehsud's Hometown." UPI.com, 24 October
    2009.
"Pakistan Closes Torkham Border Crossing, Shuts Down NATO's
    Supply Line." By Bill Rogio. *Long War Journal,* 6 September 2008.
    As retrieved from its website, www.longwarjournal.org, on
    19 November 2009.
"Pakistan Conflict Map." From BBC News Online, South Asia section,
    22 June 2009. As retrieved on 16 July 2009 from the following url:
    http://news.bbc.co.uk/2/hi/south_asia/8046577.stm.
"Pakistan Cuts Deal with Anti-American Taliban." News Briefs Wire
    Reports (AP). *Jacksonville Daily News* (NC), 20 October
    2009.

"Pakistan Project." International Center for Religion and Diplomacy (Washington , D.C.), n.d. As retrieved from its website, www.icrd.org, in July 2009.

"Pakistan Reels Under A Jihadi Guerilla War." By B. Raman. South Asia Analysis Group. Paper No. 3462, 15 October 2009. And *International Terrorism Monitor*. Paper No. 568, n.d.

"Pakistan Trims Top ISI Chairs." From PTI Islamabad. *The Economic Times* (Chennai), 13 August 2009.

"Pakistan Troops Seize Radical Cleric's Base: Officials." From Agence-France Presse, 28 November 2007. Pakistani Government. From its website, pak.gov.pk.

"Pakistani Commandos Break Siege on Army Headquarters." By Bill Roggio. *Long War Journal*, 10 October 2009.

"Pakistani Islamists Sign Deal With China." By Farhan Bokhari. CBS News "World Watch," 18 February 2009. As retrieved in late November 2009 from the following url: www.cbsnews.com/blogs/2009/02/18/world/worldwatch/entry4809534.shtml.

"Pakistani Madrassahs: A Balanced View." Report for U.S. Institute of Peace, August 2005. As retrieved in June 2009 from the following url: http://www.uvm.edu/~envprog/madrassah.html.

"Pakistani Military Hits Taliban in Orakzai." By Bill Roggio. *Long War Journal*, 17 November 2009. As retrieved from its website, www.longwarjournal.org, on 19 November 2009.

"Pakistan's 'New Zone of Militancy'." BBC News Online, 12 October 2009.

"Peace Pipeline Progress." *Asia Monitor,* June 2007. As retrieved from its website, www.asia-monitor.com, on 1 September 2009.

Pennington, Matt. "Afghanistan Stops Paying Farmers to Give Up Growing Opium." From Associated Press, 25 August 2003.

Pennington, Matthew. Associated Press. "Pakistan Unsure If Target Is al-Zawahri." *Jacksonville Daily News* (NC), 21 March 2004.

Peters, Gretchen and Aleem Agha. "Weary Taliban Coming In from the Cold." *Christian Science Monitor,* 14 December 2004.

Peterson, Scott. "Shiites Rising—Part One." *Christian Science Monitor,* 6 June 2007.

Petraeus, Gen. David. On NPR's "Morning Edition" News, 29 May 2009.

"The Presence of U.S. Troops and Alleged Support for the Insurgency." Afghanistan Project Themes: Iran and Afghanistan, Institute for the Study of War. Washington, D.C., n.d. As retrieved from its website, www.understandingwar.org, on 20 December 2009.

"Profile: Pakistan's Military Intelligence Agency." By David Chazan. BBC News Online, 9 January 2002.

Raman, B. "The New Trojan Horse of Al Qaeda." South Asia Analysis. *International Terrorism Monitor.* Paper No. 301, 10 November 2007. As retrieved from its website, www.satp.org, in July 2009.

"Reluctance to Slate Suicide Bombing." By Kunwar Idris. *Dawn Newspaper Group Online* (Karachi), 21 June 2009.

"Renewed Hope for Afghan Pipeline." By Raouf Liwal. *Asia Times Online,* 23 November 2004.

Rice-Oxley, Mark and Owais Tohid. "British Keep a Wary Eye on Pakistan." *Christian Science Monitor,* 27 July 2005.

Risen, James. "Reports Link Karzai's Brother to Afghan Heroin Trade." *New York Times,* 4 October 2008.

Risen, James. "U.S. Inaction Seen After Taliban P.O.W.'s Died." *New York Times.* Asia Pacific edition, 10 July 2009.

Robertson, Nic. "Pakistan: Taliban Buying Children for Suicide Attacks." CNN Online, 7 July 2009. As retrieved from its website, cnn.com/asia, on 1 October 2009.

"Russia's Georgia Invasion May Be About Oil." By Rachel Martin, ABC News Online, 16 August 2008.

Samander, Rahimullah and Rahim Gul Sarwan. "Concern That Jihad Chieftains Will Set Political Agenda." Institute for War and Peace Reporting. ARR No. 88, 18 December 2003.

Samanta, Pranab Dhal. "India Wants Him, Pak Uses Jaish Chief to Defuse Mosque Tension." *India Express* (New Delhi), 7 July 2009. As retrieved from its website, indiaexpress.com, in July 2009.

Santoli, Al. "The Panama Canal in Transition: Threats to U.S. Security and China's Growing Role in Latin America." American Foreign Policy Council Investigative Report, 23 June 1999.

Sarhadi, Zia. "Turning Pakistan into a Sectarian Battleground." *Muslimedia* (London), 1 February 1998. As retrieved from its website, www.muslimedia.com, in July 2009.

"Secrets of Brigade 055." By Daniel Eisenberg. *Time,* 28 October 2001.

"Sergeant Alvin York." By Dr. Michael Birdwell. Great War Society. As retrieved from its website, www.worldwar1.com, on 15 October 2009.

Sen, Chanakya. Review of *Karachi: A Terror Capital in the Making,* by Wilson John. *Asia Times Online,* 17 January 2004.

Slavin, Barbara. "Iran Helped to Overthrow Taliban." *USA Today,* 10 June 2005.

"Smoking Al Qaeda Out of Karachi." By B. Raman. South Asia Analysis Group. Paper No. 519, 14 September 2002.

"South Waziristan's Maulvi Nazir: The New Face of the Taliban." By Hassan Abbas. The Jamestown Foundation. *Terrorism Monitor.* Volume 5, issue 9, 14 May 2007.

Straziuso, Jason. Associated Press. "Afghan Bomber Deadlier." *Jacksonville Daily News* (NC), 3 June 2007.

Straziuso, Jason. Associated Press. "General Says Troops Need New View Of Afghan War." *Boston Globe,* 25 June 2009.

"Suicide Attack Kills 30 in Pakistan." World News in Brief. *Christian Science Monitor,* 28 May 2009.

"Suicide Attack on Afghan Ministry Kills Five." From Indo-Asian News Service. *Thaindian News,* 30 October 2008. As retrieved from its website, www.thaindian.com, on 19 January 2010.

"Suicide Bomber Kills Peacekeeper, Civilian in Afghan Capital." World Brief Wire Reports (AP). *Jacksonville Daily News* (NC), 28 January 2004.

"Suicide Bomber Kills 22 Border Guards at Torkham Crossing in Pakistan." By Bill Roggio. *Long War Journal,* 27 August 2009. As retrieved from its website, www.longwarjournal.org, on 19 November 2009.

Tahir, Muhammad. "Iranian Involvement in Afghanistan." Jamestown Foundation. *Terrorism Monitor.* Volume 5, issue 1, 21 February 2007.

"Taliban Attack Afghan Presidential Palace, Ministries." From Indo-Asian News Service. Kerala News (India), 18 January 2010. As retrieved from its website, www.newkerala.com, on 19 January 2010.

"Taliban Claim Pakistan Army Raid." BBC News Online, 12 October 2009.

"Taliban Group Chooses New Name." *Daily Times* (Pakistan), 27 April 2008.

"Taliban Launches Brazen Attack on Kabul." From Associated Press. MSNBC Online News, 18 January 2010. As retrieved from its website, www.msnbc.msn.com, on 19 January 2010.

"Taliban Leader's Death Confirmed." News Briefs/Wire Reports (AP). *Jacksonville Daily News* (NC), 11 February 2010.

"Talibanism: Pakistani-Style." *The Friday Times.* Volume XI, number 52, 25 February-2 March 2000. As retrieved from www.afghanistannewscenter.com in July 2009.

"Terrorism's Pacific Gateway." By Patrick Lloyd Hatcher. University of San Francisco Center for the Pacific Rim. Report No. 38, June 2005. As retrieved from its website, www.pacificrim.usfca.edu, in November 2009.

"Terrorists Hit Pak N-Sites Thrice in 2 Yrs." *Times Global* (Chennai), 12 August 2009.

Thomas, Lt.Col. Timothy L. Thomas and Lester W. Grau. "Russian Lessons Learned from the Battles for Grozny." *Marine Corps Gazette,* April 2000.

Tohid, Owais. "Al Qaeda Supporters Strike Back in Pakistan." *Christian Science Monitor,* 25 March 2004.

Tohid, Owais. "In Death, As in Life." *Newsline,* October 2003. As retrieved from its website, website, www.newsline.com, in June 2009.

Tohid, Owais. "Pakistan Gains in Al Qaeda Hunt." *Christian Science Monitor,* 16 March 2004.

Tohid, Owais. "Pakistan Marks Pro-Al Qaeda Clan." *Christian Science Monitor,* 23 March 2004.

Tohid, Owais and Faye Bowers. "U.S. Pakistan Tighten Net on Al Qaeda." *Christian Science Monitor,* 22 March 2004.

Tran, Tini. Associated Press. "Tape Targets Clerics." *Jacksonville Daily News* (NC), 25 November 2004.

"Trio Sign Up for Turkmen Gas." *Upstream* (International Oil and Natural Gas Newspaper, Norway), 25 April 2008. As retrieved from its website, www.upstreamonline.com, on 1 September 2009.

"The 'University of Holy War'." By Haroon Rashid. BBC News Online, 2 October 2003.

"U.S. Puts Afghan Drug Lords on Hitlist to Disrupt Taliban Finances." By Richard Norton-Taylor and Jon Boone. *The Guardian Online* (UK), 10 August 2009.

"U.S. Turns to Drug Baron to Rally Support." By Syed Saleem Shahzad. *Asia Times Online,* 4 December 2001.

Varma, K.J.M. "PoK Also Banns Jihadi Outfits." From *PTI* (Pakistan). As posted at www.rediff.com on 5 December 2003 and retrieved in early 2005.

Walsh, Decian. "Pakistan Bows to Demand for Sharia Law in Taliban-Controlled Swat Valley." *Guardian* (UK), 14 April 2009.

"Waziristan-Based Terror Group Takes Credit for Lahore Assault." By Bill Roggio. *Long War Journal,* 30 March 2009.

Whitlock, Craig and Karen DeYoung. "Attributes Suggest Outside Help." *Washington Post,* 28 November 2008.

"Who Really Killed Daniel Pearl." *Guardian Online* (UK), 5 April 2002.

"Why West Africa Cannot Break Its Drug Habit." By Rose Skelton. BBC News Online, 21 June 2010.

Yousafzai, Sami and Ron Moreau. "Rumors of bin Laden's Lair." *Newsweek,* 8 September 2003.

Yusuf, Huma. "Taliban Rising? Ask the Women." *Christian Science Monitor,* 24 May 2009.

About the Author

After 28 years of commissioned and noncommissioned infantry service, John Poole retired from the United States Marine Corps in April 1993. While on active duty, he studied small-unit tactics for nine years: (1) six months at the Basic School in Quantico (1966); (2) seven months as a rifle platoon commander in Vietnam (1966-67); (3) three months as a rifle company commander at Camp Pendleton (1967); (4) five months as a regimental headquarters company (and camp) commander in Vietnam (1968); (5) eight months as a rifle company commander in Vietnam (1968-69); (6) five and a half years as an instructor with the Advanced Infantry Training Company (AITC) at Camp Lejeune (1986-92); and (7) one year as the Staff Noncommissioned Officer in Charge of the 3rd Marine Division Combat Squad Leaders Course (CSLC) on Okinawa (1992-93).

While at AITC, he developed, taught, and refined courses on maneuver warfare, land navigation, fire support coordination, call for fire, adjust fire, close air support, M203 grenade launcher, movement to contact, daylight attack, night attack, infiltration, defense, offensive Military Operations in Urban Terrain (MOUT), defensive MOUT, Nuclear/Biological/Chemical (NBC) defense, and leadership. While at CSLC, he further refined the same periods of instruction and developed others on patrolling.

He has completed all of the correspondence school requirements for the Marine Corps Command and Staff College, Naval War College (1,000-hour curriculum), and Marine Corps Warfighting Skills Program. He is a graduate of the Camp Lejeune Instructional Management Course, the 2nd Marine Division Skill Leaders in Advanced Marksmanship (SLAM) Course, and the East-Coast School of Infantry Platoon Sergeants' Course.

In the 18 years since retirement, John Poole has researched the small-unit tactics of other nations and written ten additional books: (1) *The Last Hundred Yards,* a squad combat study based on the consensus opinions of 1,200 NCOs and casualty statistics of AITC and CSLC field trials; (2) *One More Bridge to Cross*, a treatise on enemy proficiency at short range and how to match it; (3) *Phantom Soldier,* an in-depth look at the highly deceptive Asian style of war; (4) *The Tiger's Way,* the fighting styles of Eastern fire teams and soldiers; (5) *Tactics of the Crescent Moon,* insurgent procedures in Palestine, Chechnya, Afghanistan, and Iraq; (6) *Militant Tricks,* an honest appraisal of the so-far-undefeated *jihadist* method; (7) *Terrorist Trail,* tracing the *jihadists* in Iraq back to their home countries; (8) *Dragon Days,* an unconventional warfare technique manual; (9) *Tequila Junction,* how to fight narco-guerrillas; and (10) *Homeland Siege,* confronting the 4GW assault by a foreign power's organized-crime proxies.

As of May 2010, John Poole had conducted multiday training sessions (on 4GW squad tactics) at 39 (mostly Marine) battalions, nine Marine schools, and seven special-operations units from all four U.S. service branches. Since 2000, he has done research in Mainland China (twice), North Korea, Vietnam, Cambodia, Thailand, Russia, India, Pakistan (twice), Iran, Lebanon, Turkey, Egypt, Sudan, Tanzania, Venezuela, and Sri Lanka. Over the course of his lifetime, he has visited scores of other nations on all five continents. In preparation for this book, he spent a few days in Karachi in May 2010.

Between early tours in the Marine Corps (from 1969 to 1971), John Poole worked as a criminal investigator for the Illinois Bureau of Investigation (IBI). After attending the State Police Academy for several months in Springfield, he was assigned to the IBI's Chicago office.

Name Index